HUMAN RIGHTS AND
THE BORDERS OF SUFFERING

ONE WEEK LOAN

New Approaches to
Conflict Analysis

Series editor: Peter Lawler
Senior Lecturer in International Relations,
Department of Government, University of Manchester

Until recently, the study of conflict and conflict resolution remained comparatively immune to broad developments in social and political theory. When the changing nature and locus of large-scale conflict in the post-Cold War era is also taken into account, the case for a reconsideration of the fundamentals of conflict analysis and conflict resolution becomes all the more stark.

New Approaches to Conflict Analysis promotes the development of new theoretical insights and their application to concrete cases of large-scale conflict, broadly defined. The series intends not to ignore established approaches to conflict analysis and conflict resolution, but to contribute to the reconstruction of the field through a dialogue between orthodoxy and its contemporary critics. Equally, the series reflects the contemporary porosity of intellectual borderlines rather than simply perpetuating rigid boundaries around the study of conflict and peace. *New Approaches to Conflict Analysis* seeks to uphold the normative commitment of the field's founders yet also recognises that the moral impulse to research is properly part of its subject matter. To these ends, the series is comprised of the highest quality work of scholars drawn from throughout the international academic community, and from a wide range of disciplines within the social sciences.

Human rights and the borders of suffering

The promotion of human rights in international politics

M. ANNE BROWN

Manchester University Press

MANCHESTER AND NEW YORK

distributed exclusively in the USA by Palgrave

Published by Manchester University Press
Oxford Road, Manchester M13 9NR, UK
and Room 400, 175 Fifth Avenue, New York, NY 10010, USA
www.manchesteruniversitypress.co.uk

Distributed exclusively in the USA by
Palgrave, 175 Fifth Avenue, New York NY 10010, USA

Distributed exclusively in Canada by
UBC Press, University of British Columbia, 2029 West Mall,
Vancouver, BC, Canada V6T 1Z2

British Library Cataloguing-in-Publication Data
A catalogue record for this book is available from the British Library

Library of Congress Cataloging-in-Publication Data
A catalog record for this book is available from the Library of Congress

ISBN 13: 978 0 7190 6393 0

First published 2002 by Manchester University Press

First paperback edition 2009

Printed by Lightning Source

CONTENTS

v

Contents

PREFACE

This book grew out of some years spent living and working in China. There I experienced the complexities, challenges, frustrations and richness of communication, affection and work across differences of various kinds. One does not have to go to other places for such experiences, although it helps. But at moments I also stumbled across what was not really recognisable, despite the threads of similie upon which one draws. (I am not referring here to any acts of abuse, which often seem strangely cross-cultural.) These in a sense shocking moments offered a glimpse not so much of another world as of the vast cloudy constructions of one's own collective universe.

While in China I worked for the Australian Government. One of my tasks was to regularly raise matters of human rights with officials in relevant Chinese ministries. These were strange encounters in quite a different way, and some time after returning to Australia I decided to reflect on the questions that they raised for me. This book grew, first as a doctoral dissertation, out of those questions. In some ways it is a continuation of conversations with friends, colleagues and interlocutors that took place in China, Australia and elsewhere – it is at least written as an offering in a larger conversation and a moment in a longer exploration.

Many people have contributed to the process of writing this book. I am particularly grateful to Nancy Viviani for her patient and thoughtful reading of drafts and for her encouragement of my work. I would also like to thank Rob Walker, Andrew Linklater and Ann Kent for their much-valued and insightful advice – as well as Roland Bleiker, Pam Christie, Ian Hunter and Peter Jull for their support and comments. Andrew Linklater and Tim Dunne were particularly kind in regard to advice on publishing, while the University of Queensland allowed me the time to complete the manuscript. I thank, too, all the people at Manchester University Press. And many thanks to my partner Richard Llewellyn, for good humour and support beyond the call of duty.

This book is dedicated to the memory of my father Leslie, whose way of being in the world was perhaps an early inspiration for it.

I

The question of human rights

1

Opening up conceptions of rights

T HIS BOOK'S ARGUMENT takes as its point of departure the question of
how to promote human rights observance in international life. The
whole complex business of international human rights promotion is not
approached here as a particularly 'innocent' enterprise. On the contrary, the
various philosophical and ethical claims of rights promotion, its actual as well
as proclaimed political functions, outcomes and implications – what could be
summed up as the 'virtue' of the enterprise in entirety or in part – can be readily
questioned from many directions. Nevertheless, for this work the aim of questioning human rights promotion is ultimately practical and the standpoint
of the question 'committed'. This commitment, however, is not to advocacy of
the idea of human rights *per se*, when that idea refers to either a universal
transcendental attribute thought to be inherent in individuals or to a socio-
legal attribute considered essential to the proper functioning of states. The
commitment is rather to human rights, and its crucial category of abuse, as an
available language and tool for articulating suffering in a political voice, for
asserting the value and the vulnerability of people, and for grappling with the
on-going question of how we value each other in the complex circumstances of
our different and interwoven lives.

For reasons that will become clearer as the argument progresses, the
understanding of human rights emphasised and explored in this work is
an open-ended one. Rather than aiming for definitional clarity – often a
valuable goal – the concern here is to open out discussion by stepping aside
from some of the categories and models that dominate much promotion
of human rights, particularly in the international arena. Ways of talking
about human rights and systems for defining and implementing them have their
own complex histories and particularity. The argument here, however, proceeds
from the understanding, or the presumption, that questions of human
rights are also part of the much broader context of people's repeated efforts
to work against the systemic infliction of suffering in political life and to

3

create conditions of life that do not turn upon the generation of such suffering.

'Suffering' is used here (though the more common terms 'abuse', 'injury' and 'harm' are also used) as an element of this open-endedness. John Donnelly (1999), a leading theorist of human rights, emphasises the importance of keeping definitions of human rights focused and of recognising that not all suffering is a matter of rights. While agreeing that not all suffering is a matter of rights, or is political, here I want to take a different approach – to question the scope of the term 'human', to draw attention to the shifting range of what is counted as 'political', to offer a reminder that there is suffering that we have not seen and do not see and of the sometimes acutely political nature of this 'not-seeing'. The 'overlooking' of the suffering of others, and the denial that such suffering could claim any part in the dynamics of our collective political orders, has a long, highly respectable and continuing record. All suffering is not political but the line between what is and is not, is not settled and demands attention.

'Suffering' is also an evocative term. Whereas the language of rights and abuse, of claim and obligation, can appear to offer a proper balance of settled equivalences and hoped-for justice, 'suffering' can work as a reminder that the reality of pain, loss and trauma, even within indisputably political exchanges, can pose dilemmas not easily contained within our moral languages (Connolly, 1993).

In the first instance, however, human rights are approached here as particular kinds of conceptual and practical tools, as bundles of social, institutional and legal practices and complex ways of talking and doing for practical, if often general and recurrent, circumstances and purposes. That is, the task of understanding human rights is not presumed to be one of capturing an entity intrinsic to the person, where rights are sometimes cast as markers of transcendental individualism, or of grasping a specific body of rules or capacities intrinsic to all possible forms of civilised political order. As tools that shape us as we shape them, specific practices and models of human rights have their own histories and modes of operation. They are dynamic and evolving, as traditions and languages are. Moreover, as the following chapters argue, particular models of human rights can work differently in different contexts and can not be presumed to be invariably beneficial or emancipatory.

Though not a fixed entity or a categorical imperative, the subject matter of human rights is not therefore understood as lightly malleable. Physical pain, which is frequently the mechanism or imprint of abuse and the means by which dominance is directly or indirectly claimed and enforced, has a powerful, even overpowering, reality. As Elaine Scarry (1985) makes clear, for the sufferer pain is a form of certainty intrinsic to being a body – which for others is transformable into a political weapon. For those who use it as a weapon pain is an assertion of domination which, because never able to be genuinely certain

4

or secured, must be asserted again and again. As an instrument of political organisation, suffering is an obdurate reality, however unwieldy and evasive its boundaries, forms and significance can be.

To draw attention to human rights practices as *tools* is also not to cast them as purely mechanistic, existing only in their specific institutional forms within the state or in inter-state regimes, in laws, regulations or established norms. Despite the crucial significance of these institutional forms, it is argued here that it is part of the practical value of the idea of human rights that it is not quite reducible to them. If the language and practices of human rights are tools, they are fluid, with often difficult and unsettling purposes and potentials. They can work to register and respond to the intolerable,[1] to engage with the deep-rooted patterns of injury that we inflict on each other, and so are as capable of confounding norms of proper action as they are of confirming them. Whether or not notions of human rights are the 'best' tools for such tasks is perhaps beside the point – they are part of what is to hand.

The forms of 'rights talk' most prevalent in human rights promotion and debate, particularly in the domains of interstate politics, take a somewhat different approach. There are indeed many ways of understanding and talking about human rights. In terms of conceptual framework or of particular cases and causes, human rights are routinely a matter for debate by philosophers, legal theorists and practitioners, political theorists, social and political activists, religious figures, state and foreign-policy makers, and so on. They are an arena of both passionate contention and relentless scepticism and, for those of us in liberal democratic traditions and social institutions, they touch on some of our most potent political icons and foundational reference-points – points so foundational that they are elusive and naturalised almost to invisibility. But patterning this quite diverse field is a repeated motif or model or story (albeit with many variations) of the genesis and nature of rights. This is a story of rights that draws on the idea of the social contract, particularly in its Lockean form. It is an account that dominates much of the effort to articulate abuse and to stop or restrain its repetition, particularly in the international arena.

In the following chapters, the argument considers critically this dominant 'story' of rights, touching briefly on some of the other approaches to human rights, or the sub-themes, with which the Lockean account is in practice interwoven. My purpose here, firstly and most importantly, is to step aside from the certainty with which the central organising categories of the dominant accounts of rights, particularly those of the human individual and of the community, are held. This is not because the ways of talking and acting made available by these categories are bankrupt or particularly poor – they have in any event deeply shaped the forms of our political communities. It is rather because these categories are limited while too often claiming to be limitless; they can be destructive while claiming to be liberatory; and they certainly exhaust neither the questions with which abuse confronts us nor the complexity of human life. And, secondly, the purpose of reflecting on the Lockean story is to explore at least some of the effects that our dominant constructions of human rights have had on efforts to work with cases of abuse or suffering as an instrument of political organisation. Questioning categories of the human, the individual and the community is an underlying if sometimes distant theme of this work, – just as it is a challenge thrown out by confrontation with suffering and abuse. Challenging the categories in which so many claims to moral certitude are grounded need not destabilise the basis for working with human rights. A preparedness in the context of practical engagement with human rights issues to question vigorously these categories can enable debate to shake loose from some of the sterile dichotomies (the 'individuality' of the West in contest with the 'communitarianism' of the East, for example) that suffocate exchange on questions of how we live our collective lives. And it may encourage the growth of working rights practices that are more responsive to the forms of suffering, exclusion and exploitation that we both inflict and endure.

As a set of conceptual and practical tools, notions of human rights are a very mixed bag. It is part of many classic accounts of rights (John Donnelly's work is notable here) to say that the idea is essentially a Western and liberal construction; that however universally applicable or otherwise the idea of rights may be argued to be, it was forged and reforged in the struggles and debates of sixteenth–eighteenth-century Europe and the United States – struggles from which the modern liberal state, the modern market economy, the modern individual and the ascendancy of what are seen as 'secular' and 'civic' rather than 'sacred' virtues took shape. Indeed, notions of human rights were one, deeply contentious, thread in the long effort to piece together a political *modus vivendi* well apart from the bloody divisions surrounding the relationship between sovereignty and the various versions of ultimate truth that marked the Wars of Religion. As R. B. J. Walker (1993) has suggested, through the slow elaboration of the sovereign state as the central organising principle, this *modus vivendi* enabled the simultaneous assertion of the state as both a universal, self-consciously secularised form of collective order and progress and a principle of radical differentiation.

Certainly the early modern debates and their elaborations and revisions in the following centuries seam deeply the ways we construct human rights and the sort of tool we make of them. In very general terms, these debates tend to cast concrete struggles for greater freedom from the violent or degrading exercise of power in terms of an abstract tension between conceptions of universality and of differentiation. (The 'Asian Way' debate is one example of this circular dichotomy.) Or categories for recognising and responding to the systemic infliction of suffering are conceptualised in terms of the relationship between the individual as a rational calculator and the state as an ideally neutral and homogenous political space. Or people's diverse desires to live according to their own collective ways, as James Tully (1995) has pointed out, are packed into the confined vocabulary of the independent nation state, as numerous entrenched and bloody separatist conflicts demonstrate.

The past few centuries of struggle, debate and administrative efforts around questions of human rights represent a protean and in many ways rich inheritance. The traditions and language of rights that have slowly taken shape in these on-going debates are called upon both to communicate a potency of aspiration that is in no sense peculiarly Western and also, on a more immediate level, to sustain a significant network of local, national and international practice that is not always reducible to the pressure of Western institutions or 'paradigms from the Centre'. However, as the later chapters of the book argue, the instruments that at least the dominant traditions of rights bequeath, and in particular the categories of 'community' and of 'person' in which understanding of human rights is routinely embedded, have also carried their own forms of damage, their own significant myopias and exclusions. The language of human rights has at some junctures given expression to and been shaped by otherwise silenced voices – of indigenous and colonised peoples, women, alienated minority peoples, urban and rural workers and the propertyless poor; at some junctures it has acted to deepen the deafness which has systematically excluded the voices of those constituted as inferior or as outcasts.

Approaching human rights as tools with significant but ambivalent potential places them as part of a broader conversation, across as well as within cultures and communities, on how to live well together. The significance of this is threefold. First, if we are considering whether and how we might work with a particular area of abuse, it helps to clarify which matters we are trying to pursue and which problems we are trying to make progress with. There are often many agendas at work in human rights promotion, certainly in the international arena. It is important to recognise which of any given set of circumstances is being accorded priority. Second, this more general approach to human rights allows discussion to step aside from the assertion of or the search for certainty that drives much work on human rights. And, third, a reduced preoccupation with certainty can encourage greater openness to the idea, and the task, of listening. For in the effort to shift those social and political practices in which systemic injury is often embedded it can be more valuable to be able to listen than to imagine we always have the answer. Such an approach enables the work of grappling with the concrete reality of abuse and suffering to step back from the assertions of ideological rectitude which often characterise rights talk. This is the core of the 'commitment' of this work and its ultimately practical standpoint.

Despite considerable differences of perspective, much of the theoretical work on human rights is an endeavour to anchor them; to define for them not only particular evolving shapes in particular political traditions but an essential role in a model of the good state, in legal reasoning, in logic, in an established realm of moral or human nature. Rights are often seen as close to the heart of the good life, particularly in liberal democratic perspectives, and yet our understanding of them is troubled by the anxiety 'that we do not as yet have a firm rational basis for pursuing rights and attempting to protect and uphold the rights claims of ourselves and others' (Bernstein, 1993: 19). Thus much theoretical elaboration of human rights is motivated by a search for certainty – the endeavour to shape our understanding of rights according to a rigorous logical imperative from which a systematic analysis of their nature and scope can be extracted, defended and promoted. Understanding the truth about human rights – or about some of the ways in which we can live well together – becomes an endeavour to secure a fixed propositional representation of the nature of things or to define permanently the conditions under which interchange can take place. Armed with a possessable truth, the hope goes, we are in a better position not only to expose without prejudice the hypocrisy and brutality of exploitative or violent practices but to insist on the enlightenment of less perceptive others, and, perhaps most importantly, to protect ourselves against the problems posed by our own collective histories of exploitative or violent choices.

People claiming universality for human rights can mean different things – most simply and perhaps frequently that no one should be subjected to the kind of violence to which many people are relentlessly subjected. But in the more sustained elaborations of human rights the character of the universality that is claimed is commonly defined by the push for epistemic certainty (as the demand for certainty presupposes a certain construction of universality) – by the notion, criticised most notably by Wittgenstein, that epistemological grounding is the only reasonable basis for certainty and that with it one is armed with a truth that will fit any tangle of circumstance. Moreover, in this context, to assert the universality of human rights is generally to claim the (eventual) universal applicability of a particular model of the individual situated in the rational, secular space of the Westphalian state[2] – of progress towards a particular, if broadly conceived, model of social order. That is, the character of the universality and the certainty sought by many approaches to human rights is one embedded in the historical emergence of the modern state.

And yet the effort of recognising and responding to abuse and the social practices in which it is embedded can raise profoundly difficult questions – questions that are liable to shake certainties as much as secure them. The massacres of the twentieth century, for example, of which for Westerners the Holocaust remains emblematic, raise questions that have no clear answers. The recognition of suffering can throw deeply embedded assumptions about the workings of political and social life into critical doubt; it can demand of us that we see our collective or individual selves differently – perhaps as inherently vulnerable, or as potentially complicit in abuse, or both. Hence the resistance of many immigrant states, for example, to acknowledging the persistent violence towards and suffocation of indigenous peoples and cultures which deeply mark, and perhaps made possible, their own history – their own immigrant stories of the struggle and survival of the human spirit and ideals of fairness and opportunity for all. Hence, too, the 'invisibility' of much systemically inflicted injury and the belief, common in many societies, that abuse, as opposed to the 'natural justice' by which the victims inevitably bring their fate upon themselves, is something that only happens somewhere else. Or the confusion which confrontation with sudden overt abuse can call forth – as in the case of the Tiananmen Square killings in 1989, which in some quarters at least elicited a momentary uneasiness that the working of the market may not lead naturally to political propriety. Questions of rights can interrogate the validity of our own collective and individual responses and intuitions across boundaries of culture, context and place.

Apart from the most general of injunctions and orientations and from the accumulated if often ambivalent lessons of our various histories, there are no clear answers to these questions. Indeed, the demand for a general, always intelligible, answer to such questions, for an overarching structure of philosophy or political theory which can guarantee that we will get it all 'right' seems a more than dubious enterprise. A propensity to generate unsettling questions may be central to the potency of ideas of human rights. It may be that such questions neither can nor need be fully resolved on a conceptual level, or that they will not be answered 'once and for all'. We resolve these questions well or badly, and again and again, in our intermittent practical efforts to live well together.

Indeed, one way of understanding the idea of human rights, at its most basic, is as a particular kind of question – the question or the web of questions with which the realisation of serious and systematic harm confronts us. At this most general level, human rights turn on the recognition of the suffering of another or of oneself, and they throw down the challenge of how to act so that this pattern of injury does not repeat itself. That is, they turn on the recognition of or identification with others across the barriers, among others, of suffering, marginalisation and abuse. The power of the idea of the universality of human rights draws strongly on the recognition across cultures that people are profoundly mistreated and that this should not happen. This response to the fact of abuse – persistent if hardly literally universal – is itself an assertion of the value of people, or more simply a recognition of the pain of the victim. And it remains a powerful response despite the fact that the recognition of the intolerable is perhaps rarely, if ever, a total and immediate grasp of the harm that is done and the harm that we do, but a dynamic understanding that learns and revises – with some forms of harm seeming irreducible and others, often those within one's own social matrix, rendered almost invisible.

In this sense working with human rights in practice and in theory is one fertile way of grappling with some fundamental questions – how do we go about valuing each other, not solely as particular social agencies or roles but as people who, like oneself, are vulnerable beings (Fromm, 1960; Turner, 1993)? How do we build and sustain relationships and communities of mutual respect? What is it to live well together and how do we constitute the dynamics of power by which social agency is produced so that we do live well together? The idea of human rights thus addresses questions about power and participation, respect and the ways we construct the boundaries of exclusion and inclusion by which our identities and our communities take shape. The facts that the terms of such questions are not themselves clear and give rise to further questions, and that in the practical circumstances of our lives and at any but the most general level the answers may be not fixed, but shifting and partial, do not undermine their potency.

But if human rights can be understood as a kind of question and a way of working with those questions just posed they can also, and frequently are, understood as a quite definite set of answers – a set of answers that took shape as an element integral to the emergence of the modern liberal state. These two approaches to rights, as question and as answer, need not be mutually exclusive: awareness of both is important, but which of the two is given primacy makes a significant difference. For in this case the answers given, while substantial, do not exhaust the question.

Human rights promotion and the 'foreign analogy'

The approach to human rights taken here is to a large extent shaped by a focus on some of the problems of working with questions of suffering across national borders. By contrast, discussions of human rights set directly in a 'domestic' context or analyses that assume rights to be the jurisdiction of the liberal democratic state tend to place considerable emphasis on the definition and structure of rights – not surprisingly, since within a specific legal jurisdiction some of the fundamental questions raised by the subject can be taken as already settled, and sometimes quite reasonably so. Frequently, however, as the later discussion of the health of Indigenous Australians indicates, such analyses assume or demand a crucial zone of uniformity, whether within the state or more broadly – a realm of public discourse that is declared to be neutral and open to all citizens and others, but one that is repeatedly exclusionary. Moreover, it is easy to overlook or forget these practices of exclusion, simply because within states they have proved relatively effective, so that, for example, marginalisation can appear to be the consequence of the 'natural' characteristics of those marginalised. In international life, however, confronting questions of human rights can underscore the reality of difference (in forms of understanding and practice) – and difference that, in the form of a state, can wield power. Particularly if the intention is to have an effect on a certain practice in a certain place rather than simply to denounce it, response to abuse often involves concrete engagement with other forms of social practice in other political and legal jurisdictions. Thus, in an inversion of the domestic analogy, working with human rights in international life brings to the foreground the need to take difference seriously – something that is arguably essential to the ways we understand human rights more generally.

There are, of course, well-established ways of handling difference in international life. The formal conception of the state system according to the principles of Westphalian order – particularly that of non-interference in the sovereign affairs of another state – is itself one set of ways of conceptualising and containing diversity. The traditional realist image of states as billiard balls, albeit of many colours, points vividly to what remains a dominant approach to difference in international life – that is, homogeneity more or less within states and difference among them, while all are subject to the same immutable dynamics of the struggle for survival and power (Tully, 1995: 10). In regard to human rights, then, difference may be seen as reason enough to reject the possibility of responding to forms of injury across borders. Here the discontinuity of the domestic political and legal jurisdiction between states is understood as paramount, and efforts to respond to abuse as threatening principles of non-interference, or (paradoxically) as threatening the vast welter of cross-border dealings which constitute the rhythms of contemporary life. Or, conversely and most powerfully, dealing with difference in the context of international human rights issues can be reduced to a confrontation between the evil empire and the forces of light.

As is discussed further in chapter 3, the assertion of difference between states but homogeneity within them establishes the billiard ball principles of identity around which the universalist versus relativist debate endlessly turns. It thus defines the standard cultural relativist defence by dominant political groups of their power to define the social, political and cultural realities within their state. But as later discussions in this text make clear, states (and cultures) are not homogenous. Thus engaging with human rights issues across borders draws attention to the need to work with diversity not only between but within states. Moreover, while borders are a blunt statement of difference and jurisdictional discontinuity, the corollary of this is that they are constantly crossed in myriad ways. They are a working part of networks of interaction, they are intersected by various patterns of relationship and solidarity (ethnic, cultural, religious, familial, commercial and so on), and as a statement of boundary and sovereignty are less a condition of autarchy than of membership of complex systems of state interaction.

Or difference can be downplayed or ignored by efforts at rights promotion internationally. It can be assumed that human rights are universally intrinsic to the person and that therefore difference is secondary or even a camouflage – here, however, the person who is the locus of rights is often constituted from across a reasonably specific and narrow set of characteristics, as discussed in chapter 2. Or, more commonly, it can be assumed that whether or not human rights are intrinsically universal, they are part of the process of modernisation and of the evolution and expansion of the market that will gradually eradicate all but, again, a secondary difference. Or notions of human rights can be argued to be essentially specific to the liberal democratic state as epitomised by Western Europe and the English-speaking nations, but that this form of government is evidently the best, thus casting the problem as one of whether or how to ensure its reduplication in all countries.

When difference is downplayed the promotion of human rights in the international domain is approached like the delivery of a message – a message concerning known and established truths that may nevertheless require the use of significant pressure on the part of those delivering it. The message is, almost without exception, assumed to be one from 'us' to 'them', from West to East and North to South, from Athens to Persia. But, as was suggested earlier, questions of human rights do not simply ask us whether we should or how we can extend the rights observance in 'this world' here to 'that world' there. Rather, trying to respond effectively to abuse in another, as well as our own, place raises questions about what we mean by 'community' and 'identity', and how we work with and across difference. Approaching response to abuse as essentially the delivery of a message is mistaken in a number of ways. It is to assume, at least for a moment, not only that our liberal democratic traditions have valuable, if also profoundly mixed, historical experience and bodies of practice on the question of how to live together without generating significant systemic infliction of injury, but that these traditions have resolved such matters in an almost final form. It is to overlook the reality that 'this world' also generates abuse at home and abroad. It is to assume that the dominant models of rights and their categories of 'human' and 'community' represent the only or the superior forms within which these questions can be approached and that theories of liberal democracy are the only viable basis for a human rights practice. Most importantly, it is to assume that we have little or nothing to learn from others. And the message model of human rights promotion is mistaken not only in these substantive ways, but in its applicability: it is only in quite particular and limited circumstances that telling people across borders of state and other forms of difference what to do, even with some force, is an effective way of changing social practice.

This, then, is the force deriving from an understanding of human rights as open-ended. If notions of rights operate as a way of identifying and working with patterns of injury, of asking questions and sometimes constructing answers about how to build political community that does not turn on such injury as a basis of political organisation or the assertion of power, but, to put it positively, turns rather on relationships of mutual respect, then it is important to recollect that no one culture, society or tradition of thought has a monopoly on how to cast and pursue these purposes. Working with and debate about human rights are parts of a conversation between and within cultures and communities, including those very particular collectivities that are states. A response to injury and to the questions it raises is an act of communication. To continue the metaphor of conversation, effective communication on human rights can not be simply the delivery of a message, although messages may at times be part of the exchange; it is an activity requiring and creating mutual understanding, and which leaves no participant entirely unchanged. Such communication is not a fixed or permanent achievement but an on-going engagement. Thus, no matter how resourceful the heterogeneous body of perceptions, institutional forms and practices that make up specifically Western liberal traditions of human rights can be as models of participative civility, they do not represent a final, sufficient or exhaustive truth but are part of a dynamic exchange. The 'answer' to particular occurrences of abuse, over what are sometimes the immensely slow processes in which social change takes place, emerges – or not – through the mutuality of communication.

This approach may appear at best romantic in the face of the pressing and grave violence of much abuse. A forceful response may be appropriate, on the rare occasions a forceful response is to hand, but it is likely to be only a temporary measure or part of a broader response. Outpourings of violence do not come from nowhere: systemic patterns of abuse are embedded in often complex knots of social practice – in people's collective construction of themselves and their network of relationships, identities, tasks and values. Abuse is not limited to the sheer physical act (the killing, the moment of torture or attack or exclusion from an essential activity) but is frequently made possible by the life practices and social institutions that in large part shape people's participation and identities within the communities that they at once inhabit and construct. Abuse is thus part of a positive (if violent or humiliating) construction of community. To shift such patterns may in many cases require persistent effort across a number of lines of attack over a considerable period of time; that is, it may require a substantive long-term engagement in the tasks of social change – the kind of engagement that we might take for granted in other commercial, political or social interactions.

The recognition of difference and the need for engagement with and communication across it that is highlighted by efforts to promote rights practices in

13

international life can be applied to discussion of human rights in a domestic context. Working across borders can show us something of diversity, but diversity is not limited to or even epitomised by international borders. Nor are borders the assertion of unbreachable differences between internally homogenous cultures or states, as cultural relativist arguments suggest, or a sign of difference as necessarily exotic. Rather, the 'foreign analogy' is a reminder that boundaries and differences, and efforts to make some sense across them, are mundane realities within societies, cultures and states as well as between them. This approach builds on the tradition, deeply entrenched in liberal perspectives, of understanding rights as devices for enabling and defining participation. However, as James Tully (1995: 183) argues in regard to contemporary constitutionalism, a more open and dynamic sense of participation is needed – one that is able to listen to diverse voices and open to the practical exchange of 'limited and complementary stories'.

Indeed, lines of difference are perhaps the most common and probably the fundamental site of abuse. It seems likely that grave abuse in particular is nearly always inflicted across a deep division – of race, gender, class, belief – divisions that are significant enough to 'dehumanise' or to place those who bear the injury into a realm of non-person and outside the circle of possible empathy. Or, if they do not fit into a ready-made category of otherness, they can be construed as deficient in or as the enemy of whatever is taken to be the crucial identifying moment of humanity. Moreover, since people often display a propensity to cross the barrier, the act of abuse is itself an effort to entrench division between victim and other – as Elaine Scarry (1985) and David Grossman (1995) have argued. It is an endeavour to assert an ultimate difference of power, and a demand that any propensity to identify with the pain or predicament of another be overridden in this arrogantly declared and frightening gulf. Far from being limited to the extreme moments of torture, however, the process of division may be entirely routine and scarcely visible, as, for example, Jane Elliott's race discrimination exercises make plain.[3]

As Fromm (1977), Scarry (1985) and Grossman (1995) have in quite different ways explored in their discussions of torture and war, the relationship between the infliction of extreme pain on another and the exclusion of that person from the referential world of interchange, of self and other, is powerful. The ultimate exclusion of the person not just from life but from language, exchange and personhood by 'breaking him or her down' is not merely an additional consequence but one of the crucial objects of torture. It is an extreme but pervasive form of the organisation of political community and the assertion of power through the infliction of suffering. This dynamic of asserting one's own collective reality and potency on the destruction, pain, exploitation and exclusion of others may be at the heart of abuse of human rights. If abuse is a fundamental and constitutive act of exclusion, the effective recognition of

14

human rights may turn upon people's mutual acceptance of each other as part of the world of exchange and communication – to move, in Patricia William's words, from 'human body to social being' (quoted in Brown, 1995: 96).

The notion of *human* rights can be understood as a demand or a reminder of the need to find some way across the division around which the particular injury in question is being generated, sufficiently at least to arrest or restrain the abuse. This is not to suggest, however, that if a way across a particular gulf becomes plain one arrives at a permanent territory of the human, or that there is any territory of the human. The category of the human is deeply paradoxical, appearing with the power of both innocent description and moral norm. Once the category settles and acquires stable content it frequently operates as an exclusionary mechanism patrolling the divisions between self and alien, addressed above, while at the same time appearing to maintain reference to an unimpeded universality. This enables a more powerful, or insidious, form of exclusion. As Richard Rorty comments in one of the numerous discussions of this very common phenomenon, the Serbs carrying out 'ethnic cleansing' 'take themselves to be acting in the interest of true humanity by purifying the world of pseudo-humanity'. Meanwhile '[w]e in the safe rich democracies feel about the Serbian torturers and rapists as they feel about their Muslim victims: They are more like animals than like us' (1993: 112, 113).

Human rights talk is deeply imbued with this paradoxical sense of the 'human'. On the one hand, it calls to include all people simply by virtue of their humanness. On the other hand, rights talk becomes easily trapped into the moment of judgement – in identifying and condemning the perpetrator and the clean confronting the unclean. The confrontation of abuse can have, perhaps always has, great value in the dynamics of change: the naming of the destruction, the attribution of responsibility, even if in parts mixed, may be an essential step in moving past a climate of violence. Such, at least, is indicated by the response of relatives of many of those killed during the apartheid regime to the proceedings of South Africa's Truth and Reconciliation Commission. In a process still far from being played out, that Commission has endeavoured to step back from the dynamics of condemnation. While it has its own moment, condemnation leaves untouched the problem of recreating social relationships and identities in ways that do not simply recycle the abuse. Moreover condemnation can obscure the difficult reality that the perpetrators are as 'human' – as much like us – as the victims, and that today's victims can be tomorrow's perpetrators, and vice versa. Indeed, the act of condemning can itself be an effort to expel the perpetrators from the realm of the human and the possibility of exchange – a potentially dangerous though much-repeated move, if distinguishing 'ourselves from borderline cases' is indeed a fundamental element characterising abuse.

Within international politics, and according to the Westphalian order, a distinction, indeed a complex opposition, is commonly drawn between the proper domain of politics and that of ethics, with human rights standardly classed with ethics. Questions of human rights are overtly ethical, in that they are concerned with the perennial questions with which abuse confronts us – with responding to the patterns of harm that we inflict on one another and with how to live, in the concrete circumstances of our collective and individual lives, in ways that do not require such patterns of harm. This is to draw on Indonesian poet and journalist Goenawan Mohamad's suggestion that a sense of rights starts with the face of the victim (1995). It does not start, that is and according to this understanding, with a theory of a fixed transcendental reality or of the state but from some movement towards and identification with the victim. Thus questions of rights are not necessarily ethical in the narrow and epistemologically driven sense of ethics that demands anchorage in a definitive ground of substantive, propositional truths or the actualisation of an idealist agenda. Questions of rights do not stand in opposition to, or take priority over, the mundane dynamics of politics, power and practicability but are part of the same knot of problems – 'the conduct of living and the living, is itself already ethical' (Gordon, 1991: 8).

This argument does not aspire to be visionary. Visions, whether of better futures or of permanent truths, can offer valuable energy; they can capture or inspire movements – most importantly, they can suggest to people that there are other ways of looking at things. However, if one of our senses is to be given precedence as a metaphor for understanding here it is listening, or a more general attentiveness to the forest of voices, rather than sight and its traditional association with an abstract grasp of crisp and timeless truths. As a culture we tend to focus on sight as a metaphor for knowledge and understanding: we see through to underlying truth or reality, envisage the future, seek new theoretical visions, and so on. Moreover, as a literate culture we associate sight with knowledge through the written word. Walter Ong's reflections (1982) are instructive here. 'Writing fosters abstractions that disengage knowledge from the arena where human beings struggle with one another. It separates the knower from the known' (44). 'Whereas sight situates the observer outside what he views, at a distance, sound pours into the hearer . . . [Vision] comes to a human being from one direction at a time . . . A typical visual ideal is clarity and distinctness . . . The auditory ideal, by contrast, is . . . a putting together' (72). 'For oral cultures, the cosmos is an ongoing event' (73). Sound is essentially evanescent and is sensed as such; vision 'favours immobility' (33). Metaphors of listening may assist more interactive, more open and less bordered ways of enacting knowing. Rights are traditionally associated with the activity of claiming, but they could be equally associated with listening. If notions of human rights and rights more generally are a way of recognising and taking part in the

16

on-going interchange and negotiation among self and other, of requiring that one be properly heard, then they demand not only the ability and 'space' to claim participation, but also the ability and willingness to accord others attention.

However valuable models of human rights may be, we can carry to them only the understanding we develop, through application, in the more or less mundane obscurity of our own backyards. Following Robert Cox's notable critique, criticism is often made of the 'problem-solving approach' adopted in much international relations or political theory.[4] Indeed, as Cox made clear, 'problem solving' can merely be a code-word for recycling problems, moving them from one beat to the next, without addressing their deeper causes. But if a concrete problem is actually resolved, the world changes a little and the field of possibilities, at once practical and theoretical, shifts. It may be worth treating with a little caution efforts to place a higher value on theory and its emancipatory potentials (with its promise of the capture of a truth behind mere activity) over people's efforts to shift the conditions that are to hand. Such work carries its own emancipatory possibilities. While the approach taken here is certainly not to attempt to 'solve' the case studies it considers, it nevertheless takes as its model the possibility of incremental work across many fields that can shift abuse by reconstituting fundamental social relationships.

The following two chapters explore some of the theoretical questions that have been touched upon in this introduction. Chapter 2 considers the Lockean account of human rights, as a leading model in international rights promotional activities, focusing on its construction of the categories 'human' and 'community'. Discussion then moves, rather briefly, to some of the dominant institutionalised ways of dealing with human rights made possible or illuminated by certain major theoretical approaches to international politics. Chapter 3 addresses more directly the universalist versus relativist debate which so characterises contemporary international discussion of human rights issues. In doing so, the chapter touches on the writings of some of the more critical analysts of ethics in international life, although essentially within the context of the debate on the nature of the grounds of rights.

Part II is a consideration of three case studies: the Tiananmen Square massacre of 1989; East Timor; and Australian Aboriginal health. The case studies were not chosen as examplary of the arguments put forward here – indeed in many respects they challenge those arguments. All, in their own way, are high-profile issues internationally or on a national stage, referred to repeatedly by the media in terms ranging from bell-like clarity (Tiananmen) to moral ambiguity and political confusion (Indigenous Australians). All occupy public as well as specialist imaginations. The case studies do not draw on original research or new empirical insights – this is not the nature of the argument. As well as drawing on the theoretical discussions of chapters 2 and 3, however, the case studies bring forth their own pattern of reflections. In particular, questions of citizenship rights mark all case studies, but are explicitly engaged in the examination of Indigenous Australian health. The conclusion endeavours to draw together more clearly the main themes to emerge from the earlier discussions and to indicate some of the contributions of this approach to a working human rights practice.

Something that this argument sets out to do, but perhaps does not always succeed in doing, is to be critical of certain streams of liberalism and modernity, without slipping into the position of rejecting them out of hand – in their totality as it were, as if they had a totality. 'Liberalism' is a broad term covering a complex range of traditions and debates while 'modernity' is at least as slippery. But, even more importantly, liberalism refers to a raft of social, political and economic practices, experiments and modes of government that grew out of particular historical circumstances, in response to particular problems and which are not necessarily reducible to theories of liberalism. The modern liberal state is 'an historically constituted form of community, one that has been subject to considerable variation across time and space' (Walker, 1993: 77). At the same time the effects of certain models and motifs – 'human', 'community' – are pervasive and powerful, and can be traced. This is the significance of using the language of tools and mechanisms. What is sought here, if not always found, is a sufficient distance to allow an appreciation of the tools we have to hand, and that avoids either a condemnation or an embrace of those tools, thereby enabling us to be more attentive to how well or how badly they may be working in the circumstances faced.

NOTES

1 'The primary ground for ethical reflection no doubt remains a capacity to identify the intolerable' (Walker, 1993: 52).
2 References to the Westphalian state system in this text are in line with usage in the study of international politics, where the phrase refers broadly to certain aspects of the modern state system, rather than with the tighter definitions more common to the study of history.
3 Jane Elliott has been running race discrimination exercises, mainly in the US, since the 1960s. The exercises turn on the attribution of identity – of capacity and incapacity – on the basis of a single physical characteristic.
4 Robert Cox draws a distinction between critical theory and 'problem-solving' theory, which 'takes the world as it finds it' and sets out to make already given relationships and institutions 'work smoothly by dealing effectively with particular sources of trouble'. By contrast, critical theory 'is directed towards an appraisal of the very framework of action . . . which problem-solving theory accepts as its parameters' (1981: 128f.).

2

The construction of human rights: dominant approaches

T HE IDEA OF human rights covers a complex and fragmentary terrain. As R. J. Vincent comments near the beginning of his work on human rights in international relations, 'human rights' is a readily used term that has become a 'staple of world politics', the meaning of which is by no means self-evident (1986: 7). After glossing the term as the 'idea that humans have rights' (1986: 7) – a deceptively simple approach – Vincent notes that this is a profoundly contested territory, philosophically as well as politically. This is not surprising, as notions of human rights draw indirectly or directly on some of our most deeply embedded presumptions and reference-points – for those of us in liberal democracies, particularly those cosmologies concerning the nature of the person and of political community. Questions about and concepts of the human as individual, of what is right, the state, justice, freedom, equality, and so on, flicker like a constellation of stars just off the edge of our fields of analysis – fading in and out, holding much, promising or claimed as anchorage, yet elusive and obscure. For many, the assertion of human rights has become a kind of repository of secular virtue – a declaration of the sacred in the absence of the divine. In the Western liberal democracies, human rights are claimed as political home or as a principal 'instrument of struggle' by the libertarian right, by liberals of various persuasions, by socialists who feel the traditional socialist agenda has been overtaken by events and by 'post-liberal democrats'. To declare in a debate that the matter at hand involves rights can be to 'trump' discussion, drawing the limits beyond which exchange may not go, in a way that Ronald Dworkin (1977, 1984) probably did not intend. The language of rights thus carries great power while being potentially deeply divided against itself.

The purpose of this chapter is to draw attention to some of the orders of thought that dominate human rights promotion and shape the meaning of this powerful, complex and in some ways contradictory tool of rights and 'rights talk'. In particular, I want to underline the limitations of these orders of thought, the narrowness of some of their central categories and the disfiguring consequences of these limitations. This does not mean, however, that they are understood as having nothing to offer. As James Tully (1995) and Wendy Brown (1995), among others, have pointed out, the histories of and the tools offered by the dominant, broadly liberal, political configurations have been both eman-cipatory and oppressive. The question is, which potential is in play in the cir-cumstances at hand? Nor am I suggesting that we simply step aside altogether (even if we wanted to) from the more fundamental trainings and reference-points that constitute modern political life and in which notions of rights are embedded, although surely some debates and motifs are almost worn through. Rather, the effort to explore some of the general themes that seam much rights talk in world politics is offered as a basis for a more reflective understanding of what we might be trying to do when we promote rights – an understanding that is cognisant of both the value and the limitations of the tools we bring to the complexity and immediacy of deeply entrenched injury. Among its other effects, greater critical awareness can enable us to be more open to other experiences, other tools.

This chapter divides roughly into two parts. The first part introduces briefly the polarity of universalism and relativism that structures much of what it is possible to say on human rights – chapter 3 explores this theme further. The chapter then looks at the story of the Lockean social contract, as one still potent myth of the origin for human rights and more broadly as a mechanism for con-ceptualising the human political community and ethics in the liberal state. The adequacy of these constructions for responding to the complexity of systemic infliction of injury is questioned. The second half of the chapter considers briefly the dominant theoretical accounts of international politics that have formed a central platform for the debate and, to some extent, for practice regarding rights in the international arena. Constructions of politics 'inside' and 'outside' the state (to use R. B. J. Walker's 1993 phrase) are interlocking, and together they articulate a range of accounts of ethical possibility in contemporary life. The dominant notions of rights provide models of the state as much as they make claims regarding the integrity and autonomy of individuals. And questions of rights in international relations quickly become matters of whether or not and how to ensure that key elements of this configuration of state and individual – and, to a shifting extent, this model of the state – pertain in all states. This discussion points to the aridity of the ways for conceptualising ethical con-cerns in international life made available by the dominant accounts, which remain significantly characterised by the see-sawing polarity of idealism and realism. The discussion of Lockean contractarianism is not an effort to explore the history of the emergence of rights practices or of notions of human rights, although reference is made to that history. Nor is the considerable body of multilateral practice on human rights, particularly United Nations and international legal practice, analysed in any detail.

We commonly grasp human rights issues in terms of a series of deeply entrenched oppositions, most stridently between assertions of universal, or absolute, values and forms of cultural or communitarian relativism, between a search for something to be regarded as essentially human or an irreducible morality – a universal humanity – and an appreciation of the ambiguous tissue of local realities, the value of the particularities of community life. But this polarisation can distort the problems raised by human rights in ways that leave them irresolvable and arid. Moreover its effect is to maintain a dichotomy that feeds directly into states' competing assertions of territoriality and power and into the passions and suspicions of clashing nationalisms – to tie rights even more deeply to arenas of political contention in a way that only hinders work on specific problems of abuse.

To work with the questions raised by rights only within a polarisation of absolute and relative is to fix them within a quite particular and limited framework. For some, to reject the possibility of a definitive answer to questions about how to live well together – to reject the motif of the universal – is an assertion of relativism and therefore a declaration of non-interference or despair in the face of violence and debilitation. For others, who reject anything that might appeal to a seemingly transcendent category such as 'the human', any talk of human rights, beyond the positive rights of citizens, is incoherent or fanatical. This is to deny the persistent reality of working across boundaries – the boundaries of states and legal systems, of communities, of understanding, of supposedly coherent conceptual frameworks. It is to see fences as having only their self-proclaimed function and not, as Wittgenstein remarked, many purposes (1978: para 499).

To consider what we might mean by 'human rights' involves questioning the broad conceptions of 'the human' and of 'political community' that underpin approaches to rights. The purpose of questioning our assumptions is threefold. First, to draw attention to the patterns of exclusion that constitute the dominant figures of universal and human. Second, to draw attention to the truly limited nature of our grasp in practice of those values that form the references for human rights, whether emancipation and freedom, or compassion and justice. And, third, to point to the dynamic and open-ended nature of understanding in general. The significance of being attentive to the partiality of one's understanding is that such attentiveness can shift, radically or subtly, the way we go about working with particular issues. In particular, one is more likely to be open to a sense of the processes and of the mutuality involved in arriving at understanding – in this case, of the constitution of community and person. One is more likely to listen.

To grasp understanding as interactive may be peculiarly relevant to working with human rights abuses, since their resolution over the long term commonly involves a reconstitution of community and the relationships that comprise it. Moreover, talking about rights often operates as a way of drawing connections or of identifying threads of commonality across boundaries – whether they be national boundaries or ethnic, cultural or economic divisions. That is, it involves a process of thinking about community differently, seeing a connection, recognising some element of 'ourselves' and so disturbing and re-opening 'ourselves'. The discussion of Australian Aboriginal health issues in chapter 6 provides one example of the significance of the process of redefining and renegotiating community to progress on human rights.

Our own contemporary senses of 'the human', of 'the subject' and of 'community', are inevitably embedded in particular, if broad, complex and evolving histories. These understandings of what it is to be human are part of the stuff from which we make our lives and from which we are made – the dynamics of power, the economic formations, our experience of material and natural realities, what we deem to be valuable, what we do not see. Our approaches to human rights are shaped by these processes, often competing or simply discontinuous, of valuing or counting the human. The following discussion looks at aspects of those senses of 'the human', and also at the scope of our duties or responsibilities to each other, generated by what is arguably our dominant model of human rights, that of Lockean contractarianism.

However, it is important to emphasise here that human rights practices are not reducible to contractarianism, while the history of the notions and the practices of rights is complex and varied. In parts of Europe systems of rights, although not of *human* rights, constituted mechanisms for formulating social relations some centuries before the emergence of contract theories. Specific legally enshrined protections or claims that are now strongly identified with respect for human rights are traceable to the evolution of certain such rights practices and modes of governance (*habeas corpus* is perhaps the most famous Anglo-Saxon example) at least as much to later liberal notions of 'human' rights *per se*. The institutions that now serve as pillars of the liberal democratic state (such as the courts system) are not necessarily liberal in origin, and have long and, of course, on-going histories, predating contractarianism and varying across regions. In contemporary practice, rights traditions and means of rights promotion prevalent in parts of Europe rely less on Lockean (or comparable) motifs than is the norm in the English-speaking world. Nevertheless, these motifs remain pervasive and significant.

Moreover notions of human rights are frequently understood as originating, historically and philosophically, not in the social contract but in earlier traditions of natural law.[1] Chris Brown (1999) considers that all notions of universal human rights must presuppose some idea of natural law (although some scholars reject this attribution, e.g. Minogue 1989, Donnelly 1989). At the least, natural law doctrines are to be seen as offering human rights advocates some of their principal themes – the inherent value of the person and the

22

universality of underlying moral truth, even if they are classically obligation-rather than rights-based cosmologies. Lockean contractarianism can itself be regarded as a subcategory of natural law, but also as constituting a radical break with these already heterogeneous traditions. The notion of the rational and in some cases transcendent individual standing outside society, discussed in the following section, was predicated on a virtual revolution in the fundamental categories of understanding which made up the earlier Thomistic approaches. This figure represented a rationalist break with the world where all dimensions, including visible and invisible orders, were understood to be interwoven in immanent as well as transcendent patterns of meaning (Tully, 1991).

Contemporary variations on natural law traditions may also have more in common with and be more open to the social, political and religious traditions of non-Western societies than social contract theory. They may, for example, suggest a variety of ways of constituting 'universality', from the dogmatisms often favoured by the magisterium (which guards doctrinal purity within the Catholic Church) to the fluid, interactive and contextual approaches that flow from an emphasis on a shared 'affective inclination towards the whole concrete human good' (Kelly, 1993: 209). This may be precisely what leads to the rejection of natural law theories as sources of human rights practice by theorists such as John Donnelly (1989) or Eugene Kamenka (1978), who (quite accurately) consider all the varied 'traditional' approaches to political ethics to be offering not conceptualisations of human rights – when these are limited to the articulation of the relationship between individual and state – but concepts of human dignity, justice and the recognition of suffering. But this may be to retreat into a kind of rights fundamentalism that assumes that there is one and one only form underpinning practices of mutual respect within political community which emerged in seventeenth-century Western Europe and America and which for the good of all must be systematically applied to the rest of the globe.

In addition to these various sources of human rights, both the theory and practice of rights promoted by the liberal democracies also draw strongly on utilitarianism. Unlike contractarianism, utilitarianism is not a rights-based theory. But it can nevertheless 'deal with' rights, offering a pragmatic and more 'technocratic' approach that is in some ways at odds with the language of fundamental social principle and the more evocative rhetoric of the social contract. Whereas the contract theories speak of *human* rights, in the strong forms appealing directly to a figure of the universal human being as the ground of rights, utilitarianism focuses more readily on rights of the citizen and takes conventional and positive rights as the model from which assertions of moral or non-positive rights may be derived. Contractarianism and contemporary utilitarianism are therefore often regarded as offering opposing accounts of liberal society (e.g. Dworkin, 1977). But as currents of liberalism essentially occupied with questions of the proper relationship between the individual as citizen and the state, utilitarianism and contractarianism also share much in common and in practice work often in tandem. Standard diplomatic treatment of the Universal Declaration of Human Rights (1948) gives some indication of this practical complementarity between contractarian and utilitarian approaches to rights. The language of the Universal Declaration is contractarian. The more frequent justification within UN and national policy-making bodies for upholding the rights standards set out in the Universal Declaration, however, is that most states have signed it, this signatory process being part of the essential procedures for establishing reasonable parameters of international order. The fund of imagery is contractarian while the language of operational power is utilitarian. Discussion here will focus on the social contract, as it proposes the crucial imagery of rights, but will later touch on utilitarian approaches to rights as they feature in international politics.

The social contract

Social contract theories developed from Protestant natural law schools in response to the on-going crisis of the wars of religion and the impact of the scientific and economic revolutions of the Enlightenment upon the fundamental concepts of the human, the social and knowledge. The universalist structures and claims of medieval Christendom fragmented into savage religious wars contained eventually by a number of treaties, most famously the Peace of Westphalia in 1648. From these treaties and compromises the Westphalian system of individual sovereign powers, which in principle recognised no power above their own purview, gradually emerged. It would seem a mistake, however, to think that the universality of Christendom had simply given way to the particularism of Westphalia. The Westphalian state system is perhaps better understood as a reworking of the relationship between universal and particular (e.g. see Walker, 1993). The seventeenth-century Protestant schools were preoccupied with the problems posed by the religious wars – how to have stable political community in the face of unrelenting religious difference coupled with the pursuit of moral or religious uniformity. They sought to elaborate a 'science of morality' independent or tolerant of the different confessions. This 'science', naturally concerned with questions of viable community, became an exploration of the conditions for and management of proper or enlightened states.

Social contract theories (of which there was a range) offered a reconceptualisation of the universal, away from being located in a 'spiritual' and all-encompassing community of mankind, dogmatically interpreted by competing Churches, to a mechanism which related the new figure of everyman to a bounded and sovereign political community. This relationship, it was hoped, represented 'the discovery at last of the proper basis of social and political life' and a desperately sought 'rational solution to all human conflict' (Minogue, 1989: 6). Recasting the universal in terms of the relationship between individual and state legitimised, in the moral codes of the time, the move away from the destructiveness of a long evangelical war between competing claims to ultimate truth and offered a remarkably effective means of resolving the dilemmas of the time. At least as important, it also established the zone of the 'secular' as the proper sphere of political life and envisaged the possibility of a secular, rational and knowable truth and a secular, rational and knowable ethics. In establishing the zone of the secular, this construction of individual and state radically redefined the boundaries and the place of the 'spiritual' or metaphysical. Moreover, while the particularism of the state was asserted in the face of universalist claims to spiritual, and thus under Christendom temporal, power, the conditions for the proper state, the 'science of morality' and secular truth became in different ways potential new grounds for universalist claims.

Not all theories of the social contract furnish a strong case for rights, however. Of the seventeenth-century theories, the Hobbesian social contract is an argument for absolutist government in which people barter all their rights (except that of self-defence) in the state of nature in return for the protection of the sovereign (Hobbes, 1968). And Pufendorf, for example, sought to distinguish not so much the rights of man but those social duties 'which render him capable of society (*sociabilis*) with other men' (Tully, 1991: xxiii).

It is the Lockean version of the social contract that is the theory of social relations most closely associated with ideas of human rights. This reflects partly the nature of Locke's arguments (particularly in *The Two Treatises on Civil Government*) and partly the historical consequences of the fact that these arguments had such a powerful impact in the American colonies and France. The following discussion, then, addresses aspects of Lockean contractarianism, not in terms of a history of seventeenth-century thought or state practice but as a still powerful way of imagining political relationships. Lockean contractarianism provides a fundamental point of reference for contemporary theoretical departures concerning rights, as in the writings for example of John Rawls, Ronald Dworkin or John Donnelly. But it appears also to be a vein of political imagination at work in the US foreign policy community and to a lesser extent similar circles in other Western states. Arguably, it acts as a pervasive cosmology and set of trainings for constructing notions of the state and the person. This does not mean, however, that the Lockean social contract is always underpinning Western understandings of human rights issues, or that the specific operation of specific rights practices can be simply 'read off' or reduced to the Lockean story. Nevertheless, it is to propose that Lockean contractarianism provides a persistent, powerful and deeply embedded set of conceptual linkages for

Western constructions of human rights and ideals and the rhetoric of political community.

The social contract is conceptualised as a narrative[2] addressing the proper basis and form of rule. To briefly recapitulate: the human person, understood as 'man', exists originally in a state of nature, that is, a condition of existence before entry into political community. In the state of nature relationships belong either to the family, to women and children or to the domain of sustenance, wealth creation and spontaneous association ('civil society'), and are conceived as 'natural' or intrinsic. The state of nature is a state of perfect freedom. But this freedom is marred by the threat of violence to person and property and (in Locke's account) by the lack of an impartial mechanism for judging crime and adjudicating disputes. Insecurity in man's natural relations thus creates a need to establish an order beyond the pattern of nature. In what became a major theme for certain streams in later sociology, man is incomplete in nature and must complete himself, making the state distinct from, yet necessitated by and logically founded upon nature. So natural subjects agree to join together to establish a form of rule which will provide security and just judgement of crimes and conflict. The state thus emerges from, and is answerable to, civil society as the zone of natural relations between men. This is the contract – not a directly 'divine' act of creation but a human act of rational choice and negotiation whereby man exchanges some degree of his natural freedom for a government that guarantees reasonable security.

The political society that emerges from this negotiation represents the proper or essential ordering of power – an ordering which is deemed to take place on the basis of the reason and freedom of the rational subject in the state of nature. Societies may vary in particulars, but the underlying logic of the story by which particular political orders are constituted and bound to the subject does not vary. For Locke (here in sharp contrast to Hobbes), any society which is not constituted as the product of and as *answerable to* the union of rational persons is not truly a political society but merely a degenerated state of nature. For Locke, then, absolute government (such as Hobbes advocated), in which all are subject to the will of one without the protection of institutions of impartial justice, is neither the state of nature nor true political society, but is a degraded nature where people are neither free nor secure. Thus, although political organisation is not intrinsic to the state of nature, one form of political organisation, the liberal state, constitutes the rational, universal and 'natural' progression from nature itself.

It has often been observed that the historical emergence (and endurance) of the social contract as a powerful normative and explanatory metaphor for civil life is closely tied to the rise of the middle classes and the revolutions in social and political structures that accompanied the development of capitalism. The idea of the social contract was a vital lever in the reconceptualisation of knowledge and authority that constituted the figure of Enlightenment man; its account of political life was intimately bound to the development of the modern state, by providing a mechanism that shifted the ultimate source of authority for government from God to an abstract 'man'. Through its elaboration of the essentially new categories of nature, society and the individual, it was indirectly part of the movement away from the belief that knowledge of the one creation was accessible through spiritual intuition mediated by the Church, to a belief that man was an observer of a segmented universe, knowledge of which was available through observation and experience. In the same fashion the story of the contract has played a seminal role in delineating at least one ideal form of the modern subject, a form that fashions assumptions across a chequerboard of disciplines and institutional practices.

The social contract imagines an idealised subject who is essentially prior to political community, who enters fully formed into the contract that establishes the state, who is motivated by the rational recognition of fundamental self-interest, and who is naturally equipped to take part in the negotiation and bartering that constitute the contract. This metaphor is rich in implications. The subject is individual, autonomous and disembedded from social context. His grasp of interest, value and rationality is cast as prior to and independent of questions of power and political community and thus is arguably prior to the fabric in which one learns one's self. His ability to project and negotiate his self-interest exists independently of socio-political or psychological formation. His relationships with others, at least in the zone of public life, are instrumental. His relationship to himself, the relationship that makes possible the initial exchange of absolute freedom for relative security, is also to a significant extent instrumental. At the same time, he is a heroic figure who straddles the two realms of nature and society, encapsulating the particular within the universal. He is a quasi-divine subject in a Newtonian universe, creating by will and beyond the contingencies of circumstance or mutuality. Compared to, for example, an understanding of the individual as having a potential for acting autonomously within the interplay of social relationships and a fluid world of meaning, this is a radical assertion of individuality. We are in effect given a quite particular political, emotional, epistemic, moral, economic and gendered figure. It is *this* figure that defines the universal man.

In the battleground of early modern political life, this new figure of man-as-citizen (or universal as particular) laid claim to the authority of being grounded in the atemporal, primary and 'scientific' space of nature, as a fitting counter to the king, who claimed the atemporality and primacy of divine authorisation. While in one sense the category of nature signifies the unbridled jungle, it also serves to assert a rhetorical space that stands as the ground of the universal and the normative. In this case nature is not essentially defined, for example, as the domain of the family and its affective relations but rather via faculties of reason and the calculation of interest, that is, via categories that serve epistemic functions. 'Nature' remains a fundamental rhetorical manoeuvre in the way we think about political life, functioning as a space upon which we are invited to cast our imagined ideal selves, supposedly purified of partiality or identities shaped in actual power relationships.[3] This is a quite particular way of imagining the category of 'universal', establishing it as static, a world beyond the mess of history, separate from the webs of close relationships and outside the transactions of power. It is also a quite particular way of imagining ethical questions and their relationship to political life (within the state), as both foundational to but severed from it.[4] Moreover the supposedly depoliticised and neutral rationality which marks the category of man in nature defines also the character of the negotiation upon which political society is founded. The notion that there is a space of political participation, as conceptualised by the Lockean contract, which remains fundamentally accessible to all, that it is neutral, spontaneous and universal in form – a 'science of morality' that is normative but also 'secular' or free of 'denominational' or partial values – and moreover that we have it, remain powerful assumptions within contemporary political debate. These assumptions can be distinguished from a recognition of the need of mechanisms for the adjudication of disputes.

Marking a sharp disjunction with much premodern (and modern absolutist or legalist) European political thought, the rights of the citizen were not understood as the gift of the sovereign, to be extended or withdrawn at will. This remains a critical defining feature of the notion of human rights. For the story of the contract, human rights are rooted in the citizen's universal nature. They are given shape or articulated, however, by the process by which he enters the sovereign state and which binds him to his fellows. Rights are in a sense the guarantee that everyman will not lose more than he agreed to barter in becoming a citizen. They are what he holds against the state or the majority as a protection of his natural freedoms. Thus rights are the definition and expression of the universal subject as he enters the political order; they constitute the linchpin between nature and the state. Within the domain of the state rights express the individual's universal nature, but they express nature in a way that requires and calls upon the existence of the state.

When derived from the Lockean account of the contract, rights are what the universal individual carries as he transverses nature and the state. But, as it is now commonplace to point out, not everyone crosses these zones so unambiguously: 'the unchecked individualism of the state of nature does not extend to all persons' (Brown, 1995: 148). Family relations, whereby it is the right of 'the father to exercise alone in his family that executive power of the law of Nature which every free man naturally hath' (Locke, 1966: 153), are part of the natural domain. Man is thus conceived to be free and equal in nature, but it is precisely gendered males who occupy the category of man. Women and the family are already from the beginning under the 'executive power' of the 'father alone'. Women belong to a different ontological zone – the private realm and the affective life, not to the public domain of autonomy, political exchange, calculation of interest, universal rationality and rights.

Property and the broader resources needed to sustain it, and thus fundamental relations of production and economic power, also belong to the domain of nature, and not to the state. In contrast to familial relations, however, relations of production *are* part of 'civil society'. For Lockean contract theory all men are understood to have a natural right and equal access to what they need; it is the difference in men's industriousness that determines the differing value of their property. Differential accumulation of the otherwise common resources of property or wealth thus reflects free choice or merit – 'the consent of men have agreed to a disproportionate and unequal possession of the earth' (Locke, 1966: 140). Only European-style agriculture, however, established land as property, with disastrous consequences for indigenous people. Equal access to sustenance is claimed to underlie and be accommodated within the unequal distribution of wealth and productive capabilities. The exclusion of economic relations from the zone of the state establishes the disjunction of political and economic rights, while prioritising political rights and identifying economic relations as not so readily open to rights practice.

The inclusion of relations of production and exchange and of gender and reproduction within the state of 'nature', and their parallel exclusion from questions of political power, have some profound consequences. The first is that these relations are acknowledged, indeed they are seen as fundamental, but they are acknowledged in such a way as to exclude them from discussion – to put them aside from the questions, reflections, negotiations and struggles that are part of the social ordering of power relationships. They are cast not as part of our collective political choices and possibilities but as the putatively natural foundations of those more contested relationships. Moreover, as Wendy Brown notes (1995), writing of the division between the family and civil society, the division and indeed opposition of one domain and the other – the political from the economic, the political and economic from the familial, the public from the private – leads to quite specific characterisations of each zone. Thus, for example, the protracted struggle for domestic violence to be recognised as a crime is in part a consequence of this pattern of divisions.

The second implication of the exclusion of family relationships, and of the child and childhood, from questions of power and political society is both epistemological and political. To set aside the child from negotiation of the contract that marks (for this story) entry into the political is to exclude from consideration those processes of the formation of the capacity for reason and judgement that are epitomised by childhood. It is thus to give no place to contexts of uncertainty, mistake, experience, play, experimentation, and so on in which the growth and shaping of capacities, including those which enable people to participate in political and social community, take place. Indeed there seems no space given to what is arguably the dynamism and mutuality of understanding. Reason and judgement appear to be at best an already formed trajectory simply awaiting achievement when the child finally reaches adulthood. This implies that reason and understanding are essentially abstracted from people's actual efforts to work with the world. It also indicates a particular model of reason – the disembodied *cogito*, the unattached rational legislator, who is other than and contrasted with the affective relations of the family. This model of reason is implicit, for example, in Lawrence Kohlberg's oft-cited work on the development (in individuals) of universal moral competence. Female subjects in Kohlberg's tests scored relatively poorly – an outcome that, according to Carol Gilligan and others, reflects the partial and gendered character (in particular the formal and hypothetical character) of what was being counted as 'universal'.

'Man' could be understood as a technical term that functions on at least two levels – an overt and a hidden level. Overtly, man is the fully rational individual, equal and free. He is the universal subject, able to stand outside the particularities of his circumstances and so to observe their essential ground – an everyman, able to travel to the American woods or to an interior space of rationality and autonomy. The category proclaims itself all-inclusive. It is significant that this is the category that stands as the basis of both universality and community for Lockean contractarianism. But, even within the terms of its own narrative, man simultaneously *occludes* many people who do not have such powers. 'Man' excludes women, who remain shadowy and dependent within the family, and children, whose capacities epitomise change and fluidity. The category effectively excludes those people who render the state of nature insecure and whose rationality is at best ambiguous. It excludes the physically, mentally and economically vulnerable, for 'only those who could in principle exist in a state of nature make up society and this means only those who can fend for themselves' (Tugendhat, 1994). It excludes slaves, who have by circumstance forfeited their freedom, rationality and right to life. Equality of access to property, which is central to the social contract's view of the autonomous individual, accommodates hidden within itself inequality even to the extent of accepting the existence of slaves, who do not have themselves as property.

Man, as the category of universality upon which the social contract's account of power turns, is thus a notion divided against itself. It claims all and yet contains only some. But those who do not fill the terms of the generic autonomous subject are not simply not properly accounted for. Exclusion from participation in the world of rational exchange and negotiation, the world of political life, itself *constitutes* the domain that they occupy. Moreover, the 'universalisation' of the subject of the contract not only attempts to universalise something that is partial, thereby acting as an impediment to understanding: it suppresses those constructions or experiences of the subject (and the state and the community) which also do not fit. Thus disembodied rationality, possessive individuality and economic security become the standard of the human. Critiques by feminists, indigenous and Third World activists, theorists and others often turn on this point. Third World and indigenous experiences of the 'universal man' have been at best mixed and often extraordinarily destructive. In its literal manifestation as North America, the nature that Locke imagined as the terrain of the rational individual was in practice cleared by force of its indigenous inhabitants, a practice repeated in many parts of the world.

The double life of man is also reflected in the category of equality. Entering the state, all are equally sovereign. But, as argued above, certain categories of people are systematically excluded from participating in shaping those processes which in turn shape the essential contours of their own lives. Thus the contract recognises the equality of citizens in a way that 'overlooks' but also reproduces the substantive inequalities of people's lives. As Marx pointed out:

> The state abolishes, after its fashion, the distinctions established by *birth, social rank, education, occupation,* when it decrees that [they] are *non-political* distinctions; when it proclaims, without regard to these distinctions, that every member of society is an *equal* partner in popular sovereignty ... But the state, none the less, allows private property, education, occupation, to *act* after *their* own fashion ... and to manifest their *particular* nature. Far from abolishing these *effective* differences, it only exists insofar as they are presupposed; it is conscious of being a *political* state and it manifests its *universality* only in opposition to these elements ... Only in this manner, *above* the *particular* elements, can the state constitute itself as universality. (1972: 31)

This self-contradictory and self-concealing construction of society marks deeply the accounts of political community and of human rights that the story of the social contract generates. It can be argued that the original overlooking of certain categories of person simply reflected the prevailing social realities and that this should not affect the emancipatory insight of the idea of the social contract itself. The idea can be applied more liberally and the pattern of inclusion broadened in keeping with the original intention to widen social and political participation. And in some significant ways that has happened – partly as the middle classes themselves became wider and in some respects more diverse. The story of human rights is often told as a story of the gradual expansion of the zone of application, with the implication that this progress will be continued (e.g. Donnelly 1999).

There is some force in this point. Rights mechanisms have operated historically as both a powerful emancipatory vehicle and 'as a mode of securing and naturalising dominant powers – class, gender and so forth' (Brown, 1995: 99, 100). The emancipatory potential can be, and at times is, used as a tool against the naturalisation of exploitation. Yet the 'violent founding' of the community of autonomous individuals, and the constitutive exclusions in different ways of women, indigenous peoples, the vulnerable and the 'developing' world, continue to reach deep into the shape of contemporary political community – both within liberal states and more broadly in the structures of international interaction (Connolly, 1995). The difficulty that the social contract faces is not simply that various categories of people, activities and relationships have not been included, leaving them untouched. It is that they have been excluded – in the most extreme form from universality, from community, from full rationality – and this exclusion has been a powerful and formative activity. In ways ranging from subtle to gross, categories of people are still shaped by these exclusions, as chapter 6 explores.

The contract ignores, too, the formation of the self-possessed individual to whom it is addressed. That means it ignores, among other things, the role of the excluded in the production of the fully participating agent. The economic role of the unpropertied – women and the impoverished at home or in distant places – in the production of the autonomous individual is perhaps only the most obvious labour of production that is overlooked. The social contract ignores equally but tacitly the social formation of the excluded, and the ways, direct or subtle, that these zones of existence – one of which is constituted as visible, universal, fully rational and community, the other as invisible, partial, emotional or childlike and a threat to community – are entwined, mutually constitutive and interdependent. In this way, by entrenching a kind of myopia, or a 'politics of forgetting' (Connolly, 1995: 138), the idea of the contract can itself reinforce and naturalise those social dynamics which marginalise, impoverish and disempower.

It follows from the story of the social contract that rights are essentially understood as political and civil liberties – the so-called 'negative rights' of non-interference in life, liberty and property. The continuing power of a narrow definition of rights (despite active criticism by some leading rights theorists) is indicated by the fact that political and civil rights can still be regarded as requiring simply non-interference, and are classed as 'first-generation' rights, while economic or subsistence rights, although given increasing credence, still 'seem strange' (Shue, 1980: 27). 'A standard assumption in liberal theory is that there is only moderate scarcity. This has the effect of assuming that everyone's subsistence is taken care of. You must have your subsistence guaranteed in order to be admitted into the domain of theory' (Shue, 1980: 27). This excludes one-fifth of the world's population from the ambit of liberal theory, as Henry Shue points out.

The idea of negative rights is underpinned by a remarkably persistent assumption that rights can be secured essentially by the state refraining from certain (oppressive) activities. When understood in this fashion, observing rights appears a relatively easy matter. 'There is nothing essentially difficult about transforming political and civil rights' into legally enforced rights, according to one, still widespread, view (Cranston, 1973: 66). Upholding political rights seems effortless because it is simply a patrolling of the axiomatic boundary between civil society and the state and allowing people to go about their 'natural' business. The complex balance of social forces that may be holding abuse in place can be simply erased. Because rights are understood as a limitation to protect the natural activities of already fully formed subjects, only political rights, conceived of as limits on government (or majority goals), carry strong conceptual links with notions of obligation, justice and universality. By contrast, issues of sustenance or of enabling people to participate effectively in their world do not fall unproblematically into the public domain.

'Second-generation' or positive rights, in this view, require active governance – the provision of social goods of all kinds. In practice they are often approached not as rights *per se* but as a form of welfare that dilutes the concept of rights, for they involve actively intervening in the domain of nature (economic activity, people's social and family lives). Or they are cast as 'welfare rights' (and part of the terms of citizenship in capitalist industrial societies) in contrast to those rights that enable autonomy or liberty. The point is often made that the fulfilment of welfare claims is beyond the scope of all but the wealthiest governments. And what is beyond the power of an individual or a government to provide cannot be reckoned a duty of that person or government. Thus, while positive rights are understood to express social goals or justifiable moral claims, they are not counted as 'something of which no one may be deprived without a grave affront to justice', and thus they 'belong to a totally different moral dimension' (Cranston, 1973: 66) which is not universal and lacks the insistent moral force of negative political rights. Their implementation is often seen as immensely complex (which indeed it is) as opposed to the illusory simplicity of changing political relationships and arrangements.

This view remains deeply embedded, despite the practical evidence that the social and political infrastructure required to routinely deliver and guarantee political and civil rights is significant and complex. In practice, no civil or political right requires 'simply' legislation to be observed unless it is already widely practised. Observance of a right that was not substantially observed previously requires not only systems of enforcement and review but a major change in social attitudes and the constitution of relationships. Liberty, if it is understood to include the physical security, nutrition, education and, importantly, respect that enable people to cross a threshold of participation in society, rather than simply not suffering undue interference, could be the most costly and (in Cranston's terms) impracticable right of all.

The social contract thus provides a minimalist account of the state and political community, and of the scope, nature and subject of rights. The state and the political order are understood as boundaries – not as producers of or participants in the dynamics of power and meaning across which people's lives are shaped, but as a form around the pre-given content of the individual. This produces a curiously apolitical view of government and the state wherein government becomes 'political' (or ideological), as opposed to purely instrumental, only when it oversteps its role as neutral facilitator. In this constitution of things, the political order can be peeled away, leaving the assemblage of rational individuals virtually untouched. This is an inadequate account of power and the social production of categories and relationships across which people live their lives. It is also a narrow and rationalist account of the dynamics of much abuse, which are often not only the oppression of the already autonomous individual but the positive constitution of violent or grossly exploitative social dynamics and deformed lives. While nothing could be more profoundly 'unreasonable' than severe and persistent abuse, such abuse is not essentially a failure of rationality. Much human rights abuse is maintained and embedded in the entrenched social, economic and psychic processes that generate extreme racism, sexism and widespread practices such as torture, habitual violence and near-slavery. For many 'the sources of injustice and exploitation lie in the social structure rather than in the framework of the state' (Kothari, 1991: 21). The persistence of extreme violence against women within the context of the family in many countries is simply one example of this.

The economic abundance assumed by liberalism during the period when the major lineaments of liberal theories of the state were taking root was underpinned by colonialism. Arguably, the complex patterns of accumulation that have been part of the 'natural' rights assumed by the social contract have often entailed the impoverishment of others, particularly in the Third World. As Henry Shue, among others, has pointed out, our classical construction of rights, in particular the prioritisation of (an interpretation of) political and civil rights itself assumes and is made possible by this abundance and its patterns of enrichment and impoverishment. This is a point argued with some bitterness by a range of non-Western human rights activists.

> By equating human rights to civil and political rights, the rich and powerful in the North hope to avoid coming to grips with those economic, social, and cultural challenges that could well threaten their position in the existing world order . . . [If a struggle for economic transformation is] presented as a human rights struggle . . . it is not inconceivable that the North, which dominates the global economy, will be in the dock. (Muzaffar, 1993: 31)

It has been argued (by Donnelly, 1989, 1999, for example) that the colonial and post-colonial history of interaction and exploitation has itself acted to universalise the value of the Lockean contract, although it is not universal in any inherent sense. Human rights practices, grounded in the idea of the social contract, have developed in the West 'in response to social changes associated with the rise of modern markets and modern states. However, similar changes in virtually all areas of the world have given human rights a near universal contemporary applicability, despite their obvious historical contingency and particularity' (Donnelly 1989: 2). Modernity has, in practical terms, become universal.

To tell this as simply a story of progress is to ignore the experience that modernity, like other cultural forms before it, is a history of both civilisation and barbarity (following Walter Benjamin's aphorism). The rise of modern markets and modern states on the back of colonialism indeed 'opened up new vistas for many, particularly for those exploited or cornered within the traditional order' in the colonised societies. But these promises of and potentials for 'a more just and equal world' have brought their own 'genocides, ecodisasters and ethnocides', as Ashis Nandy, among others, has pointed out (1983: ix, x). Donnelly's approach assumes that the modernising experience is sufficiently unproblematic to support the unquestioned precedence of one particular conception of human rights as (a construction of) the individual holding rights against the state. 'So-called non-Western conceptions of human rights are in fact not conceptions of human rights at all, but involve alternative conceptions of human dignity and seek to realise that dignity through devices other than human rights' (Donnelly, 1989: 2). Certainly the modernising experience seems highly generalisable, so that 'the West is now everywhere' (Nandy, 1983: xi). This is not coincidental, and is anything but 'neutral' as the processes of modernisation, of which liberalism is a part, participate in the suppression of other conceptions of dignity. Despite this, however, it seems clear that modernisation has not rendered the 'historical specificities and community contexts that define human roles' (Kothari, 1991: 27) so irrelevant. In seeking to universalise a particular model of rights we may be promoting not only the political virtues articulated by the contract but its patterns of exclusion while promoting a tool which is not equipped to respond to many forms of systemically inflicted injury. We may again be turning away from 'the plurality of critical traditions and of human rationality' (Nandy, 1983: x). To dismiss 'alternative conceptions of human dignity' is to fail to grasp the potential for change towards a greater respect for the person that may be present in the circumstances at hand; it is to consider that one has nothing to learn, and it is to continue to 'overlook' other cultural traditions in a way that is characteristic of the profoundly Eurocentric conceptions and interests that dominate international politics.

Contractarianism has exerted a powerful effect on ways of thinking not only about the internal constitution of states but about international politics, although the form of contractarianism more commonly associated with international politics is that of Hobbes, not Locke. Contractarianism is founded on the polarity between the sharply conflicting fields of possibility inside and outside the state ('nature' in one form or another). Despite the optimism of the liberal versions of the contract, the accounts of what is possible outside the state or between states 'in nature' that its own cosmology of political community generates are dominated by insecurity and tragedy. This is a paradox of contractarian, but more broadly of dominant Western, models of the state. It turns on a dichotomy lying at the heart of our political thought, as Martin Wight has most famously pointed out, between the search for the good life, progress and well-being within the sovereign community and the lack of community, fragmentation, and conflict that characterise our grasp of sovereignty in international relations (Butterfield and Wight, 1966). This is not, however, a dichotomy patrolling two separate zones of being. Both dimensions of political life are generated by the dominant modes of grasping the modern (Westphalian) state, and both rooted in the story of political origin set out in the contract, with the notion of state sovereignty standing as the hinge articulating their movement (see Walker, 1993).

The rhetoric of rights is addressed to the universality of humankind. But contractarianism, from which much of the contemporary rhetoric is derived, is not about people as such. It is a theory of the state and of citizenship which takes as its foundation a retrospective ontology of 'Man'. Within the debates and social realities in which the theory of the Lockean contract took shape, the language of rights worked to counter particular forms of rule, privilege and abuse, championing in their place and under the banner of the universal quite particular conceptions and *subjects* of freedom and equality. The particular character of universal man, the split between private convictions and affective life on the one hand and public rationality on the other, enabled a move away from the violent claims fuelling the religious wars and opened a space of relative tolerance and autonomy. There is continuing value in the model of the unattached legislator. But as an Everyman it has naturalised its own oppressions and exclusions. When we recirculate arguments about the universality or otherwise of human rights standards, it can be the scope and applicability of this broad but particular picture of the human and of community that we are discussing, not whether and how it is possible to work against particular patterns of violence, degradation or suffering.

To draw attention to such division and potential for ambivalence in the language, and also in the practice, of rights is not to argue for the abandoning of the idea. It is simply to argue the need for persistent and collective attention to *how* rights may be operating or may be used in particular circumstances. The idea of human rights is not a guarantee. At its broadest the idea of rights refers to a protean set of tools, practices and orientations, imperfect, uncertain and evolving, upon which we can draw when grappling with questions of how to live well together.

The international domain

It is realism, as a twentieth-century theory of international relations, that has articulated most powerfully the possibilities of international life proposed by the story of man in nature. It is realism, elaborating perhaps freely from a Hobbesian rather than a Lockean account of the social contract, that captures both the overriding emphasis on the state as a principle of exclusion and inclusion and the ahistorical conflictual zone of 'nature'. The writings of Locke and Hobbes (let alone other social contract theorists) on the nature of the relations obtaining between states do not lead directly to realism as a theory of international politics. Nevertheless, realism finds its source in an echo of this story of the state's origin. Even in the Lockean version, nature stands as both the space of universal rationality and the anarchical absence of government. Rationality moves forward into government and the state and defines the zone of the study of political community. Realism's scope, however, is the dimension of nature as anarchy that forms the flipside of the 'science of morality' and the principle of sovereignty.

In both (of what could be loosely called) its 'strong' and 'softer' forms, realism has been the dominant mode for understanding world politics at least since the Second World War, although, clearly, it is the inheritor of much older modes of address and their preoccupations and maxims. It has not only formed the core of theoretical discourse concerning the world of states: often coupled with a changing selection of other themes, it has acted as a persistent thread patterning the view of international life prevailing in bureaucracies, journalism and everyday commentary. Thus the various forms of realism constitute a basic context for the handling of questions of rights in international life.

Inevitably, any discourse which has been so broadly and persistently persuasive will exist in diverse forms. Indeed realism interweaves powerful, but also contradictory, themes of Western political thought. There have been, among the variations, at least two fundamentally different, even opposing, orientations in realism. The first is a critical voice exemplified best perhaps by E. H. Carr. In this voice, realism operates as an antidote to a particular kind of hubris – the rather nasty complacency of power mistaking itself for virtue. It is a sceptical exercise that draws on historical analysis and sets store by good seamanship (in Michael Oakeshott's sense) rather than in the promise of arrival at a final port. For Carr, at least, realism remains in need of the opposing and balancing convictions of idealism, with the two fixed in a permanently see-sawing relationship (in which realism dominates).

By contrast, the second orientation of realism (and neorealism) emphasises its claim to be the voice of an inexorable reality while also defining itself through its opposition to idealism. Its tendency is to identify with the power it claims to describe.

It may be unsurprising that realism is therefore, at the least, the de facto preferred theoretical stance of major international powers. It seems that, over time, the latter tendency has become dominant (though one piece of work may move between the two voices) and it is this tendency, found in 'hard' realism (and more prevalent in the work of, for example, Hans Morgenthau or Kenneth Waltz) focused on here. Nevertheless, the variations of realism share key themes to a greater or lesser degree. Realism could also be regarded as including much pragmatic foreign policy analysis, analysis that indeed takes as common sense a number of realism's principal observations without, however, necessarily endorsing the breadth or assertiveness of the theoretical framework.

Its exponents claim that, as an intellectual tradition, the roots of realism can be traced to Thucydides and other, non-Western, ancients. This claim is based partly on the assertion that, as a theory of world politics, realism grasps the essential realities of power and conflict that form the enduring bedrock of political life. Realism is thereby often portrayed as part of a deeply rooted 'common sense' about the facts of power. Realism does offer insight into the dynamics of power, conflict and the behaviour of states, but it arguably focuses on one, albeit significant, moment in the complexities of international life and freezes it. Its claims to common sense are perhaps strengthened by its mirror fit with liberal accounts of political community within the state. Realism provides a pervasive context within which questions of human rights in international politics are framed. As a dominant political theory, it has been analysed and criticised frequently and from a variety of positions. What follows is a discussion of some of its effects on the way we approach human rights issues internationally. In particular, questions of change and timelessness, and of the relation of power and ethics, will be discussed.

Realism is a theory of states operating under conditions of anarchy and mutual mistrust (nature), their interactions constrained and ordered by the shifting balance of power and the more or less mutual recognition of their common fate.[5] Its claim to span so much of history is grounded in a belief in the essentially unchanging nature of the dynamic it describes – 'the striking sameness of international life for millennia' (Waltz, 1979: 66). In effect, this is a reduction of history to 'nature' – not the dynamic, teeming nature of the natural sciences, but the separate and immutable domain of early modern social theory – whether it is human nature or the systemic inevitabilities of the inter-action of states. As a theoretical structure realism turns on an elegantly formal dichotomy – that is, the paradox between states' necessary effort to maintain security and, because security is achieved at the expense of others, the inevitable tendency of this effort to produce insecurity. This pattern, of a damaging *a priori* dichotomy that can not be resolved but is at best contained or managed, provides one of realism's key analytical mechanisms. Realism thus endeavours to explain the workings and the logic of an all-but closed system and examines how, sometimes despite people's best efforts, that system reproduces itself.

For realism, therefore, particularly 'hard' realism, the history of relations between communities is essentially repetitious and driven by necessity. This establishes the character of realism as an explanatory system. It is hardly equipped to throw light on change in the world it describes, nor is it concerned to elucidate the possibilities for acting otherwise that can emerge from actual historical contexts, for these are registered as simply shadows on the face of what is the same and unchanging. Because realism focuses on states (and therefore on the many) it can be seen as particularist. However, the timeless and inexorable quality of nature or system constitutes the universalism of realism. It allows little scope for individual human endeavour to do other than bear one's load with or without determination. Preoccupied as it is with Thucydides's maxim that the strong do what they will and the weak do what they must, historically realism has failed to recognise the scope for action by the 'weak'. The later discussion of East Timor explores some of the consequences of this particular oversight.

Realism describes a world pessimistically founded on the idea of the onto-logical incompleteness of the human being. However, unlike accounts of onto-logical incompleteness within the state, for the international arena there is little hope of the humanly constructed completion offered by society. Realism, par-ticularly in its more classical expressions, thus often carries a sense of tragedy; indeed, it draws explicitly on the motifs of tragedy as a literary form, insofar as it is populated by figures conscious of moving inexorably towards a doom stemming from ineradicable flaws in their own condition – in this case flaws grounded in the relentless, often violent, struggle for power that is seen as fun-damentally shaping international life. George Kennan's description of states-men as 'actors in a tragedy beyond their making or repair' (quoted in Garnett, 1992: 66) captures this clearly. Realism's claim to kinship with the ancient Greeks, and therefore to a timeless common sense, may work more through its use of the compelling and socially embedded dramaturgical mode of Greek tragedy rather than any particular continuity of political judgement. But realism's claim to historical continuity and its pessimism also rest on the use of certain Christian motifs. It stands as a political theology of the Fall and the unredeemed, where the good can by definition only be what is beyond reach. This has immense consequences for thinking about the ethical fabric of life.

Power is the principal explanatory concept for realism in international rela-tions theory. It defines the particularity of the political arena and supplies the essential structure through which phenomena are intelligible. Power is thus irreducible, marrying the core of political life with the acuity of theoretical insight. The struggle for power defines the nature of an imperfect, incomplete, 'fallen' world. But this reference to imperfection does not denote simply the messiness of life; nor is it to forgo the assertion of the ontological primacy of abstract principles with which 'perfection' is often associated. On the contrary, 'imperfection' is an assertive claim as to the essence of things, and sets the relation of 'power' to 'ethics'. While the dynamics of power establish the reality of political life, 'ethics' belongs to a realm of perfection. Those who seek to structure political life according to 'ethics' are idealists. In practical terms conflict between the apparent dictates of morality and self-interest can be a common enough occurrence, but what realism proposes here is a deeper truth. Ethics is elsewhere, by definition, a world of seemingly static principles, and in the 'real' world of power seen only in its shadow of hypocrisy or an arrogant, self-righteous idealism. According to this dichotomy, questions of power are what cause moral truth to slip from our grasp, as if ethical problems concerned a world other than human, including political, experience. As Walker has pointed out (1993), this dichotomy sets the terms within which much international relations theory is constructed. Those more optimistic voices that ask how to bring ethics to bear on international relations are already accepting that 'international relations' is predicated on the abstraction and separation of the two domains.

This produces a strangely abstracted version of both power and ethics. Indeed, despite claiming to reject all belief in utopian abstractions, realism is itself an idealist and explicitly normative (if distopian) doctrine. Power and ethics tend to be understood not as ways of grappling with the complex and fluid movement of life but as two actual domains, patterned by their own laws. 'Realism is a clear recognition of the limits of morality and reason in politics'[6] (Harland, quoted in Garnett, 1992: 66). The problem here is not the recognition that one can reach the limits of fixed principles and abstract reasoning, but the equation of these frozen standards with 'morality and reason'. In an extreme form of this polarisation of power and ethics, Morgenthau states that 'the political realist maintains the autonomy of the political sphere . . . He thinks in terms of interest defined as power . . . the moralist, of the conformity of action with moral principles' (Morgenthau, 1978: 12). Even the early Bull (1977) sees justice epitomised in violent revolution or in the maxim 'Let justice be done though the heavens may fall', and thus in fundamental conflict with 'order'. Rather than an inevitable part of the process of shaping our collective lives, ethics becomes, really, another claim to power, as perhaps it must in this doctrine of our collective exclusion from disembodied perfection.

Thus, for realism, while power is emblematic of all that is significant in international life, the prism through which all else makes sense, the conception of power is divorced from questions of what people value. More broadly it is divorced from the processes by which 'valuing' – forming the categories by which we understand and live our collective and individual lives – takes shape.

By understanding ethical and political questions as belonging to fundamentally different abstract domains, realism mystifies ethics and empties politics, offering little insight into how to deal with those numerous practical conundrums in international life which are simultaneously political and ethical. The effect of explaining so much in terms of power while at the same time shearing history of everything but the timeless clash of contending forces, of stripping everything down to the underlying interest, is that the category of power itself becomes almost emptied of content. It is a negative (if nevertheless important) conception of power as the bending of one agent to the will of another – a conception that overlooks the constitutive and enabling senses of power as well as the notion of power as resistance explored by Michel Foucault and feminist writers (e.g. Bernice Carroll).

The cultural dichotomy between power and ethics, might and right, upon which realism draws and which it reinforces, is deeply entrenched. What the dichotomy does not describe, however, is the dynamic nature of both power and ethical direction, the complex, perhaps mutually constitutive, interaction between the two categories and the contingent, rather than essential, nature of any distinction between them. It is not only that the demands of power and ethics can sometimes coincide. The development over time of the shared sense of what is right, desirable or ideal, shifts the limits of the possible and the parameters within which interest and power are calculated as well as ethical directions adopted. The relentless polarity between power and morality (or order and justice) that realism (and utopianism) propose takes these non-dual currents in the life of human communities and turns them both into 'fixed and absolute standards' outside of history.

This has a number of rather different implications for approaches to human rights issues internationally. Questions of rights are marginal to the core concerns of realism. Realism is concerned with states, and (in line with liberal constructions of rights) understands rights as belonging primarily to individuals. The narrow category of power and the lack of ways of thinking about political change hardly prepare realism for questions of response to systemic infliction of injury. Within a strictly classical realist framework there is really no place for notions of human rights – they belong to what could be called the 'private life' of states, and their pursuit across borders threatens international order. In practice in Western states, however, such a simple dismissal has been contentious since the end of the Second World War and for some decades has not been feasible – the framework of what constitutes order in international relations has been shifting. But realism can also be divided against itself. Realist goals of power maximisation and the more Westphalian tenet of non-interference (or carefully managed interference) can be in conflict with each other. Thus realist approaches *can* mean that questions of rights are simply not taken seriously since they belong in the category of 'ethics' – they are included on the foreign policy agenda as a result of pandering to elements of the domestic electorate. But realists can also take human rights very seriously indeed.

For some states in particular, human rights in international politics have become part of the currency of self-assertion. Under these conditions, rights in effect come to be treated principally as elements within the on-going competition for supremacy, or 'edge', among states. International reputation and occupancy of the moral high ground are valuable commodities. Under such conditions, the goal of a reduction of violence or improved conditions of respect for excluded groups can become rather less important than the process of achieving it, which is another complex step in the efforts of governments to assert or resist pressure. Even when respect for human rights is upheld as a serious commitment in itself, the tools of realism are implicitly competitive, confrontational and threatening.

Of course, such an approach can be effective and at times may be the only available tool that promises any success. It can produce important results – the release of prisoners, a constraint upon a sadistic regime, a timely warning of the costs of a destructive policy direction. But it has, as it were, one tool in its kit, and that is the graduated scale of confrontation. Moreover, the purpose of the task is often highly ambivalent – and that inevitably skews its execution. Some of the sharpest criticisms of this approach come from the more sceptical traditions of realism itself.

> There is a certain tendency in the Western countries to believe that . . . the human rights problem is essentially the problem of how Western countries are to use their influence to bring the Socialist countries and the countries of the Third World into line on this matter. Indeed, one can say . . . that the public appeal of human rights as an objective of foreign policy derives in large measure from this belief that the guardianship of human rights in the world as a whole is a special vocation of the Western countries. It helps to restore our flagging conviction of our own virtue, and at the same time enables us to give vent to long pent-up feelings of frustration and aggression towards our critics in other parts of the world. (Bull, 1979: 84)

Curiously, it may be precisely that approach to rights which pursues them primarily in terms of conflict, confrontation and national or cultural self-aggrandisement which most easily slips into casting the pursuit as a moral crusade. Here, in the practice of great powers in particular, the mechanics of realism can slide into a selective rhetoric of liberal triumphalism and the aggressive export of 'the truth'.

If human rights are indeed a way of asking or of answering the question 'How do we live well together?', they are a demonstration of the enmeshment of politics and ethics. The assertion of human rights is part of politics as it questions the constitution of relationships and agency and the circulation of power. And, in the same way, notions of human rights address the processes, slow and invisible or explicit and direct, by which we come to value things. Abuse is often embedded in damaging social practice and relationship. It is generated not only through that exercise of power that is forcing others (unreasonably) to your will (although that is a significant form of abuse) but through that power which is the systematic production of deformed, marginalised or malnourished lives. Moreover, these two strands of abuse are frequently entwined. Realist analysis does not equip you to engage with these realities; indeed it can obscure them.

The classical constructions of human rights are liberal in origin, and it is not surprising that support for human rights in international politics is more easily associated with liberal than with realist orientations. The growth of an international human rights regime since the Second World War can be understood as reflecting a reduction in the power of the 'radical statist logic' of realism (Donnelly, 1999: 71) and a consolidation of liberal influences. When discussing human rights, liberalism can thus be cast as a clear alternative to realism. The emergence of human rights as a topic for international relations over the past fifty or so years is a significant development in international politics, as Donnelly notes (1999). Liberal perspectives have contributed substantially to enabling and shaping this process. As suggested above, however, realism and liberalism can also slide into each other. If realism has best captured the story of man in nature in the international domain, it is liberalism, as a family of sometimes contradictory political motifs and trajectories, that in Western states at least underpins our conceptualisation of political community. The international arena and the state are not separate ontological zones but interdependent effects of the way sovereignty has been constructed (Walker, 1993). In practice, the two are utterly entangled.

Liberalism has a broad agenda and within the international arena is characterised by a number of interweaving streams, some more communitarian, some internationalist, some highly critical of various elements of contemporary international life. The more dominant forms of liberalism in contemporary international politics – interdependency and regime theories, neo-liberal institutionalism, and so on – draw on largely utilitarian traditions and are associated with the effort to construct institutions, regimes and norms. These traditions have undoubtedly contributed to the construction of a framework of international human rights mechanisms. Debate about human rights is frequently couched in terms of a conflict between the principle of non-interference in the domestic affairs of another state and the international promotion of social and political norms. The principle of non-interference has stood as a basic element contributing to order in the Westphalian state system (if often ignored when the demands of other forms of 'order' become more pressing). However, various international norms may also themselves be regarded as fundamental to orderly relations between states, as Hedley Bull pointed out (1977). The promotion of norms, in this context, could be regarded as an essentially liberal endeavour; it could also be seen more broadly as a response to the relative increase of diversity within the state system as a result of colonisation and, subsequently, decolonisation following the Second World War. The principles of order articulated by the treaties of Westphalia, the boundaries within which difference was to be tolerated, occurred within a reasonable level of cultural consonance – sovereignty is both a definition of separateness and a commitment to a level of conformity.

This suggests a considerable interlinking of realism and liberalism in the international sphere, a relationship which interdependency and regime theorists acknowledge (e.g. Donnelly, 1986: 640; Keohane and Nye, 1987: 728). Moreover, it is a relationship that sets the themes in the management of rights issues in many multilateral fora, as well as in bilateral interstate relationships. The approaches described by interdependency and related theories are a major element in the everyday workings of many national foreign policy agencies and related national and international organisations. In practice, a division of labour in many theory and policy circles between realist and certain liberal approaches creates only occasional friction.

Within that complementarity, however, important differences between realist and dominant liberal tendencies in international relations theory remain – differences relevant to questions of rights. Liberal theorists focus on the interleaving of national and international interests as states find benefits in acknowledging and exploiting multiple channels of information, bargaining and exchange. Whereas realism is concerned to explain conflict, liberal theories explore conditions under which cooperation occurs in a world understood to be both anarchic and interdependent; whereas realism emphasises the systemic constraints that determine the underlying dynamic of relations between the state and the timeless nature of power relations, liberalism proposes the significance of human agency and its capacity to shape developments and history as (at least potential) progress. Again, whereas realism casts international relations as its own autonomous domain of investigation and activity: 'the realm of recurrence and repetition' (Butterfield and Wight, 1966: 17), of competition and distrust in contrast to the rich possibility of relations within political community, liberalism sees the boundary as more fluid and the patterns of interaction outside the state as potentially analogous to domestic processes. Moreover utilitarian liberalism does not echo realism's epic tone but reworks it into a pragmatics and a search for workable bureaucratic norms.

While fundamentally state-centric, liberalism emphasises the processes by which state and non-state actors build habits of interaction, establish patterns of conformity and constrain uncertainty. The architecture of UN standard-setting on rights, the various regional rights regimes and less formal multilateral clustering or solidarities on particular rights issues could all be understood (although not reduced to) examples of such cooperative and constraining webs. Self-interest remains, for these approaches, a fundamental concept and the defining characteristic of both rationality and human agency. But liberal theorists draw attention to some of the processes by which patterns of interest are defined and shift and so cast interest as a more interactive, heterogeneous and negotiable construct than strong realism allows. Central to this interactive self-interest is the idea of learning. For interdependency theory, for example, learning occurs when rational agents change how they think about their interests, a change that follows new experience or a redefinition of the context within which interest is recognised. Learning is thus a process of changing perceptions of interest brought about through interaction and the effort of mutual adjustment. Self-interest can also contain 'empathic' elements (Keohane, 1984: 111) where the line between enlightened self-interest and what might be called intelligent self-sacrifice becomes blurred. These are important features, serving to distinguish liberalism from realism. However, despite the potentially fluid and dynamic nature of interests defined through institutional bargaining and the blurring of the distinction between the 'games and coalitions' shaping the agenda inside the state and those crossing state boundaries, the self defining the 'interest' remains a given and essentially unproblematic category.

Prevalent liberal approaches thus offer points for helping build or for assessing certain kinds of practical coalitions on human rights issues internationally. The view that states can change over time in their dealings with each other as well as within their own community stands in sharp relief to the belief that international relations is an inevitable recurrence of necessitous behaviour. In contrast to the intense polarities of realism, the dominant strands of liberalism propose an understanding of cooperation that does not exile conflict. Within limits, both become part of the normal processes of interaction. This acknowledges an approach to human rights not only through state to state confrontation but through seeking shared solutions to common problems through norm building and learning. In keeping with this more flexible appreciation of interaction, power is approached from a broader, more complex perspective, as multivalent and fluid. Joseph Nye speaks of 'soft power', as 'the ability to structure a situation so that others develop preferences or define their interests in ways consistent with your own' (quoted, Van Ness *et al.*, 1992: 30). Peter Van Ness argues, with some force, that 'soft' power captures well the success of various NGOs, such as Asia Watch, in the field of human rights. These are important reflections on and contributions to the dynamics of international politics and the potential for progress on questions of rights.

The effort to build a shared vocabulary in the face of difference, to draw on resources of 'soft' power to construct at least the context within which common norms can emerge, and the potential for learning may illustrate both the strengths and the limitations of the major streams of liberal theory in the field

45

of international human rights. At a simple but significant level, this approach reiterates the immense importance and day-to-day reality of cooperation, reasonableness and the slow persistent effort to build connections that mean something to the participants. Regional rights regimes or institutions and above all, the complex array of UN rights machinery stand as the classic examples of the construction of multilateral norms in this most difficult field. Norm building is founded on the commitment to dialogue – dialogue across different political, legal and social cultures, different economic realities, different histories and simply different sovereign claims about what actually are accepted as the worth and reach of norms, and about actual cases and whether they contravene those norms. In practice, dialogue is important because of its capacity to consolidate norms, but also because of its potential for open-endedness, for movement into unknown or unpredictable territory, a potential that seems little considered by utilitarian traditions.

Despite these strengths, however, liberal approaches seem deeply constrained by the character and the pervasive dominance of the models of 'the person' and 'the community' within which they operate. Claims to universality for human rights covenants provide one way of reflecting on these limitations. International rights machinery is regularly celebrated by the assertion that effectively universal standards on human rights have now been created by the work of the UN and are expressed in the rights charters and the body of international law. 'Governments, working through the United Nations, have been successful in establishing universal standards for civil and political rights as well as economic, social and cultural rights' (Van Ness *et al.*, 1992: 48). 'The universality of the Universal Declaration of Human Rights and the International Human Rights Covenant is now the real starting point for discussion' (Donnelly, in Van Ness *et al.*, 1992: 48).

The UN charters indeed represent significant achievements and have acquired the status of customary international law. They can indeed work as a starting-point for certain discussions. And it might even be true that the international rhetoric of rights represents 'an implicit, submerged, or deflected expression of a sense of moral interdependence' (Donnelly, 1989: 617). But this is a long way from the assertion that universality of standards has been achieved. What does such a degree of apparent self-confidence reflect? 'Universality' is here based on an appeal to a pragmatic and utilitarian, not an ontological, justification – it literally means that, for whatever reason, most governments have signed the relevant declarations and more or less participate in the relevant multilateral fora. Yet the word suggests a greater power and reach, and a deeper acceptance. The fundamentally state-centric nature of most forms of liberalism allows the pragmatic to slide towards the ontological, as do the unreflective 'thin' notion of the self and political community and a 'negative' narrow construction of the forms of systemic harm that can be embedded in sociopolitical relationships. All three elements enable the signature of governments – significant though that can be – to stand somewhat too easily as a crucial sign of the direction and the character of international life and our attentiveness to the patterns of suffering institutionalised within it. Perhaps, too, the declaration of universality implies that human rights standards are already well in hand and, despite some occasional slips and blind spots, unproblematic, at least for the liberal West. This is the 'message' approach to rights promotion: we have the truth (even if we are not always perfect); let us teach you. It rests, in this case, on an unreflective category of the self, including both the self as bearer of that message and 'the other' who receives.

What are some of the elements of this unreflective self? One is simply a failure to look critically at ourselves and our tools. The self-confident assertion of universality suggests a pervasive belief in the progress of modern rationalism – that the globalisation of Western liberalism represents the natural, if not inevitable, path of evolution of human history and that the onward movement of modernisation is ultimately an innocent, transparent and emancipatory process. But as this chapter and the discussion of Indigenous Australians' health suggest, not simply the application but actually the constructions of human rights themselves in developed states can be ambivalent, myopic and exploitative. In the international arena, the persistence, for example, of widespread starvation as a feature of our political and economic lives – a phenomenon that is sometimes ruled out of consideration under the category of 'human rights' – raises at least some questions about our collective constitution, let alone implementation, of rights standards.

Without critical self-reflection, however, and thus armed with the belief that those of us in the West already know the story of human rights and human wrongs (to use Ken Booth's phrase), difficult conversations, particularly across cultures, sovereignties and histories, can become both more elusive and less productive. Yet without such dialogue norm-building exercises may rely increasingly on the 'hard' power of realism. When struggling with the need to respond to a particular atrocity, of course, self-reflection may seem neither appropriate nor tactically wise; within the context of a broader engagement on the patterns of harm we find acceptable within and across our communities, it may be fundamental. Liberalism hardly predetermines complacency on the part of negotiators and the institutions of which they are a part. But it does support categories of rights that 'overlook' much entrenched and systemically imposed suffering. Nor does it make available the tools with which to consider what those of us in the liberal states may have to learn about respect for people.

Despite emphasis on intersubjectively created meaning, much liberal theory starts from a strong presumption of universality – not necessarily regarding human rights but of the nature of knowledge and the person. Here the self is the ideal bearer of a process of calculation, operating a universal method. This self – the subject which defines the universal – is in many respects the same construction as contractarian man, discussed earlier: technocratic and rationalistic, self-possessed and self-interested, alienated and gradually accumulating knowledge in order to improve technical control of the matter at hand. Or he is the object of those disciplines. This is a highly specific and limited construction of the person, of interaction among people and of knowledge. It is apposite, then, that this instrumentalist understanding of human interaction so often takes as the real subjects of its theory the 'elites' of the state – national leaders, decision makers in the relevant area and the world of international diplomacy. For this world is itself in many respects a modern technocratic construction, and its movements are suited to the insights that interdependency theory offers. For interdependency theory, what people think is an important dimension of political reality. But the kind of human agency that is proposed is of a quite limited order – bureaucratic bargaining.

The premature optimism of the belief that universality has been achieved can thus also come from taking the world of multilateral diplomacy – the field of operations upon which interdependency theories, for example, focus – as the icon of and the gate to the reality of international life. This reflects the assumption that the task at hand is to a significant extent one of capturing the assent of an (in practice rather narrow) elite, through a combination of rational argument and political pressure. (Such agreement, of course, can provide important tools to international bodies or movements for change within the state.) This is a misreading of both multilateral diplomacy and the obdurate complexities of international life and political change. The patterns of suffering or harm which our political and economic systems impose on each other can be rooted in some of the basic forces which shape human identity – political, economic, cultural, and emotional. International institutional machinery is indeed an important tool in working on questions of rights. But the achievement of 'universality' across societies in the form of real dialogue and significant agreement on and commitment to working with the forms of abuse embedded in collective life seems as yet some way off. To capture the agreement of elites is precisely the task for a range of international issues for which regime and interdependency theories offer valuable analytical tools. For human rights, effective change that does not simply substitute one form of abuse for another is a more arduous task.

Interdependency theory proposes a model of interaction and interdependent interests. This has the potential for presenting communication as a two-way street and for emphasising that societies in fact have something to learn from each other regarding respect for people. Yet in practice the greater emphasis seems to remain on declaratory standards, which while important can give a false promise of clarity, rather than on the shared activities normally associated with learning. Despite the work of a range of UN organisations, as well as various bilateral and multilateral bodies and programmes, opportunities for learning at the sites of abuse – and so for changes in both behaviour and understanding among those engaged in abusive relations – remain relatively unexplored. These are areas of dialogue and practical cross-cultural engagement, supported by a range of non-governmental and international organisations, where practice is likely to run ahead of theory and offer new sources of theoretical insight.

This is certainly not to argue that utilitarian liberal approaches have nothing valuable to contribute to questions of human rights. Even less is it to suggest that international rights regimes are doomed to inadequacy. On the contrary, work on interactive learning and the construction of shared understandings and standards could be taken far more seriously and applied in a more exploratory and probing manner. Such work could more regularly reach beyond the world of multilateral diplomacy to the actual sites of the social practice generating abuse. (Or, at least as contentiously, international processes themselves could be explored for the extent to which they maintain or create conditions for severe abuse.) And theoretical engagement with such work could be open to richer understandings of the subject and the constructions of political community. But to inflate the achievement of current practices and orientations is to imagine, wrongly and with increasing difficulty, that 'we' in the West have emancipation more or less in hand.

But just as liberalism is unable to deliver on the promise of political salvation in which it has schooled us, neither is it the epitome of disaster that it is sometimes painted. Liberalism is not an ideal essence, predetermining and completely containing its various moments. It is a complex history of administrative and governmental practice dramatised and summarised as a story of multiple parts about how people live together. This story is spoken in different contexts, as part of different communications. The idea of a neutral public service, for example, is part of a different battle, and it carries a different significance in China from that which it has in Canada, while an emphasis on standard setting may have a different resonance in post-apartheid South Africa than it does in Bonn. Technocratic liberalism and its search for global norms may be unable to provide the approaches necessary in order to engage with the 'historical specificities and community contexts that define human roles' (Kothari, 1991: 27) and in which abuse is often embedded. The task is well beyond realising in practice the values we already largely share. It may also require greater critical reflection on what we mean by 'rights' than simply the more widespread institutionalisation – implicitly *from* here *to* there – of standards that are already given. Our shared understanding of the need to refrain from systematically injuring each other, let alone of how to go about that task, is not secure or given or complete. If anything, it is intermittent and recurrently under threat.

Realism and liberalism form dominant complementary voices addressing human rights issues in international politics – at least in policy and academic circles. But there are other, related, voices: a more specifically legal emphasis; attention to the historical development of an incipient society of states; idealism or utopianism; and the critical insights of Marxism. Marxism has not formed one of the dominant approaches to rights, and so will not be explored here; but it has nevertheless had a major and on-going impact on thinking about rights. As well as denaturalising liberal notions of rights (evident in the quotation of *The German Ideology* earlier in the chapter) through its analysis of the global dynamic of production, Marxism enabled quite a different appreciation of the international dimension of rights from that offered by liberal and interdependency theories. Various Marxist approaches have offered a critique of the dynamic structures of enrichment and impoverishment, and so have given substance to the idea of patterns of abuse and the assertion of rights beyond the boundaries of citizenship. Moreover, drawing on Marxism's emphasis on the primacy of human production in the continuing transformation of the social and material world, later interpretations of Marxism (neo-Marxism, critical theory) have questioned the production of fundamental categories of identity, power and social reality, thus making possible subtle critiques of liberal notions of rights and of specific patterns of abuse. However, Marxism's other great impact on questions of human rights to date has been, not as a critique, but indirectly through the rigidities of the communist states and the unyielding political and strategic structures of the Cold War. It is difficult to assess the impact of the brutal and confrontational simplifications of the Cold War on the development of international practice and understanding of human rights at a time when questions of rights were being explicitly constituted as international. Nevertheless, an extraordinary amount of energy was diverted into sterile competitive debates and to efforts to control any access to rights by clients of both states.

Utopianism, or idealism, is a marked presence in any discussion of human rights. In contemporary political terms, idealism is perhaps most closely associated with the impulses and language of human rights activism. And yet, in another sense, the actual conceptual terrain which has since the seventeenth century generated and dominated our models of human rights is itself idealist. For it is idealism, as a thread seaming various approaches to political life, that asserts the truth and defines the ground of the universal – idealism that identifies goodness or truth in a realm of its own. In one way or another, the theories of politics and international relations that have been discussed here situate themselves in relation to the tenets of this mode of understanding. In some ways it would make more sense to start this consideration of dominant approaches to rights in world politics with idealism, for realism initially defined and situated itself through the rebuttal of idealism, by turning idealism's hope for a 'perfected' world on its head.

> Again we are drawn to understand that the dominant theoretical tradition in inter-national relations theory is not political realism but idealism, for it is the possibility of universality proclaimed by idealism that makes possible the discursive linkage between difference, relativism, anarchy, tragedy and violence. (Walker, 1993: 74)

Idealism stands as a kind of alter ego to realism while including the relent-lessly optimistic notes and the constitutive assumptions of some branches of liberalism.

As a philosophical move, idealism posits an ultimate truth, as an essence or an idea, hidden beyond or behind the processes of living. It searches for or assumes possession of a metalanguage that expresses this perfect reality. Thus idealism sets in motion the bifurcation between experience as the 'dark glass' which both expresses and hides, is passing, fragmentary and misleading, and the abstract essence which is whole, timeless and true. This is the quandary of true and absolute versus fragmented and unreliable on which we have strung our understanding of how to care for each other.

Idealism not only describes a range of overtly idealist philosophical posi-tions but remains a powerful dimension in theories, some versions of Marxism for example, or realism itself, that endeavour to expunge it from their work. At the same time, and closely related to idealism as a philosophical move, the term also describes a strong emphasis on the driving force of moral values and a rejection of 'pragmatism', or the morality of the 'lesser of two evils', and an impatience to arrive at and judge situations in accordance with ultimate moral realities. Strong realism is idealist in its presumption of ownership of a metalanguage. In their depiction of 'power' versus 'ethics', idealism and realism are mirror images, locked into the kind of struggle in which, like the mythic generational battles, each side needs and reproduces the other as parody of its worst fears.

Idealism draws on those veins of thought which belong to the ontological traditions of natural law and variations of Kantian transcendentalism. In its more Kantian form in international relations theory, it is associated with a belief in the universality of ethical principles that express the unity of humankind (or the harmony of all fundamental interests) and that can be recovered by rational thought. It looks for a natural cosmopolitanism, now artificially constrained by structures of power and deception and by parochial or non-rational divisions of creed or culture. In this aspect, idealism offers a sharply different conceptuali-sation of international life than either realism or utilitarian liberalism – here the state is at best a temporary means or at worst an obstacle to the proper end of politics. Being universal and transcendent, the principles put forward by a utopian movement are often understood as unchanging, and in theory have been available throughout history, or they may be evolving as an increasingly complex whole; they are amenable to universally applicable proposition as might be the laws of physics. The purpose of reflection here is to lay bare the transcendent truths obscured by the divisions of history in order that social relations or institutions can be reconstructed in their light.

Utopianism or idealism may serve two contradictory functions. In the politics of social movements and social change it can refer to a moment which may be simply an energy for asserting the importance of ethical principles or the possibility of change – an emphasis on aspirations for personal goodness and non-exploitative community, however those may be conceived – in the face of efforts to exile 'values', or particular values, to an inarticulate periphery where they cannot distort the facts of the matter. The power which utopian theories or personalities have exerted can (at best) reflect their ability to give expression to belief in the possibility of goodness in the social and political domain and to the suggestion that things could be other than they seem. Vision and imagination are the faculties favoured by this form of political address. 'Idealism' can be the tag given to those who refuse the strange attraction of the foreclosure offered by the more brooding versions of realism by drawing attention to the need to recognise that the present has potentials for different futures.

But idealism as a politics of universal truth has a very different register. The inspirational moment regularly hardens into its own powerful foreclosures which offer not openness but implicit or explicit blueprints – the 'attempt dogmatically to prefigure the future' (Marx, 1972: 8). Like realism, idealism turns on posing an intense ontological split between what is and what ought to be, fact and value, practice and theory, policy and principle, power and truth. This divorce establishes the deformed character of both terms of the antinomy. It sets in motion the polarities and quandaries contained in the tension between universal and relative in which we generally grasp issues of respect for people. The antinomy may be managed by using the language of time to project what ought to be into the future. There it can seem to be the goal, reachable through actions in time. But it is more likely another country altogether, an otherworld.

In an inversion of realism, what ought to be, theory and principle are given pre-eminence in this antinomy, so that social change tends to be imagined as a process of actualising a vision, of displacing the messy present with a correctly imagined and ordered future. The right account, the right theory, the right formula seem themselves to promise a liberatory power. Truth is located in theory, where it can be claimed and possessed in propositional form. For extreme utopianism, 'reality' must be made over in the image of theory, the slate of history wiped clean and fresh words written. Or the antinomy may not be managed at all, leaving only a sour cynicism preoccupied with exposing the ways in which actual people and events have again failed ideas. The vision of emancipation founders and returns as a metalanguage of nihilism and romantic despair.

A persistent criticism of the political theories discussed in this chapter – their failure to grasp that their visions are embedded in their own histories and context of social practice, their mistaking of the partial for the absolute – is directed at their idealist dimensions. From conditions of 'imperfection', utopian theories or moments imagine the lineaments of a perfect world – either explicitly, by prescription, or implicitly, by wholesale condemnation of things as they are now. But our understanding of what is and what ought to be 'are in actuality mutually constituted: our world view constructs our definition of human nature and vice versa, whereas any preferred state necessarily derives from the givens and aspirations embedded in our understanding of the nature of reality and the range of what is possible' (Peterson, 1990: 307). Partiality of itself does not devalue insight or little would be valuable. And, indeed, all the approaches discussed here form a dense ground from which we draw: tracings of our collective efforts to grapple with difficult circumstances. But the abstraction and hubris of then ignoring one's own humble origins can serve to mislead by obscuring what is also rooted in practice – that is, the tools for change that may be available or emerging, the kinds of change that may be needed, and respect for the unfamiliar contributions of others, for circumstances and for 'problem solving'.

NOTES

1 European natural law doctrines have been current in medieval, enlightenment and contemporary times. Theories of natural law may be theistic or non-theistic (and within the Christian theologies, Catholic, Calvinist or Lutheran), rationalist or mystical, flexible or highly doctrinaire. Thomistic natural law doctrines posit the existence of a moral order that is inherent in the nature of things and of which human beings are part, but which does not derive from human society *per se*. The moral universe envisaged by these schools of natural law is understood to turn upon certain fundamental principles, the key one often being identified as the 'law of love'.

2 Stories can be far more potent than theoretically elaborated frameworks. The dynamism of narrative allows you to experience and move through contradiction and unexplained gaps – to integrate states and events in an ordered but not strictly rational way. Theoretical explanations, on the other hand, are always trying to repress contradiction. In this way, story 'understands' language better than does theory. In keeping with the classical narrative form, the story of the contract operates through the dynamic interplay of a series of overlapping polarities which are traversed and articulated by the figure of the hero, in this case, the everyman.

3 John Rawls's veil of ignorance is a prominent contemporary example. See his (1971) *A Theory of Justice*, Harvard University Press, Cambridge, MA.

4 'Nature', like the Garden of Eden on which it is based and which it turns on its head, is by definition where we are not but where we imagine the formation of our essential self and the unchanging imperatives that shape community to lie.

5   Under conditions of mistrust security becomes a scant resource, had at the expense of others. States' competition for security and power establishes their place within a shifting international hierarchy. This competition establishes the systemic constraints that shape what it is possible for states to do under conditions of insecurity. The sovereignty of states resembles the sovereignty of man in nature, but is nevertheless a principle of order in international life, allowing the dynamic of competition and conflict sufficient equilibrium to reproduce itself. Sovereignty both defines the separateness of states and constitutes the condition for their participation in the system of states. It is an act of mutual recognition by states of each other's right to pursue internal and external security independent of interference.

6   Indeed, realist theorists can uphold particular ethical values – primary commitment to the benefit of one's national community (where 'benefit' is given a particular ambit) and, particularly in the case of early critical realists such as Carr, prudence, resignation, a certain wry toleration born of scepticism and the consciousness of human frailty, the skills of the game, a disdain for easy moralisms and a certain sense of responsibility. These are substantial values. For much realist thought they appear as pragmatism, however, while 'ethics' belongs to the different and competing domain of 'principle'.

3

The pursuit of grounds

As THE INTRODUCTION to one of the more recent human rights readers notes, the effort to establish or assert ' "some particular ground" upon which right-holders can justify their claim to rights . . . has framed the dominant discourse on human rights' (Dunne and Wheeler, 1999: 4). Indeed, any discussion of the broader issues raised by human rights seems condemned to endlessly patrol the beat mapped out by the polarities of universal and communitarian or relative grounds for rights and, as Dunne and Wheeler make clear, the associated epistemological debate between various forms of foundationalism and anti-foundationalism. It seems impossible to entirely avoid situating one's efforts to grapple with the questions raised by systemically inflicted injury on that particular compass, so that if one is not anchored on one side of the debate there is an inexorable slide along the well-travelled path towards the other pole. Yet this chapter is shaped by a profound reserve concerning the debate between universalism and cultural relativism. This reserve is not the natural impatience with reflection expressed by some activists. Rather, it is rooted in a suspicion that, at the level of abstraction in which the debate circulates, the polarity of relative and universal not only has little to offer actual problems of response to abuse, but may itself, somewhat paradoxically, remain trapped within what could be rather sweepingly summarised as a modernist Western cultural milieu. Thus it may not only be the dominant figures of the universal that are, in the end, somewhat parochial. Despite the alacrity with which it has been picked up internationally, the dichotomy itself, and the apparently logical imperative that demands a choice one way or the other, may in some important respects be generated and sustained by the history of the development of the state and of colonialism.

From this position of reserve, then, the chapter considers aspects of these two interlocking metatheoretical debates (in part through a discussion of alternative or more critical approaches to the conceptualisation of rights, or ethics). These debates have certainly been central to scholarly exchange on questions of rights (as well as on ethics more generally); they have also been prominent in the politics of international rights promotion and in the effort to understand what we do when we pursue human rights in the international or the domestic arena. Yet while it seems impossible to avoid direct engagement with questions of universal versus relative truth, or of the presence or absence of ontological grounds for knowledge, and impossible to escape positioning on those trajectories, no position on those trajectories seems entirely satisfying. This chapter is written tentatively then, in the hope that working with questions of abuse can gradually leave aside the universal-relative dichotomy. In the context of this discussion the chapter returns to some of the themes raised in Chapter 1 – the limited value of the push for certainty and the sometimes creative function of uncertainty, and the metaphor of conversation or dialogue (or multilogue, in James Tully's term). While not quite clearing a path out of the universalist-relativist debate, a rich sense of dialogue offers at least a counterpoise or a place to start the unravelling of what seems an unnecessarily confined and too all-encompassing dichotomy. The case studies in the following chapters will directly and indirectly continue to explore these themes.

Chapter 2 considered one group of universalist claims underpinning what remains perhaps the dominant liberal construction of human rights. The categories of 'human' as radically autonomous individual, of 'state' as minimalist administrator, of 'reason' as formal, abstract and segmented, but also of 'community', 'family', 'property', – the categories which are the stuff of leading liberal rights models – offer a 'particularism masquerading as the universal' (Taylor, 1992: 44). Such a construction of universality has a nasty habit of operating to exclude many people from the ultimate community it claims as its own. Richard Rorty points clearly to this danger when he warns against labelling those committing atrocities in the former Yugoslavia (or elsewhere) as irrational or inhuman – that is, as falling outside the defining criteria of membership in the moral community of the human (Rorty, 1993). It may be, as some postmodern approaches would suggest, that the identity of the universal can only be forged by the exile of what it is not; that our categories of the human, for example, must work to cast some as sub-human. Whether or not this dynamic is intrinsic to all universals, it has clearly operated on a number of levels in the dominant models of rights. As argued in the earlier chapters, the claims to universality which mark and enable these models of rights have in practice excluded and made invisible categories of person and of abuse. Rights practices are not limited to liberal conceptualisations of society, but theories of rights generally build on presumptions carried in the workings, both hidden and explicit, of those concepts. Moreover, differing, even opposed, modern accounts of society, knowledge, order, or wealth creation can share fundamental points of departure with the liberal myths of origin. It is the presumed universal applicability of notions not only of rights but for example of the interest-maximising individual, as well as the historical and material power of 'Western' modes of life in which these notions are embedded, that have ensured that the history of human rights is not one of darkness gradually overcome by light, but a more mixed and painful account.

It is not surprising, then, that disquiet at universalist claims is quite widespread, particularly, in Ashis Nandy's words, 'at the fag end of that phase of domination that we stand today, ready to pick up the fragments of our lives and cultures that survive after European hegemony and intrusion' (1998: 142). There are, however, other ways of thinking about the gesture to universality. We appeal, sometimes passionately, to the primacy of a sense of the universal or of the particular in a range of quite different contexts. The infliction of suffering, for example, is a powerful mechanism to isolate and enclose. To call upon universal principles or solidarity in the face of that enclosure is to reach out for, and to recognise, connection to what is beyond it. Such a reaching out and recognition bears little relation to the search for meta-ethical certainty. Or we support the Universal Declaration as an international agreement that can have considerable practical value in working against systemically inflicted abuse while offering a powerful symbol of an aspiration for social orders that do not turn upon violent or exploitative subordinations. Support for international frameworks on rights need not imply an ontological claim.

In a similar way, 'relativism' can draw attention to the textures of particular times and places and can note the reality of deep and incommensurable difference. It can be a call for prudence and attentiveness to what is to hand in the face of crusading moral certainty or be a protest against a long, painful and largely overlooked history of exile of our or others' ways of being from the languages that define truths and certainties. Or the polarity between universal and relative may be a way of referring to an everyday, but potentially searching, experience – the recognition of difference, even extraordinary difference, and the experience of significant communication and commonality, despite this difference, or conversely of a gulf that perhaps makes a joint enterprise unworkable, or both.

These and other gestures to what is shared widely and what is perhaps shared more intimately have strong purchase on notions of 'universal' and 'relative', and are often called in to support one side or the other. The peculiar intensity of the dichotomy, however, may derive from quite different and more limited roots in particular historical, political and conceptual accretions – shaped in the kind of dense layering that Michel Foucault's work, most famously, has studied. It is this fundamental imbrication with the dominant constitution of political community that guarantees the argument between the two terms such embedded and knotted obduracy. Here this layered history can only be suggested, rather than investigated.

Certain powerful accounts of sovereignty seem to be the primary hinge around which the terms of the debate between universalism and relativism turn. As suggested in chapter 2, the early modern accounts of political possibility that helped to conceptualise the development of the Westphalian order may not have so much replaced the universalism of Christendom with the particularism of the state system as they have provided a new way of articulating – together – both universal and particular. The state and the power of the sovereign (or of sovereignty) was particular. Its freedom to follow its own faith, or management of faiths, was supreme. The power of sovereignty was the power (in principle) of the particularist government to override all other claims to (worldly) authority. Despite radical shifts in the state system since Westphalia, this broadly constitutive element continues to serve as a powerful inscription of particularism. But within the evolving European state system this particularism and differentiation was held within the scope of both complementary and competing principles of universality and sameness. The norm of sovereignty in interstate relations is a principle of both differentiation and uniformity – the traditional realist image of states as billiard balls captures this quite well. The 'uniformity' may be understood in practical and political terms, as the result of carefully crafted criteria for sovereignty, standardised expectations regarding its operations and agreement to certain rules of the game, as well as a long history of interactions. For many powerful accounts of political life within the state, however, the underlying mechanisms by which the authority of the particularist sovereignties was seen to be founded, and which legitimised the break from the universalist claims of Christendom, were not pragmatic but themselves universal – the figure of everyman, or of a primal community, exercising reason. Even without an imagined moment of origin, the human community, in the space of the state, was understood as creating itself, guided by its new-found tools of enlightened self-interest, reason and science. The figure of the rational subject became the new seat of universality whether that subject was envisaged as prior to – and the foundation of – community or as possible only in the context of community. The rational community was particular, autonomous and co-terminous with the state, or heading towards a universalist Kantian federation of rational states. 'Man' was seeking mastery of his own natural and political universe and was becoming 'himself'. But he was doing this through the medium of the state – either as ultimate community or as stepping-stone to universal citizenship.

Clearly, states themselves, as the particular, were not understood as simply *ad hoc* fragments of humanity. Rather, state-building practices over several centuries ensured that they came to take on the mantle of fundamental unit of political community, the *sine qua non* of human community and, to a greater or lesser extent, the theatre of ethical life. Moreover, in the dominant versions at least, states came to be understood as constituted by an essentially uniform people, whether that uniformity was conceived of as the expression of ethnicity, shared culture and will, as the assemblage of atomised individuals holding identical rights, or defined around primary commitment to civic institutions and language. Thus the state identified as bounded but unified and primary political community gained an essentially ontological, rather than contingent, political significance, quite independent of the composition of actual states and leaving aside the matter of the cost of ideals of uniformity. In many discussions around ethics and rights the state retains this significance. Although either community or universality may receive priority as the context for moral growth, the pull between particular and universal seems intrinsic to, and indeed, constitutive of dominant understandings of the state and the state system.

The tenor of this interweaving antinomy, however, was given new dimension and vehemence by the extended and violent encounters with the altogether other orders of difference provided by colonialism. Colonialism was not just confrontation with difference, of course. It was confrontation in the context of battles for possession, survival and identity, of centuries of 'ethnic cleansing' and forced labour, justified through theoretical (but actively applied) hierarchies of being; and, later, as colonised people struggled to free themselves via the only route available – that offered through the state system – it was confrontation in the context of a new, mostly twentieth-century, round of state making. We may all – the 'West', as well as those regions directly or indirectly colonised – still be struggling to come to terms with Western Europe's violent encounter with difference. The nexus of universal and relative gained new dimensions, and in both practical political and theoretical work may still echo the 'problems' posed by 'pacification' of colonised peoples within empire. As Ashis Nandy, writing of India, suggests, colonialism tended to absolutise 'the relative difference between cultures'. One 'could not be both Western *and* Indian' – for the purposes of colonialism, one was constructed as the antithesis of the other (1983: 73, 71). At the same time, the clash between belief in universality and the confrontation with difference could be (and frequently was) resolved through an ascending scale of achievement, with modern Western rationalism defining the pinnacle and the standard through which achievement was measured. Nineteenth-century theories of 'separate development' categorised colonised peoples according to a complex map of how morally and intellectually capable different societies were of eventually reaching the universal standards of Western rational government (some would never make it), thus justifying a practical relativism (and autocracy) in the context of an eventual but endlessly deferred (liberal) universalism.

The analysis is sometimes offered (for example, by Ken Booth drawing on the work of Michael Carrithers and Bernard McGrane) that the discipline of anthropology, which followed in the wake created by colonialism, articulated one complex avenue for Western response to other peoples. Anthropology undertook 'to judge cultures in their own terms', to discover and interpret cultural authenticity (Booth, 1999: 50). Anthropology has gathered a rich and extraordinary store of observation, interaction and theory making. But arguably it has also constituted 'culture' as an object of discourse: an object in the epistemic matrix guiding the social sciences and an object in the world – a reified 'black box' as Booth notes (1999: 36). In so doing anthropology gave theoretical and empirical expression to a new dimension in debates about the universal and the relative. The zone of difference and potential relativity became, in practical terms, vast. Moreover, each culture regarded could be regarded 'equally'. Indeed all were equally objects of knowledge, separate and equidistant from the knowing subject, all attesting to the position of anthropologist as *cogito*, and all ideally held in the anthropologist's single gaze. This is another enactment of existence according to the terms of a 'Western' epistemic framework. Meanwhile, following the waves of post-war decolonisation, the plethora of new states at all stages of development have been straining the state system, pulling farther apart the dual poles of uniformity and particularity that have contributed to defining that system, and so (as Hedley Bull pointed out in 1977) rendering the sociality of relations between states increasingly problematic.

While certainly drawing on both older and wider ruminations, the nexus between universalism and relativism may thus be essentially built into crucial aspects and phases of the international system of states – into debates around and particularly following the early modern shaping of that system (debates that remain crucial in the ways we think about the person and political community) and then embedded in the entangled dynamics of colonialism and its afterwash. If we take this suggestion seriously, two points follow. One is that what seems so etched into the nature of things that we cannot evade it, so logical that if you are not identified with one pole you must be moving towards the other, is a lengthy set of exchanges about the state and the nature of sovereignty (exchanges which emerged in response to particular problems), and about a not-so-distant, not-so-buried history, laid like transparencies on top of each other. Moreover, neither matter is settled: the constitution of sovereignty is yet again transforming, while the significance of colonial histories is an issue of intense political and philosophical negotiation and debate in many arenas. The universal-relative dichotomy may be more an *expression* of these struggles rather than any ultimate frame for understanding them. As a result, perhaps, the terms of the dichotomy rarely seem to shed light on problems of what to make of or how to deal with actual cultural difference and genuine gulfs of understanding. Another way of putting this, and the second point to be derived, is that this dichotomy is not resolvable in its own terms. Relativism and universalism may presume and require each other, and both are going to have something to say about courses of action in the modern state system, but not as statements of permanent truths. Some of these questions will be picked up in the discussion of the Asian Way debate later in the chapter.

To approach the universal-relative dichotomy from a slightly different direction: much modern understanding of political life starts, explicitly or sometimes quite unconsciously, with a principle of radical fragmentation. This principle of fragmentation *can* act as the basis for, or perhaps the twin of, abstract universality – the 'individual' as universal human – it certainly poses sociality as a question. What we deem to be fundamental will establish what we believe needs explanation and justification – what seems to be a question. We may posit universals in part because we start from an assumption of radical separateness – of state from state, community from community, human from animal, individual from everything. Of course it makes sense to think of people as in significant ways separate, potentially autonomous, and so forth. But people can also be understood as interconnected, not only with each other but with all of existence, past, present and perhaps in some respects future, in ways that are also profoundly significant. This fundamental biological – and perhaps not only biological – reality, opens ways of thinking about the person that we have scarcely begun to explore.

The presumptions of essential separateness and universality are interdependent. To consider this within the metaphors of the (Lockean) liberal subject discussed in chapter 2, we presume ourselves to be autonomous self-interested individuals, with instrumental relations to ourselves and others. For this liberal, or simply modern, orientation to life, what balances the particularism of individual autonomy is the universality of our status as individuals. Recognising our common vulnerability and, for most contemporary renderings of this story on the basis of our individual but common autonomy, using the processes of our common reason, we join together in society. This universality may be more substantive, so that we share specific rights (to life, liberty and property) simply because we are all autonomous individuals. Or the nature of universality may be more procedural (but still essentially rational and self-interested), where we determine virtually all, or at least some level of, our fundamental rights by negotiation. Various positions of strong to weak universalism can be based on this spectrum. But it may be this construction of the self as innately separate which makes a question of why we should care for each other. In particular, it sets the question of why we should care for those beyond our borders, beyond the separate 'self' of the nation and the self-interested community of the state (since the story of the contract provides an answer for why we would care for fellow-citizens). Moreover, there is only one genre of answers that can make sense in this construction of the self and the state: somewhere on the spectrum of universal to relative. The debate between relativism and universalism is often not, then, one about whether it is better to be loving or destructive, or even whether it always and everywhere makes sense to say that it is better to be loving than destructive – as for example Booth (1999) proposes.[1]

Some theorists

This section considers the work of some contemporary theorists who have attempted in different ways to bridge or to circumvent the polarity of relative and universal, while nevertheless taking positions on the question – the first (two) relativist, the second universalist. One effort to edge outside of the framework of relativism versus universalism that structures discourses around rights can be found in the work of Richard Rorty and Chris Brown. Both writers lever their efforts through a critique of the search for epistemic certainty regarding what is essential to human nature or what grounds morality; they argue for abandoning the quest for 'premises capable of being known to be true independently of the truth of the moral intuitions' which emerge in the course of people's lives together. 'Such premises are supposed to justify our intuitions, by providing premises from which the content of these intuitions can be deduced' (Rorty, 1993: 117). Rorty is particularly concerned to reject rationality as 'the shared human attribute which supposedly "grounds" morality' (Rorty, 1993: 116). The traditional consequence of eschewing ultimate grounds for morality is to find yourself classified a relativist, and Rorty and Brown are no exceptions here.

However, in somewhat different ways, both Rorty and Brown support a 'human rights culture', which Rorty declares morally superior. Rejecting the search for a rationalist basis for morality or understanding, Rorty proffers a fundamentally pragmatic view of knowledge, where all inquiry can be understood 'as practical problem-solving . . . [and] every belief as action-guiding' (1993: 119). Debates about abstract human nature lead us away from the practical problems of people's political interactions. More dangerously, the work of discerning and upholding such abstract categories tends to function by excluding certain groups of people from the 'pure' category of human – from 'people like us'. The emergence and growth of a human rights culture does not reflect a proper grasp of an essential truth, but rather the increased material and physical security in the wealthy developed states and the growth of a kind of empathy. Here Rorty, like Zygmut Bauman or Bhikhu Parekh, emphasises the importance of feeling, in sharp contrast to the dismissal of feeling and the prioritising of rationality and reason in modernist philosophies. For Rorty, empathy is the product of a 'sentimental education' in which people hear 'sad and sentimental stories' that slowly lead them to identify with the plight of others (1993: 119). It is the potential gradual emergence of such fellow-feeling that would enable a 'progress of sentiments' and a way to approach living better together. 'This sets aside Kant's question "What is Man?" and substitutes the

question "What sort of world can we prepare for our great-grandchildren?"'
(1993: 121, 122).

While drawing on Rorty's work, Chris Brown emphasises the contextual
nature of the qualities that have made various Western societies 'the freest and
generally most congenial' of communities (1999: 111). Respect for rights has
been possible *because* of these qualities, but rights themselves do not express or
contain the complex tissue of these qualities in essential form. Thus the export
of the formal structure of rights to other communities may have little beneficial
impact, as it is not rights in isolation but the whole web of community relationships and ways that makes freedom and congeniality possible. Neither writer
appears to believe that one can not make moral judgements about practices in
one's own or others' culture – the work of both clearly makes such judgements
and claims. Both consider that such judgements do not depend on the existence
of universal grounds.

The reflections of both writers, barely sketched here, are instructive. Chris
Brown's insistence on the contextual nature of ethical possibility is a valuable
reminder of the immense complexity of effective political and social change. If
systemically inflicted harm is not solely a matter of the relationships between
government and citizens but is embedded in social practice and in the social and
political institutions and forms in which identities take shape and value is
assigned, change is not simply a matter of legislation, less intrusive government
or the 'correct' principles. Nor is it achieved largely by formal international
norm setting arrived at by elites (although this can play a role). Rather, the
movement away from violence and oppression may involve a subtle, lengthy and
difficult process of renegotiation of political, economic and social relationships.
The difficulty of this process, however, seems no good reason not to engage
in it. Indeed, and here I move away from Chris Brown's more communitarian
emphasis, we are already engaged inextricably with each other; the choices
concern how we pursue and conduct those engagements.

Chris Brown prioritises the role of community, and community here, as in
most such discussions, appears to be co-terminous with the state. Moreover, the
sense of state-as-community (an ideal model, as Brown makes plain) presumes
an already high level of shared cultural and political norms – the ideal uniformity of the state, usually underpinned by ethnic uniformity or close complementarity, as mentioned above. But, as with the category of 'culture', there is
little that is unproblematical about 'community'. While the significance of community is not questioned here, communities themselves are multidimensional,
open-woven webs, with unclear, overlapping boundaries. The state as community, while again critical to contemporary forms of life for those of us who live
in working states, is a highly attenuated chequerboard construction of recent
origin. Many states are already a patchwork of significantly different ethnic and
cultural communities. With the pace of international migration, this phenom-

enon can only increase. The need for difficult negotiation between communities or across cultural difference within the state is already a reality. Nor, in practical, lived life, does community – as a sustained process of mutual responsibility and deliberation, to borrow loosely from the terms of Brown's Hegelian construction – stop at the edges of borders. Family, ethnicity, religion, work, trade are some of the factors that can nurture ties of mutual, collective obligation of greater or lesser power irrespective of borders. Even when they are not classifiable under 'community', people's individual and collective enmeshment with aspects of others' lives in other places are often extensive and significant. The political, commercial, ecological and conceptual structures of our lives are often already densely transnational, whether or not we are aware of that.

In similar fashion, Rorty's essay notes the lack of any 'morally relevant transcultural facts' (1993: 116). Rorty seems to be talking philosophy here – his argument at this point is concerned to reject the existence of ultimate grounds for morality (without rejecting morality itself). But the situation may be far more deeply entangled than either simply denying or asserting transcultural moral facts would allow. It is true, for example, that infanticide is a quite different proposition in poverty-stricken rural western China than it is in Australia, or indeed Beijing. But if one were thinking prosaically about living in Vietnam, marrying a Czech, doing business in Bangladesh, or more pointedly, working on peace building in Bougainville, a denial of morally relevant transcultural 'facts' would be perplexing indeed. Rorty's statement seems to be caught in the closure of the bounded state versus unbounded reason – to deny the one is to be thrown back to the other. The possible lack of ultimate, or ahistorical, grounds for morality seems no reason to assert the complete incommensurability of cultures or even a clear line of demarcation between cultures. The texture of living and communicating in a distinctly different culture, or across different cultures, seems hardly touched by such a simple opposition. However imperfect, the reality of communication and exchange seems at least as notable as that of an incommensurability of or conflict between value systems. Both are negotiated every day by many millions of people.

The rejection of transcultural moral facts also seems to turn upon a sharply delineated division between self and other – a division that is not itself an inevitable consequence of rejecting an ultimate ground in which all things can be freely translated into each other. This clear either-or alternative perhaps falls under the enchantment of dualisms that belongs, at least in part, with the rationalism Rorty disowns. But, in practice, relations between communities and cultures, and across places (and perhaps also, in a different way, across times), are often densely interactive, although also difficult. To use the metaphor of conversation, they are dialogic relations, while, to borrow from an early theorist of dialogue, '[t]rue differentiation presupposes a simultaneous resemblance and difference' (Karcevskij, in Holquist, 1990: 25).

Rorty's essay begins by referring to the savage conflict between Serbs and Bosnians. The reference serves as a warning about the cost of counting some people as inhuman, but it is sometimes read as an assertion of the impossibility of judgement across cultures (e.g. by Dunne and Wheeler, 1999: 9). To use the essay and that perhaps inaccurate reading as a springboard – the reference is a reminder of the inadequacy of notions of 'culture' in grappling with some of the deepest gulfs and the sharpest breaks between worlds thrown up by violence and extreme abuse. As so-called 'low intensity' – but high impact – conflict around the world has demonstrated, protracted violence reshapes cultures and leaves instead a 'culture of violence'; studies of the former Yugoslavia, Sri Lanka, Northern Ireland, Mozambique, and so on (e.g. Kaldor, 1998), depict it quite clearly. The need for revenge, and feelings of hatred, fear, anger, powerlessness and grief, among other factors, can create 'differences' and gulfs – not only between those locked on opposite sides of the dispute but between those inside and outside the experience – in the face of which notions of 'culture' have little to offer. It is not traditional culture that has 'legitimised' the savagery in the Balkans. Nor do notions of culture necessarily shed much light on the collective capacity to not see or not register extreme and violent forms of abuse happening in your midst – the 'states of denial' that Stanley Cohen has documented (2001).

While rejecting transcultural moral facts, Rorty's argument is also clearly shaped by a belief in caring for each other and an optimism about where such 'capacities for friendship and intermarriage' and for 're-creation of the self, through interaction with selves as unlike itself as possible' can lead us (1993: 132). Such capacities surely suggest their own forms of morally relevant trans-cultural *regard*. Rorty suggests that there is no need to ground these capacities in anything beyond themselves, only to cultivate them more assiduously. The 'sad and sentimental stories' that he recommends to that end may be more than anything else a way of emphasising a sense of moral obligation grounded not in a narrow construction of reason but one that has everything to do 'with love, friendship, trust, or social solidarity' (1993: 122). Elsewhere, Rorty has argued (1989) that human similarities (in particular our capacity for pain and humiliation) outweigh our differences. Solidarity grows, although not inevitably, out of the awakening of feeling rather than via the instructions of reason. This is clearly not an argument for 'anything goes'.

Discussions of human rights in the international context often (directly or half-unconsciously) address liberal societies as if they already had matters of human rights, or of the embedded infliction of suffering, essentially sorted out. Perhaps because of their concern to make it clear that they do not judge 'all contexts to be equally moral' (Brown, 1999: 113), Brown and Rorty make this assumption of moral superiority explicit. Rorty, for example, while maintaining a critical edge in certain references to his own society, makes the extraordinary assumption that liberal societies care more for others and takes for granted that a human rights culture, which he implies is essentially a culture of care, is 'our culture'. The problem of rights in the international arena thus slides into one of whether and how we can transfer our moral superiority, or crucial elements of it, to others; the task for others is to become 'rich, lucky and liberal' like us. Whatever the undoubted achievements of the liberal state and the culture of reason pursued by the Enlightenment, this form of address remains deeply self-delusory. It overlooks, among other factors, the persistent violent marginalisation of significant groups within liberal societies (and systemically imposed exclusion and humiliation, and the violence that accompanies them, can be just as lethal as more overt political abuse). It fails to question the historical and contemporary nature of the engagement of various liberal states and entities with other societies. What role have 'we', in the safe, wealthy and often powerful liberal states played in the insecurity, impoverishment and disempowerment of others? While not clear-cut, the answer to this question would not allow us such simple and superior innocence. How is an ethic of care to be given shape? Through a 'human rights culture' (which, if it is a liberal rights culture, is caring in certain contexts but *not* in others), or is it through 'our culture' (which is even more ambiguous)?

It is ironic that after drawing such a sharp line between 'our culture' and those of others, between self and other, the value of interaction seems to suggest the remaking of others in our image. Such self-regarding ethnocentrism undermines communication. This is partly because we are suffering delusions not only about ourselves, but also about others. The sweeping presumption of superiority slides down the familiar paths by which the 'West' has traditionally handled the difference of other societies, regarding itself as containing the criteria of achievement. As a result, despite the central place of sympathy in the argument, there is little space for actual engagement across cultures. This counters the essay's chosen path of practical problem solving, which depends precisely on engagement to make sense. Pragmatism by itself offers no clear highway through the din of circumstance (and a pragmatism which turns on an autonomous, self-interested subject may differ from a pragmatism with a different understanding of the person in the world). Even while Rorty questions the gulf drawn between 'us' and 'them' and suggests that the source of much violence is being 'deprived of . . . security and sympathy', the sense of superiority counters this work by erecting a powerful barrier between 'us' and 'them'. It implicitly reduces the density of life in 'other' places to the casualty lists presented on the world news, and it allows in through the back door precisely that crude and widespread form of relativism which Rorty's essay exposes: that 'other people' do not care so much about each other, and that abuse is what, after all, they are used to. This is the relativism that calls forth equally assertive and simplified universalisms. This careless reductionist glance at other places supports the essay's elitist, culturally reified and narrowly determinist account of the mechanics of political change – that morality rests with the rich and powerful. The charge that change comes from above may not be such a problem – change comes from all directions. It remains significant, however, that people respond in different ways to evidence of others' suffering – that it is not only the safe and secure who object to or act on other's abuse; that the safe and secure may often do little.

It seems that the essay can be read as leading in two different directions: relativist, but also universalist. This reflects in part Rorty's efforts to uncouple moral possibility from the presumption of a singular underlying truth or a formal ontological principle – in particular (for Rorty), from reason. 'Sympathy' could perhaps be cast as an alternative ground, or as too fluid and mutable to serve such a purpose. But the relativism and the universalism of the 1993 essay also reflect the inability to step aside from the broader conceptual architecture within which the dichotomy operates. Is this to say that, in this text at least, Rorty is a closet universalist? Perhaps, in both the better and the worst senses of the word; but it may also suggest that the dichotomy is not adequate for talk about the complex interweaving of difference and continuity that makes up both cross-cultural interaction and moral life.

An effort to recast the spectrum of relative and universal, rather than to step outside it, can be seen in the work of Andrew Linklater. Drawing on Marxist and critical theory (particularly Habermasian discourse ethics) as well as Kantian perspectives, Andrew Linklater's work is highly attuned to the patterns of exclusion associated with the operation of claims to moral universality. The comments here will focus on aspects of his 1998 text *The Transformation of Political Community*, which arguably provides one of the richest elaborations of Linklater's vocational commitments. While 'unapologetically universalistic', his work is an effort to elaborate a conception of universality that escapes the shadowed side of exclusion and occlusion – one that does not exile difference. Complementing this is a concern with the transformation of community, away from the formation of identity through the construction of aliens and enemies without and the marginalised within. Dialogue is both the mechanism for and the goal of this refiguring of community; engaging with others, in particular the excluded, concerning 'the ways in which social practices and policies harm their interests' is central to Linklater's vision (1998: 7). Both 'community' and 'the universal' are thus re-oriented and refocused, away from an essentially static core of identity towards a commitment to inclusiveness, community building and the process of widening boundaries. This is an effort both to conceptualise a *universalised* or open community and to find within cosmopolitan ethics a place for the intimacies and loyalties of community through new constitutions of citizenship 'which bind sub-state, state and transnational authorities and loyalties together in a post-Westphalian international society' (1998: 8). Linklater is thus pursuing a 'new articulation of universality and particularity' which harmonises both within a reconstitution of political community (1998: 49).

In order to revive universalism as an orientation capable of referring to a complex of non-exclusionary practices, political forms and institutions, Linklater understands the core universal principles as procedural rather than substantive. What constitutes the universal here is thus less visions of the good life than what needs to be in place for true dialogue to be possible. (This goal, it would seem, is likely to involve a subtle web of substantive principles.) Universality is the 'responsibility to engage each other . . . in open dialogue', in particular about the welfare and interests of the interlocutors (1998: 101). Such exchanges need not imply consensus – people may engage in dialogue without achieving 'any lasting resolution of ethical differences' (1998: 96), while many may seek to 'cooperate to eradicate unjust exclusion without assuming that they will ever converge around one universalistic conception of the good life' (1998: 99). Presumably, however, they must all be committed to open communication and its preconditions. While critical of Rorty's relativism, Linklater also draws on Rorty, particularly on the understanding that we have to start from where we are. He combines this, however, with critical theory's insight that diverse social arrangements already contain the resources with which to work towards their transformation.

This is a vision of some power. It can be read on two levels, although Linklater himself may not make much of this distinction. At one level, the 1998 text appears to be addressed to a nest of quandaries, and opportunities, facing Western Europe for the foreseeable future. The populations of the European Union member states are grappling with the need for new institutional frameworks capable of responding to the revolutions of political structure, citizenship and sovereignty in the region. As Linklater, discussing Western Europe, notes:

> [W]hile the majority of states may remain committed to pluralist principles [i.e. agreement on the basic norms pertaining to order and co-existence within the state system], . . . a small minority may embark upon collaborative projects which breach the sovereign principle which has been central to international relations since the Peace of Westphalia. (1998: 7,8)

However, EU member states have not only embarked on the extended experiment of the union, with its attendant reshaping of democratic structures and forms, transnational justice, the relationships between capitals and restless substate regions, and so on. At the same time rapid changes in both international migration flows and European demographic patterns have meant that immigration and refugee movements may substantially affect the ethnic and cultural fabric of Western Europe over the next fifty years. How to deal with so-called 'third-country migration' is an extraordinary and potentially explosive challenge for the EU and its member states, with significant ramifications for the nature of political community and citizenship. 'Accepting cultural diversity while not "losing" the essence of the established culture has stimulated widespread interest in the foundational values of citizenship in [the EU] states' (Gowers, 2001: 23). *The Transformation of Political Community* is turned towards contributing to this 'collaborative post-Westphalian project' and the debates around 'foundational values' it generates. The motif of dialogue is an effort to provide conceptual underpinnings for an approach to the transnational dynamics changing the form of citizenship in the EU that is positive and expansive while remaining sensitive to the needs of local communities.

This is not to suggest that the 1998 text engages directly with policy debates or the practicalities of social arrangements. Rather, it articulates an orientation to political life that supports a dynamic concept of citizenship – one that may be particularly relevant to Europe's contemporary and fundamental problems. Linklater's text provides a careful intellectual grounding of the potential for dialogic communities in the major traditions of European philosophy and, to a lesser extent, European and 'great power' history – that is in debates about the nature and constitution of the modern state and of moral community. Through tracing key debates on political community, and on the claimed necessity of modes of (violent) exclusion to the operation of community, this discussion contextualises and relativises the belief in the inevitability of violent conflict and exclusion as integral to political life. This is 'starting from where we are', where that place is understood as a confluence of (indigenous) intellectual traditions and public philosophies around the state and morality. Linklater's emphasis on dialogue is of course applicable beyond Western Europe. All broadly liberal or democratic states face issues of citizenship, migration and cultural and political diversity. But the sense of the human and the models of dialogue that take shape in Linklater's text are deeply rooted in the contending Westphalian traditions of the rational universal subject, even if that subject is conceived in procedural rather than overtly substantive terms. This is a vision for the radical reform of elements of modern liberal states, particularly those undertaking the collaborative experiments of the EU, which is effectively addressed to European policy and scholarly circles.

While grounded in the context of debate over Western Europe, the universalism of Linklater's argument can stand as a commitment to inclusive and participative political frameworks, a dynamic concept of citizenship and openness to the circumstances and societies of others. The text makes claims at another level, however, which according to its own logic is that of the true ground of its argument, and so moves from exploring underlying principles for policy orientations in particular fields to a search for deeper justification at the level of ultimate things. This second level of Linklater's text, and the second way in which universalism figures in the text, thus refers to universal reason and a universal communication community, where 'all individuals should be regarded as if they were co-legislators in a universal moral community' (1998: 37). As with the patterns of idealism discussed in chapter 2, a central role is given to theory as the transformative agent and vehicle of truth. This is a vision of arrival, instructed by theory: 'a philosophy of ultimate ends' in which the shape of the world will, not necessarily but ideally, come to embody theory (1998: 40). Linklater endeavours to counter the fixity of visions of arrival by presenting ultimate things as procedural. But leaving aside the question of how far procedural and substantive can be kept separate, what is presented may be less a 'thin universalism' than a thin and quite particular sense of people and of dialogue. It is important, however, that neither level of the text cancels the other.

What appears to be the 'thinness' of this conception of 'people' may be suggested by Linklater's discussion of dialogic communities. Dialogic communities do not demand convergence; they emphasise listening, a self-critical openness to learning and sensitivity to social context and difference, as well as awareness of the inequalities of power and wealth and concern to reduce such inequalities: 'cultural differences are no barrier to equal rights of participation within a dialogic community' (1998: 85). As advice on comportment, these principles are excellent. But even as an ideal of open community they seem too severed from the reality that we are already part of a long, difficult history of 'communication'. This multilayered history of exchange has been very different from the open community imagined above, but it is the history – including the configurations of power, of resistances and, for many, of suffering – in which collective and individual psyches have taken shape. Differences between cultures (among other differences) have been and are being shaped and reshaped in significant part through their long experiences of imperium. Differences of wealth and power have been and are a crucial effect of these histories and on-going experiences. Entering dialogue we are already complex and fractured, and already interwoven with each other, in ways that 'equal rights of participation' seem quite unequal to disentangling. This does not mean that communication is not possible, that societies are entirely captives of their histories, or that histories are only about hegemony. But it would seem necessary to acknowledge and work with these histories and their patterns of trauma. The abstraction of the communicative ideal offered seems to bear little relation to the actual lives of 'concrete others' – it is difficult to ground it in something other than a convergence of theoretical architectures. This abstracted idealism is itself a 'thinness' and perhaps a way of not encountering the rawness of people's lives.

This vision of dialogue suffers from problems similar to those of certain early social contract theorists: to enter into true dialogue, unimpeded by real differences in power, or inhibitions of other kinds, would seem to demand the qualities that could only be the result of already inhabiting a nearly perfect dialogic community (e.g. see Connolly on Rousseau, 1995: 138). Are only those cultures or individuals which are already 'cosmopolitan' and secure able to be interlocuters? Linklater seems to narrow the conception of dialogue when he notes Habermas's point that '[w]hat guides participants is a commitment to be moved simply by the force of the better argument' (1998: 92). But this is a profoundly rationalist conception of interaction. 'Argument' may be only one small part of what takes place in encounters where anything of significance is at stake or change is possible. Socratic dialogue is not a form of communication for some cultures (such as Indigenous Australian cultures). And what of feeling? Since what is being discussed is ideal exchange, those exchanges for which the need for dialogue may be most intense hardly have a place – for example, a meeting between disputing factions, or over questions embedded in hatred, grief, trauma, fear, or fragile or rigid identity, or with people who place other values above a training in argument.

Nor is it clear, despite the considerable sensitivity of the argument to others, in which 'language' or in what 'communicative space' the dialogue would take place. In a way that is broadly reminiscent of Rawls's veil of ignorance or even of the space of the original contract in Locke, Linklater seems to presume that there is a neutral communicative space, underwritten by rationality, in which we can all meet once the distortions of power have been removed and despite the particularities of culture, history and circumstance. *The Transformation of Political Community* looks forward to 'a tribunal which is open to all others' (1998: 102). But that tribunal may be life: we are already engaged, although there is no 'level playing field'. Linklater surely answers Rorty's rejection of transcultural applicability. But this observation does not need to be restated in an ontological mode of address. Moreover, this higher level of claim reintroduces the spectre of a universal that in effect excludes, and which has little chance of actually engaging with the 'wildly different' or even many 'concrete others'.

But Linklater may depart too quickly from Rorty's advice that we have to start from where we are. 'To make dialogue central to social life is necessarily to be troubled by the ways in which society discriminates against outsiders unfairly by harming their interests while denying them representation or voice' (1998: 7). Perhaps we could pause longer over this sense of being troubled – which is where many of us find ourselves – and with the harm that troubles us and our efforts to understand the causes of that harm, rather than moving so quickly to outlining an ideal world as an antidote. Perhaps, too, we could stay longer with the particularity of 'concrete others'. This is not to criticise the intentions or intuitions shaping Linklater's argument, but rather to suggest that, in moving so clear-sightedly down the road towards ultimate ends, we may be elaborating steps on a complex intellectual chessboard before we quite understand what we are saying, the context in which we are speaking or whom we are addressing. While troubled, it is still possible to work for political community that does not

systemically generate suffering, or for more participatory or open political structures. And it is possible to call for all people to be treated as co-legislators in a
universal moral community, or as our brothers and sisters, or as children of God,
or any of the ways in which people have articulated a sense of each other's
value, if we can do so without proclaiming or even hoping for a privileged
avenue to truth.

A slightly different approach to this disagreement can be made through the
epistemological framework of Linklater's text. '[H]uman subjects cannot perceive the world other than through the distorting lens of language and culture
which has already made them what they are as moral subjects' (1998: 48).
Linklater makes this point his basis for a rejection of any 'Archimedean standpoint which permits objective knowledge of any permanent moral truths' or
that 'transcends the distortions and limitations of time and place', indicating a
concurrence here with postmodernism and with Rorty's rejection of rationalism (1998: 48). Linklater's reference to the distorting lens reproduces exactly
the three-part structure that is the backbone of what could be loosely called
'classical' epistemology, that is, the world (reality, the object of knowledge), the
person, (the knowing subject) and language (or science). In broad terms, these
three zones are understood to be *ontologically* distinct, or distinct as objects in
themselves, thus positing the existence of a division far beyond the simply
observed difference between words and things. For such epistemologies, the
gulf drawn between the knowing subject and the object of knowledge is
mediated in various ways, well or badly, by language and its methodological
cousins. Language, according to this family of models, is the lens or the 'dark
glass'. The relationship of language to reality may be understood as essentially
representational or as expressive, while the quality of language as a medium
may be seen as clear or as clouded and unreliable – either way it is constituted
as paradoxically both link and impediment between knower and known. The
real tension and essential relationship here tends to be understood as one
between knower (subject, mind) and the world (reality), with language the
connective medium. It is this family of epistemologies – the meta-theories of
knowledge – that many postmodernists, following certain directions in
philosophy from the early part of twentieth century (taken, for example, by
Wittgenstein, or by the philosophers of language such as Saussure, Bakhtin,
Peirce) if not before, have questioned or abandoned.

Classical epistemology (as that term is used here) is not simply an enquiry
into knowing, or an effort to make investigative methods more reliable, stringent
or sensitive. The ultimate goal of epistemology as a meta-theory is rather to
ground knowledge in certainty or truth. Such epistemology does not simply ask
'How do you know that?', but rather 'How do you ground each level of knowledge until you reach a foundational ground, in which, ideally, knowledge
itself can be secured.' If, as in some forms of epistemology, our tools of

language or science are understood as deeply fallible, we can never attain the certainty of reality or truth but only its footprint. Only certain sorts of grounds, generally highly abstract, are accepted as potentially ultimate with various constitutions of reason (or Reason) being a leading modern contender. Thus, for example, Wittgenstein's comment: 'As if giving grounds did not come to an end sometime. But the end is not an ungrounded presupposition: it is an ungrounded way of acting' (1977: 110). This approach is not an epistemology in the sense discussed here but a critique of such approaches. Rejecting such epistemology is thus not rejecting the possibility of knowledge or the value of sophisticated investigative methodologies or explanatory structures *per se*. It does not deny the existence of the world, or make rigorous science or indeed religious training impossible. Language can be understood as having representational, expressive and other functions and manners, without constituting it as the medium through which distinct domains of being are aligned. Rejecting such epistemology is rather to step aside from a quite particular spectrum of ways by which ultimate guarantees that we are *right* in what we know is sought.

The classical epistemologies enable a range of philosophical moves that become untenable once the tripartite epistemological structure is no longer understood as fundamental. Clearly, for example, the ontological divisions between the domains support the notion that there is an ultimate truth or reality, distinct both from the messiness and uncertainties of lived life and from the eye of the observer; thus they support strong theories of foundations. They support, too, the idea that with the correct propositional form or the right system we can capture (or approximate) some part of this truth. The route to knowledge is to forge the least distorting lens or the best theory. Theory (somewhat paradoxically) thus becomes immensely important, although its importance lies in the notion that it can lead us to what is beyond it – a key with which we can in principle unlock the confusion of events to find reality behind the door. In Linklater's formulations, for example, the space of the human beyond the distortions of language and culture constitutes the edenic zone of neutrality, of reason and of perfect communication, where people can in principle, as perhaps they are not quite able to in the imperfection of life, meet without distortion. Without this epistemology, such a zone of reason becomes entirely perplexing. The ideal of the communication community rests here, in the space made possible by certain, deeply embedded forms of epistemology.

The Transformation of Political Community is in part a critique of the state as 'one of the main pillars of exclusion' (1998: 145). But is the universality elaborated in that text itself part of the same political landscape as the state? Linklater sees the impetus to political change coming from the conceptual alternative to the particularism and exclusion of states – an alternative which may be the state's intellectual twin. The numerous practices involved in 'being a state', however, are arguably not so totally consumed by particularism but may move in various directions, with only some, indeed powerful, elements dedicated to maintaining or enforcing particularism. Transformation could conceivably and perhaps does emerge also from this side of the equation.

In its effort to put mutuality at the heart of political life, *The Transformation of Political Community* deals with questions and themes that are of critical importance to the work undertaken here. Dialogue and expanding and interrogating the boundaries of community are shared underlying motifs. Linklater's text offers a systematic vision of the imperative to and nature of true dialogue, and sets about demolishing notable theoretical obstacles to such communication. Here, by contrast, there is no effort to elaborate a full theory of dialogue. Nor, however, can this more everyday emphasis on the need for attentiveness to people and circumstances throw much systematic light on the problem of real differences in power and the corrosive effects that decades or centuries of such differences have wrought on people's state of being – the kind of difference that, for example, most indigenous peoples struggle under every day.

One closely related move on the spectrum of universal and relative that can be touched on here is exemplified by those arguments that appeal to minimal universalism. Andrew Linklater's universalism is one highly elaborated form of minimal universalism. There are other, somewhat less far-reaching, arguments, put forward, for example by Bhikhu Parekh, Joseph Camilleri or Ken Booth. While developing the idea differently, all three appeal to the notion that different cultures (perhaps all cultures) and religious systems share an overlapping and general consensus according to which the most blatant abuses of human rights can be judged. Moreover, we can work at increasing the zone of agreement or shared meaning (while accepting, as Linklater underlines, that it may not be others who are most called upon to change). The comment above on the reservation with which the universal-relative polarity might best be treated is relevant here. However, when debate is captured by extreme polarities, a minimalism such as Parekh's allows the maintenance of at least some flexibility and tension between the competing principles.

One of the places that the search for signs of spontaneous agreement on values or for reassurance as to the existence of ontologically grounded universals sometimes leads is the religious or spiritual traditions. Ken Booth's 1999 essay ('Three Tyrannies'), for example, takes this route. On the ethical front, the spiritual traditions seem to offer what could be termed 'universals', though less in the form of propositional truths than of injunctions: be loving, be just, do no harm and so forth. (This is the language of obligation, rather than of 'rights claims', as Donnelly points out.) If one asked why one should do no harm, the answer might be that if you follow this injunction attentively, you will know why you follow it; there will be no need to ask why. Or the answer might be, 'Because that has been revealed to us by God', which is indeed an ontological ground but one that is frequently presented as elusive or unknowable. Or if you are asking within one of the traditions committed to the discipline of eschewing ontology (such as Buddhism), the answer might be: 'Someone who talks of such things cannot make even a cup of tea.' God, Mind, the One who Cannot be Named, the Beloved, the world as sacred, the pathless path, *shunyata* (often translated as emptiness) – these gestures do not lend themselves so easily to the language of liberal rights universals, although they can offer subtle and powerful ways of recognising and working against suffering and harm. In practical terms religions have been perpetrators of violence and abuse at least as much as other primary forms of group formation and identification.[2] This may be tied to a 'hardening' or a freezing of their ontological or their metaphysical orientations – the result of 'the ardent, murderous, moral passions' that Ashis Nandy associates with the monotheistic faiths and the modern nationalist versions of Hinduism, but could be linked slightly differently to the need to assert a superior and singular truth against all contending possibilities (1983: 98).

In *The Intimate Enemy*, and in other texts, Ashis Nandy writes of an alternative universalism to those that have emerged from the modern West. Nandy hints at, rather than elaborates, this alternative. The West 'may have a well-developed language of co-existence and tolerance and well-honed tools for conversing with other civilisations . . . But, culturally, it has an exceedingly poor capacity to live with strangers. It has to try to overwhelm them or proselytise them' (1998: 143). Presumably, the alternative universalism would not try to overwhelm or proselytise. It is not organised according to the binary principles of either-or but rather around the more fluid potentials of both-and. Thus, in the discussion of the fracturing effects of and resistances to colonialism in *The Intimate Enemy*, Nandy sets out to show that 'when psychological or cultural survival is at stake', polarities such as the universal versus the parochial, the realistic versus the spiritual, the efficient, rational and sane versus the non-achieving and insane break down (1983: 113). The directness of suffering can spark in the victim of the system imposing that suffering an

> awareness of a larger whole which transcends the system's analytic categories and/or stands them on their head . . . [so that] the parochial could protect some forms of universalism more successfully than does conventional universalism . . . and that the non-achieving or the insane may often have a higher chance of achieving . . . freedom or autonomy without mortgaging their sanity. (1983: 113)

This alternative universalism is not elaborated because it is not organised around the assertive maintenance of central principles or clear binary antonyms – like the traditional Hinduism that Nandy describes, which remained without an exclusive self-concept until a modernising reform movement in the nineteenth century, and then borrowed for its name the term used by Muslims to describe the unconverted (1983, 103). Despite this, Nandy indicates such universalism via its 'alternativeness'. It would seem to do this alternative some

75

injustice to include it without demur in those more conventional claims to universality which remain forgetful of their own history and partiality, as another sign of the underlying correctness of that more assertive universalism it rejects.

The 'Asian Way' debate

One of the more prominent public debates regarding human rights in the international domain over the past decade, and certainly one which engages the full force of the polarisation of universal and relative truth, is that gathered under the rubric 'the Asian Way'. This is the argument that the West's preoccupation with rights is for various reasons misplaced in the Asian cultural and social context. This argument has many different and not always compatible threads that nevertheless come together in strategic concord against the international promotion of human rights by many Western governments and non-governmental organisations. The most high-profile form of the debate is cast (and is discussed here) in terms of the so-called 'soft' authoritarianism of much of East Asia versus Anglo-American liberalism, but the underlying threads are more widely relevant. The scope of the debate is quite different from Nandy's 'alternative universalism'. Indeed, at its more strident and formalistic, the dispute would likely be seen by Nandy in terms of East Asia trying to beat the West at its own game.

Four themes dominate criticisms by certain East Asian governments and intellectuals of Western (or, more precisely, liberal) models of rights. These are: the individualistic focus of liberal rights; their antagonistic form, as opposed to models of harmony in, most prominently, Confucian political thought; the primacy given to civil and political rights at the expense of economic development; and the promotion of rights as essentially a means of asserting Western cultural hegemony and so undermining the national competence, sovereignty and self-determination of the state in regard to domestic conflicts. It is important to note, however, that criticism of the liberal model of rights and its operation in non-Western societies goes beyond the arguments of the 'Asian Way', which tends to be associated with governments.[3] While not canvassing the whole debate, which at least until the Asian economic crises of the late 1990s received wide if erratic public exposure, there are three elements of it particularly relevant to this discussion.

The first element is that, however little (or much) the 'Asian Way' may mean in regard to traditional shared political guidelines among the widely varying states of Asia, upholding that 'Way' acts as a counter to the context and manner in which rights and other political 'virtues' have been in large part not only promoted but more fundamentally understood. The 'Asian Way' debate is shaped by many historical and political factors: the broader history of colonialism and processes of cultural decolonisation underway throughout much of Asia; the economic success (until recent problems) and consequent self-assertion of East Asia; regional politics within East Asia itself; the standard political dynamics generated by using human rights platforms as a means of competing for international prestige; some governments' need for a self-righteous fig-leaf to cover abusive activities; plus the natural friction between areas of genuine political and social difference. But the debate is also shaped by the fact that, despite efforts to the contrary, human rights promotion internationally is coloured by the evangelical assumption that the 'West' is the holder of a unique truth which it must impart to the 'East', groping in darkness. The fundamental political questions raised by the persistence of the abuse and degradation of people in the world of interactions in which we all now, to different degrees, participate can easily be cast as a struggle between freedom and tyranny, between Athens and Persia, in which the liberal West comes to represent, naturally, freedom. The accusations and counter-accusations and arguments as to who is most to blame may act as a diversion for us all to look aside from some of the nastier realities of the world we create.

The 'Asian Way' debate is sometimes viewed by rights activists and supporters both in Asia and the West as merely a front for self-serving authoritarian and violent regimes (or actions). It often operates just like that, but the truth of this observation does little justice either to the significance of the argument or to the different levels at which it can operate. It is true, as Rodan and Hewison (1996) make clear, that the cultural patterns claimed by some Asian governments to represent the 'East' are often scarcely culturally specific but are rather expressions of a strong cross-cultural conservative political agenda and philosophy. In this sense the 'Asian Way' debate may be evidence not of a relativist 'clash of civilisations' but of a resurgent conservative convergence:

> the more interesting and profound development embodied in the changing position of Asia in the global political economy, and the attendant assertion of 'Asian-ness', is the apparent development of comparable configurations of political ideologies in the 'West' and 'Asia', a fact that is obscured by the proclaimed cultural dichotomy. (Rodan and Hewison, 1996: 30)

Or the official cultural assertion of some East Asian administrations seems part of 'beating the West at its own game [as] the preferred means of handling the feelings of self-hatred in the modernized non-West' (Nandy, 1983: xiii).

But it is also true, despite the conservatism of pronouncements by Asian political and business elites, that the charge of 'cultural imperialism' or cultural insensitivity in response to the manner of much rights promotion has weight. This is not because killings, torture, intimidation and exploitation are more acceptable in an Asian context than elsewhere (as Wong Kan Seng, Singapore's foreign minister, commented in his address to the 1993 Vienna Conference on

Human Rights, 'no one claims torture as part of their heritage') but because of a persistent Western assumption that the story we generally tell about rights and therefore about good government is the essential one – that 'they' have the problem and 'we' the answer.

The second point is that a marked characteristic of the 'Asian Way' debate is the level of generality at which it is often conducted. This generality is counterproductive. It allows opportunism to hide behind both serious questions and ethnocentric fervour, thereby weakening and confusing the possibility of response to these very different phenomena. There are significant questions regarding human rights at stake in this argument. The 'Asian Way' debate can demand consideration of the potential for diverse non-abusive forms of political organisation or it can broach the difficulties of how to grapple with the concrete problems of abuse in ways effective for differing circumstances. Must the bundle of things we mean by 'rights' flow only from liberal models of the individual and the state, or may there be a number of paths, in practice, along which social requirements for levels of mutual respect, political participation and the restraint of systemically imposed harm can develop? The real complexities of the social evolution of such practices are easily lost, however, once discussion slides into airy judgements about 'East' and 'West', with either tacit or overheated assertions of cultural (and national) superiority very close behind.

In the extremes of this argument 'cultures', of both the 'East' and the 'West' become strangely absolute, homogenous and unchanging, despite the fact that some of the traditions claimed as national touchstones are of very recent origin – inevitably, since fundamental dimensions of modern state practice in Asian states are in many cases scarcely decades old. As suggested in the discussion at the beginning of this chapter, it is less 'culture' than the state and its right to interpret culture and define community that is at stake here. In order to make the idea of culture an appropriate weapon for the fight, claims about the 'Asian Way' ignore the dynamic character of complex political community. Yet change and difference – the persistence of sometimes explosive conflict over social directions, an often long history of co-existence or struggle between different interpretations or dimensions of cultural traditions (e.g. between variant traditions of Confucianism), the economic and social revolutions of rapid industrialisation and modernisation and confrontation over specific patterns of exploitation, intimidation or discrimination – mark many Asian states. The version of the cultural iconography that is given precedence is determined by many factors, including concurrence with the contemporary dominant economic and political interests.

The reification of culture – turning it into a weapon – may be the expression, in this case, of a long history. It may draw directly on the dynamics of colonialism, where the gulf between coloniser and colonised was subject to tight internal patrol (Nandy, 1983), and also on the work of early anthropologists, who worked to delineate the absolute distinctiveness of societies and cultures. In this way the battlelines of domination and also of one form of resistance are drawn. This long history attests also to the unequal but dense and 'intimate' interaction and reshaping of cultures. Writing during the Suharto era, Indonesian poet and commentator Goenawan Mohamad asked 'are human rights the same as Coca Cola?', drawing an implicit comparison between those 'American products' that are welcomed and those that are treated with suspicion (1994: 65). Nandy reflects on this intimate conflictual interweaving by looking at the internalisation of 'Western' or modernised selves within 'Asians' – an 'adored enemy [who] is a silent spectator in even our most private moments and the uninvited guest at our most culturally typical events' (1998: 144). This modern self is pitted against frozen 'clandestine or repressed part-selves . . . These hidden or part-selves can now usually re-enter the public domain only in pathological forms – as ultra-nationalism, fundamentalism and defensive ethnic chauvinism' (1998: 146).

The third element, closely related to the other two, is that the problems of grappling with difference – which are fundamental to the challenge hidden within this debate – are reduced to an abstract, arid confrontation between universalism and relativism. Moreover, those who see the 'West' to be upholding global standards of rights tend to presume that they represent universality and so equate the 'East' with the relative or particular (or opportunistic). It is implied that without adherence to a quite particular construction of universality, only opportunism is left. The crude riposte to this charge – that Asia is different – simply converts the insinuation into a weapon for the other side. This argument works both ways, making Asian rights activists vulnerable to charges of representing foreign ways and powers and so betraying the achievements of hard-fought national liberation struggles. Notions of human rights are imported from the political culture of Western Europe, according to this position, and are therefore alien to Asia. But the problems posed by the systemically inflicted abuse of people are essentially practical, if difficult and far-reaching in their implications. To insist that these problems must be resolved principally through the abstract (and mutually constitutive) polarity of relative and universal truth distracts us from this practicality and further entrenches the generality, vehemence and impasse of the debate by asking us to think about questions of how we live together fundamentally outside the circumstances of people's lives.

Goenawan Mohamad's discussion[4] of the sexual abuse, torture and murder of Marsinah, a 23-year-old Indonesian labour activist, is one kind of response to the charge that concern with rights indicates the intrusion of Western influence and compromises national sovereignty. He argues that human rights are not essentially a matter of international precepts and principles, Western or otherwise. Rather, they start as a recognition of real harm and a 'story of violence and suffering' – from the immediate reality of the face of the victim. The workers who pressed the issue of Marsinah's murder with the authorities did so not because they were influenced by international propaganda or Western values, but because 'they found the murdered woman so close to their daily life'. 'Human rights are born not because they fall from the sky, or come from a textbook from a Western university, but because people make complaints and search for freedom from a sense of profound exploitation. In other words, human rights are born from real conditions' (Mohamad, 1994: 78). Mohamad argues that what we need is not 'lofty principles' but 'a type of history. In order to fully embrace human rights we need the experience of knowing the capacity of mankind to abuse any such limits, especially when we ourselves are in threat of fear. In other words, we have to perceive the issue from the point of view of the victim' (Mohamad, 1993).

There are real differences in emphasis and value between and within the overlapping networks of political cultures touched by this debate. And differences can also be overplayed. The dichotomies in terms of which the debate is standardly cast are those of the individualistic West versus the communitarian East, political rights and ideals of freedom versus economic rights and goals of development, and national cultural and political autonomy (often seen as giving priority to models of harmony) versus global or modern culture (often identified with conflict). However, rather than being drawn into questioning or defending the primacy of either of the contending values proposed – the individual or the collective, or harmony or conflict of interest, and so on, it is worth considering the circumstances within which the juxtaposition is being placed on any occasion and questioning the apparent naturalness of each pole of the dichotomy. The purpose of doing so is not to remove the differences but to shift them away from the zone of timeless oppositions into that of more concrete political problems.

By what processes, for example, does one group come to stand as the 'individual' in any given instance and another as the 'community'? In practice in East Asia the state has taken to itself the identity of 'community' over and above the various traditional collectivities (of extended family, village, ethnic or religious grouping) in which the individual was immured and which are called upon as evidence of a collective state of being.[5] Indeed these traditional collectivities, as spheres of power in potential competition with the state, are hardly welcomed. It makes a difference which activity of the state is being justified in terms of an identification with the traditional continuities of community. Is the individual (one of) the class of Singaporean landowners whose property is acquired peremptorily by the government as part of the provision of public housing? Again, is the individual one of the East Timorese youths who demonstrated (thereby exercising the supposedly individual right of free speech) during the Suharto era, and so faced the violent response of the Indonesian military, here representing the collective, or is the individual a worker attempting to organise an independent trade union? When is the debate one about community versus individual good and when is it about which individuals, groups and classes have the opportunity to determine the kind of community they want and for whose benefit it operates? In any society, power lies with the ability to call upon an unquestioned and so all but invisible normality as the reference points that map out community.

Again, the assertion of the 'right to development' or of the functional primacy of economic over political rights raises the question 'Development for whom?' Who makes up the community whose standard of living is to improve, and how is it constituted? It is widely assumed by figures on both 'sides' of the Asian Way debate that economic development is central to the promotion and protection of human rights (although what this can mean more specifically varies enormously) as it is also widely accepted that poverty is a direct contributor to major forms of abuse. But poverty can be sustained by patterns of maldevelopment that themselves incorporate systemically imposed repression and abuse. The expression the 'Asian Way' is often a reference to the overriding priority given by some states to economic growth at the expense of other political and social goals or values. In this context 'Asian' values means simply what is good for business elites – often simply social stability, with few standards governing the use of labour or accountability regarding economic activity. It could be argued, however, that the purpose of economic *rights* is not simply that people have sufficient to live but that they have sufficient to enable them to take part effectively in society – to take part, even at a simple and partial level, in the dynamics of power which shape their community. As the later discussion of East Timor makes plain, the question 'Development for whom?' becomes particularly pertinent if the process of growth acts to disenfranchise or further marginalise sections of the population.

The 'Asian Way' debate is one of the sharper political expressions of the polarisation of universal and relative truth, and indeed of a range of dichotomies – political versus economic, individual versus collective, East versus West – that explicitly or implicitly mould international rights talk. In particular, it may have grown out of the moment of judgement – of 'we', the virtuous and clean, facing 'you', the unclean – in which so much discussion of human rights becomes trapped. Rather than bringing clarity, however, these terms often seem to entrench our understanding and construction of rights more unreflectively into patterns of alternating competition and convergence, the shifting strategic alliances that make up the emerging hegemonies of the global political economy. Thus they obscure the problems of identifying and responding to the infliction of injury and suffering.

Dialogue

The Asian Way debate, with its contradictory trajectories of conflict, grievance and genuine questions, gives some indication of the operation of and the obfuscation stemming from the universal-relative dichotomy in practice. Writing of such exchanges as 'the existing, official mode of dialogue', Ashis Nandy traces the psychological fracturing which has been one, still living, effect of colonialism. He investigates the 'hidden or disowned selves', the 'subjugated selves' shadowing both the non-West and the West and their encounters, and so underlines the complex undercurrents and often violent histories of cross-cultural dialogue (1998: 146). (Nor is colonialism the only history of domination and conflict that is relevant here.) All these selves, he suggests, must be able to take part, or else they enter the debate as the pathologies of dogmatism, fundamentalism and ultra-nationalism. Like Linklater, Nandy outlines principles he regards as fundamental to 'an authentic conversation of cultures', principles that are entirely compatible with Linklater's. Nandy, however, does not seek to secure his principles as more than demands, advice or persuasion, grounded in centuries of conflict, exchange and reflection. Because colonialism is the focus of his work (with particular reference to India), Nandy's texts also bring to the fore a perspective that is particularly relevant to work on human rights and abuse: that is, an emphasis on working with history, particularly that history which has shaped the lineaments of the current relationship, and thus also on self-reflection. 'A dialogue is no guarantee against future aberrations, but it at least ensures self-reflexivity and self-criticism. It keeps open the possibility of resistance' (1998: 148).

Dialogue has been a crucial element in the approaches to ethics of most of the theorists discussed in this chapter, whether relativist, universalist, or neither. For the approaches to working with problems of abuse proposed here, this flexible but potent metaphor of conversation is also critical. Dialogue is put forward here not as the basis for an integrated theory but as a trajectory for reflection – a metaphor that may offer some practical, as well as theoretical insights and possibilities. In chapter 1, the complexity, density of relationship, and openness to learning implied by dialogue were contrasted to the delivery of a message, with its relative lack of engagement, paucity of relationship and one-way direction. When we consistently approach rights promotion like the delivery of a message, this tells us something about how we in effect understand rights, abuse and social change, and how we believe the significance of what is said to be established (at least as that applies to social change). It also reflects on the relationship between the deliverers and the receivers of the message. In a message the 'truth' or significance of the communication could be understood to be essentially contained in the words; by contrast, in a conversation, the significance lies also in part in the nature of the interaction over time and the character of the relationship. If human rights provide a way of working with the systemic infliction of suffering rather than being essentially a means of conceptualising the limits of government in a liberal state, then the category of abuse is not limited to the relationship between individual and state but is more generally entrenched in ways of constructing community (in which the institutions of the state are, of course, often pivotal). Response to systemic infliction of injury may thus demand less the assertion of a singular truth than long-term engagement with the social practices in which much abuse is embedded or sustained.

In this chapter, dialogue is also suggested as one way of stepping aside from the intensity of the polarity of universal and relative values as apparently contending homes for truth, meaning or rights. The hopelessly entangled knot of universal versus relative values can be understood as itself a particular kind of construction – not a spontaneous opposition or unavoidable moral choice but a product of the history of the state system. This does not mean that the polarity therefore has no weight or substance. At one level the dichotomy sets the coordinates for sovereignty. 'Universality' in this context can be understood quite pragmatically, or perhaps historically, as those (changing) areas subject to more than just national competence. Sovereignty has always in practice been a complex balance of national and international forces. Struggles over its changing reach and character are important in a number of arenas (including human rights) and are intrinsic to the system of states.

In discussions of international ethics, however, universality commonly appears as not merely another, sometimes contrasting, sometimes complementary arena of governance, but as an ontological domain of rationality, or of ethical life or the universal subject. But whether understood pragmatically or ontologically, or both, universality versus relativism is not a dispute that can be finally resolved across the board in favour of one term of the polarity or the other. It is misleading for the ontological version of this polarity to appear as in fact a debate about the nature of morality, or the last word on community, or to be expected to shed light on the problems of working across difference. The antinomy of universal and relative is an expression of the history of the state system (or elements of that history), not a master key to its interpretation. The notion of dialogue offers an alternative to elements of this overworked dichotomy. Dialogue offers a reminder that we are already working with analogy and difference, and across sometimes profound borders of one kind or another. We are already engaged with each other and '[e]xistence, like language, is a shared event' (Holquist, 1990: 28). The image of entirely discrete, separate and self-contained subjectivities, like the image of discrete, separate cultures which, without an ascertainable underpinning ground, would collapse into a cacophony of subjectivist contention is only one, quite particular, way of picturing our existence.

Reflecting on dialogue as a motif can suggest other subtle shifts of theoretical and practical emphasis and orientation. Some of these shifts are already apparent from comments quoted above by Linklater, Nandy or Rorty. There is, for example, an openness about notions of dialogue, particularly if one does not limit the word (as properly one should) to only two interlocutors. There are others engaged, and what they bring to the engagement is not predictable. Dialogue emphasises listening and attentiveness to circumstances and to others. If we are pursuing human rights, or even sustainable operations in fractured circumstances, this is a crucial orientation, if one that is often ignored. While theoretically simple to the point of naivety, attentiveness or creating the conditions for listening can be complex and challenging in practice. Conversation, and the understanding it sometimes makes possible, is a mutual achievement. The shifting of attention from the decentred interaction of dialogue to the formal conditions under which ideal communication is possible seems to move away from this openness. Moreover dialogue is not monologue or the enunciation of singular truths. An emphasis on interaction among a number of interlocutors draws attention not only to difference and otherness, but to the partiality of our insights, judgements and observations. Partiality does not appear in this context as a failure to achieve wholeness or totality, but as a natural condition of being part of interactions and exchanges. Partiality is a condition of potentially sharing, extending or changing understanding – one's own, someone else's, or both. It is a condition of learning.

Highlighting dialogue thus draws attention to the contextual and interactive dimension of our understanding. Particularly if we are thinking of slow and difficult 'conversations' over generations or centuries, rather than hours, meaning may then appear less as locked inside propositions (as the classical models of epistemology indicate) and more as existing in relation to the pattern and character of exchanges.[6] Ultimate standpoints may seem less central or less exclusive and settled. One site in which universality is regularly invested is notions of 'the human'. Tzetvan Todorov has commented that 'it is not possible, without inconsistency, to defend human rights with one hand and deconstruct the idea of humanity with the other' (1987: 190). But what might be most important for notions of human rights is to enrich, extend and open our understanding of 'the human' and 'humanity'. For this, a 'deconstruction' in which the partiality and the character of the notion becomes plain is a valuable step. This would seem both part of listening to others and the self-reflection to which Nandy refers. Such a 'deconstruction' need not leave a gaping hole where care for others and ourselves was once held. 'Deconstructing humanity' may instead equip us with a more discriminating awareness of our sense of humanity and of its adequacy to our commitment to rights, in this case, or to community which does not systematically generate suffering. It may entail a more attentive and productive regard to other ways of understanding the person, community, and of our relationship to life forms more generally. And so it may encourage a more open and self-reflective sense of the person, of relationship and of political order.

Recognising the partiality of our understanding and, in this case, the unreliability of some of our tools, also requires an acceptance of uncertainty. Abuse can be clear, and statements regarding human rights, or human wrongs, can at times be made with great confidence and power. But there is a great deal to be uncertain about. Atrocity and grave harm raise fundamental questions about the nature of political community that few communities and few states can avoid entirely, or answer satisfactorily, while at a personal level abuse interrogates our relations with each other and what is often our indifference towards and fear of each other (Cixous, 1993). The problems of responding to suffering bring us up against the limits as well as the strengths of the available mechanisms and presumptions regarding rights and ethics – whether liberal or other models. And the closer we come to the 'face of the victim' the more obdurate the problems can be. A change of government, or of particular laws, or a significant increase of resources can sometimes remove certain kinds of harm. The legal system, or a process of reconciliation, can be a public recognition of abuse, and may offer some redress. But effective response to entrenched violence and injury and – to return to the example of Serbia, Bosnia and Kosovo – the problems of the emergence of non-abusive political relationships at all levels of social order admit of no easy solution.

There seems often an element of vulnerability about our knowing. Dialogue is one response to this vulnerability. Perhaps one difference between those in the contemporary West and the German population in the 1940s, or (on a different level of intensity) people who carried out some of the more extreme forms of control and intervention in the lives of Indigenous Australians in the 1970s, is that we have had the opportunity to listen to the victims of those actions. It is not necessarily a strong difference, and it must be built upon in institutional or other forms. Nor is it the only or necessarily the most important difference, but it does remain significant. Encountering the victims can also be avoided, suppressed or delayed, as colonialism again reminds us. Notions of dialogue have little to add to the transactions of power (of which dialogue is a part), except to note, with Nandy, that exchange can keep open the possibility of resistance. History provides good reasons not to trust the processes of coming to understandings, but such processes remain both a central and a tenuous element of the tools that we have for living together.

Most fundamentally, perhaps, rights can themselves be understood as a mechanism for recognising and participating in the referential life of self and other, for constituting political relationships, in the broadest sense, that not only enable the claim to participation but support the processes by which others are heard.

Rights are a particular kind of conceptual, social and political tool with a dense and ambivalent history of both emancipation and exclusion. While rights are not grounded in some figure of the universal subject or of reason, it is equally important not to limit an understanding of rights to a function solely within the state, congruent with citizenship. It is true that the legal framework of rights rests overwhelmingly with states and that these frameworks are often a fundamental dimension of working with questions of the social infliction of injury. At the same time, patterns of abuse cross borders, and are often embedded in the structures of international transactions (as dependency theorists show); similarly, the effects of abuse are frequently not contained within the state (as refugee flows, as only the most obvious example, demonstrate). Bonds of solidarity, which can stimulate response to abuse, also cross borders. Moreover, while rights are a form of institutional or political practice, they are also aspirational. They are an available language for asking and, in part, for answering 'How can we live well together, how can we build and sustain non-injurious relationships at all levels?' We need to keep asking this question because we answer it differently at different times, and sometimes in better ways than at others. And we need to ask it not only of ourselves, but of others.

The contractarian story poses a version of this question and imagines a universal state as a response, with universal man as its sovereign. This story has at times legitimised pressures to uniformity within states and conflict among them. Questions and answers about how to live together, however, are in operation not only within states but within and across the various and intersecting communities we inhabit – of which states remain a fundamental and complex, but not the only operative, dimension. Nor need questions of human rights seek universal laws upon which to base claims to certainty or an achieved or definitive political form but rather acceptance of the uncertain processes of constructing our collective lives and the on-going need, not for a metalanguage but to work with each other.

The history of rights offers a substantial body of experience – both negative and positive, incomplete, not always relevant to particular circumstances, but valuable – while the idea of human rights offers a number of crucial injunctions. At the simplest level, it is important to remember that human rights (at least as they are understood here) are not so much 'about' individuals but are a way of approaching community and relationship – a way that gives primacy to mutual respect. It is in this sense that rights assert the vulnerability and the value of people, individually and collectively. Rights also uphold participatory ideals of collective or political life. For in order to give voice to suffering and to work against the infliction of suffering, people need to be able to take part to some reasonable degree in shaping and reflecting upon the contours of their common and individual lives – to take part in dialogue, not only to speak but to be listened to. Notions of rights are thus one way of entering into the processes of considering and of constituting what kind of society it is that we sustain; they are mechanisms by which people engage in the on-going struggle with questions of what community can be under present (or future) circumstances. There is also a dynamism to notions of human rights. This is partly because, as an ethic, participation is inherently open-ended. But it is also because ideas of human rights continue to challenge us to recognise the value and the vulnerability of people across the barriers of otherness and of suffering.[7]

In practical terms, rights make sense within the referential field of some world of interaction. The claim to human rights, however, and the recognition of abuse are always potentially efforts to move beyond the definition of group boundaries to recognise the possibility of a participation that is not exclusionary and that does not impose uniformity. The relevance of the assertion of the universality of human rights lies here – not in staking out the territories of the universal but as a challenge to look across the boundaries of state or community or worldview, to look out from where we are, often to networks of interaction and patterns of cause and effect already in place. Rights thus problematise community and its natural exclusions, as well as providing mechanisms with which to build it. In this sense, thinking about rights in international politics provides insight into something fundamental to the notion of human rights itself – the need to work across borders of one kind or another – but that is obscured by the habit of thinking within the terms of the state, with its illusory homogeneity. In a similar fashion, rights promotion can itself be understood as a participatory process and an act of many-sided communication. As a working practice and a participative civility, rights indeed have a Western history, or more accurately a range of Western histories. They may also have non-Western histories and certainly non-Western potentials which cannot be so easily dismissed after quick canters through other traditions fail to find enough of the major themes of liberalism.

NOTES

1   Booth's comment here is in danger of functioning like G. E. Moore's use of evident facts (e.g. 'The sun rises every morning') to establish the basis of a claim to epistemological certainty (Wittgenstein, 1977).

2   As Goenawan Mohamad notes: 'Unfortunately, religious principles have never been shown to drive the hearts of man away from torture, from imprisoning people for ten years or more without trial, or from remaining silent when one should properly speak up. These lofty principles can suddenly disappear the instant the prison door is closed and the joy of the exploitation of others re-emerges. These principles can even make us feel as though we are the ones-in-the-right, we are the pure ones – and therefore have a sort of licence to liquidate the opinions or presence of others' (1994: 66).

3   For example, see Kothari and Sethi (eds), *Rethinking Human Rights* (1991), the journal *Lokyanan*, the writings of Chandra Muzaffar and Beng-Huat Chua.

4   In an unpublished address to the Australian Institute of International Affairs, Brisbane, 1995.

5   The absorption of community into state is hardly surprising given the histories of inter-
     community violence, close to the surface or more deeply buried, that mark many states.
     But the processes by which traditional collectivities have come to be bound to each other
     are not natural historical continuities. There is nothing simple about the state as
     upholder of the collective good.

6   This is the sense of saying that the appeal to universals can operate differently in
     different contexts. One would not say to Aung Sang Suu Kyi, for example, that she
     should not appeal to a universal. That is in part because, on one level, she is engaged
     precisely in a struggle with a violent, extremist definition of 'sovereignty'. But she is at
     the same time protesting, with a power and integrity that is rooted in the circumstances
     of her speech, against the suffering imposed on people.

7   '[T]he awareness of death and suffering . . . [is] one of the strongest incentives for life,
     the basis of human solidarity' (Fromm, 1960: 212).

II

Case studies

Introduction to the case studies

The approach taken to human rights and rights promotion in the following case studies flows from the themes raised in Part I. Two simple ideas here are primary. The first is that notions of human rights, at their most fundamental level of significance, are one way of dealing with the perennial problems of the systemic infliction of suffering, particularly gross suffering, as a mechanism or a function of political organisation. That is, human rights practices are one way of articulating and working against the harm we do each other, and of encouraging political contexts of non-injury and mutual respect. We account for and recognize harm in different ways – notions of human rights are not a metalanguage, but they can operate as a way into the complexities and confusions of particular cases and broader patterns of injury as well as, in very general terms, asserting the value of people. The second idea informing the approach taken in the case studies is that 'dialogue' or 'conversation' – paying people and the pattern of their lives the fundamental respect of listening to them and being engaged with them – is at the core of both respecting and promoting human rights.

A number of themes follow from these two simple points of beginning. To take part in serious exchanges on difficult social and political problems often involves a preparedness to look at yourself and your tools differently. Thus, critical reflection on the methods, outcomes and assumptions of the human rights models and practices that are being promoted is essential to this approach – not in order to abandon traditions of rights practices but to recognise that they do not constitute a fixed or necessarily emancipatory truth. One of the purposes of the earlier chapters, in this context, is to provide some critical distance from the ways we tend to think about and work with human rights in the international domain. In stepping back from human rights as a definitive model of state and individual we meet again the complexity of rights as a series of questions about patterns of injury which are recurrent as well as embedded in and given meaning by concrete circumstances of time and place.

Thus, rather than being primarily an evangelical task of 'truth-bearing', or an assertion of the inevitable 'rightness' of a particular model of government, the promotion of human rights may demand long-term engagement with particular institutions or knots of social practice – with mechanisms for constructing community – across and between cultures. Response to abuse is part of a long and slow conversation between and across cultures on the nature of political community and the place of injury within it. In practical terms, efforts to change violent or injurious social practices require that cultural cosmologies not be dismissed wholesale as incompatible with the emergence of a working rights practice but be taken seriously as means of working against abuse or as potential grounds for the evolution of such practices. Moreover, it may be that responses to particular patterns of abuse that are effective over the long term emerge essentially in interaction with the people who live the situation to hand (whether that is ourselves or others) and the social and political orders they inhabit. It is this work which gives substance to and underpins international treaties and declarations.

The following three case studies look at quite different situations. The first considers an event: the Tiananmen Square massacre in China in 1989. This case study looks at the way a language of indignation that draws significantly on Lockean models of the state, political community and human rights may hinder understanding of and response to particular situations of abuse – even when that situation, in this case a textbook example of the grave abuse of citizens by their own government in the heart of the state, seems particularly suited to those models. The question of notions of 'human' rights versus citizen's rights is also touched on briefly here.

The second case study discusses briefly the last twenty-five years of East Timor's history, focusing on the context of Indonesia's violent occupation and the forced pace of nation building, and touching on some of the issues of peace builidng in the new state. The discussion underlines the persistent failure to engage with the grassroots dynamics of circumstances in East Timor in the creation and perpetuation of a pattern of severe and embedded abuse. That failure to pay attention to concrete circumstances marked the 'realism' of the prevailing international attitudes on East Timor; to what extent might it also characterise the current liberal approaches?

The third case study, which looks at the 'place' of Indigenous Australians within Australian political life, returns to a liberal rights focus – in this case not involving the language of international rights talk but rather concerning the ideals and practices of democratic political community. This study examines the politics of health in particular as a means of exploring how the construction of consent and participation as the basis of the state have worked to exclude Indigenous people. By discussing one obdurate complex of abuse within a wealthy western democratic state, chapter 6 again reflects on some of the tools the liberal democratic states bring to understanding and responding to abusive situations. It explores the notion of participation, as one that is central to liberal constructions of citizenship and also to the approach taken here, and considers what is in this case the essentially political nature of 'social and economic' rights.

The pattern of difference and similarity among the three case studies at best allows the studies to talk to each other, clarifying some points and opening up ambiguities in others. Despite the range of difference among the cases, it is important to note that they certainly do not cross the whole gamut of forms of abuse. Even across the range of three case studies, key aspects of the argument, particularly the emphasis on human rights promotion as a process of mutual communication rather than a message, apply differently. This emphasis is likely to speak directly and fully to some kinds of abuse and in practical terms only highly contextually and indirectly to certain other cases, where any possibility of effective dialogue has long passed or not yet arisen.

The topics addressed by the three case studies are far too complex to be dealt with in depth by a single chapter on each. In this sense the studies cannot bear out the argument made here in that they do not give to each set of circumstances the level of attention the argument would suggest is necessary. Nor does each chapter set itself the Promethean task of resolving the problem it discusses; rather it points, where possible, to a shift of emphasis from which resolutions may in time emerge.

4

China – the Tiananmen Square massacre of 1989

THIS CHAPTER EXPLORES, through a discussion of one instance, how the principal categories of the Lockean narrative can shape the context for the understanding of and response to political injury. In the case of much Western response to the Beijing massacre the conceptualisation of man and the state is particularly important, as is the related articulation of the realms of ethics and politics. The following discussion of the Beijing killings also questions the adequacy of the terms of the debate between citizenship rights and human rights, that is, the argument that rights must be located in (and contained by) either the institutional mechanisms of the state or in the generic individual as Lockean universal man, as a basis for responding to the complex problems of abuse. And the discussion touches on the role of the search for workable dialogue in this instance of deteriorating political conflict.

The Tiananmen Square killings can be understood as one, particularly savage, swing of the pendulum between official calls for reform and official repression of and violence towards those Chinese pushing the limits and pace of reform (with other more or less repressive movements occurring in 1978–79, 1981, 1986, 1989 and 1998). But because of the very public ferocity of the government's response, as well as the timing of the incident following some years of political openness and discussion within China, and at the beginning of the end of the Cold War internationally, the Tiananmen massacre also stands as a watershed. The massacre has etched itself sharply into Western impressions of and responses to China, on a popular level as well as in official and academic circles. But it also marked quite deeply a turning-point, or a road not taken, in China's political direction, as well, arguably, as a complex shift in the relationship between the regime and large sectors of the population. Certainly 4 June is a date that the government must keep in mind uncomfortably every year, watching anxiously to quell any disturbance. The pseudonymous compiler of *The Tiananmen Papers* Zhang Liang noted the 4 June protests (by the 1989 Democracy Movement) as 'the culmination of the biggest, broadest, longest-lasting, and most influential pro-democracy demonstrations anywhere in the world in the twentieth century' (quoted in Nathan and Link; 2001: xi). This is an expansive description; but, however the Democracy Movement is judged, the full impact and consequences of the 1989 demonstrations and of the massacre in which they culminated have yet to be played out.

During April and May of 1989, Beijing was the site of an extraordinary series of demonstrations and political actions that came to be known as 'the Beijing Spring'. Protesters called for democracy, freedom, dialogue with the government, the accountability of authorities and an end to corruption. Although initiated and in many respects dominated by students, for the first time in many years the demonstrations attracted widespread public support, most significantly from urban workers. Similar – smaller – actions erupted in hundreds of centres across the country, accompanied by the formation of a clutch of independent labour organisations.[1] For some time the central leadership was itself seriously divided on how to respond to this volatile public mix – a struggle that had the effect of sending contradictory messages to the demonstrators and delaying response. Eventually, in Beijing on the night of 3–4 June 1989, People's Liberation Army (PLA) tanks converged on the unarmed people in the streets around Tiananmen Square, the large public space in the heart of the capital. Estimates by various observers put the number of dead (shot or crushed) as a result of this action – workers, students, those caught up in the melee and soldiers – as ranging from approximately 240 to 5,000. '[N]ever before had the regime unleashed the full firepower of the . . . PLA on unarmed civilians' (Dittmer, 1989: 2).

Repressive follow-up operations were mounted throughout the country to investigate, punish and eradicate suggestions of support for the demonstrations. According to internal Party reports, 4 million Party members were to be investigated, indicating the extraordinary extent of the support for the students' activities (Mirsky, 1997: 33). An unknown number of arrests were made (at least 6,000 by the end of 1989 according to interpretation by Western journalists of official statistics) on a wide variety of charges, and forty executions were officially announced in the months immediately following the protests (400 executions according to the Hong Kong journal *Ming Pao*).

The focus of this chapter is less the events of Tiananmen Square in early 1989 *per se*, however, than some of the ways we talk about or approach those events. The Tiananmen massacre has become for many people in the West almost an icon of the violation of human rights – of a spontaneous outpouring of the desire for freedom and democracy (two of the students' principal slogans) crushed by the repressive state. The natural drama and tragedy of Tiananmen speak directly to our own stories of political heroism and destruction, resonating with some of our constitutive political images of and ideals about natural universal man facing the state-as-tank. This chapter considers this representation of events and some of its effects. It is argued that this representation, which may have given the disaster of Tiananmen some, although certainly not all, of its potency and grip over our imaginations (a grip that, for example, Chinese security forces killing demonstrating Tibetans in Lhasa the previous year clearly did not have), is also part of what obstructs the practical pursuit of human rights in China and other places. Might our assumptions about the relationship between individual and state, as articulated by a certain idea of rights, both demand and shape our response to certain instances of grave abuse *and* hinder our understanding of events like the Tiananmen massacre and our ability to work with the infliction of injury? It is important, in the light of this question, to look more carefully at some of the terms of the drama and in particular to question the simplification of the roles of the students, the leadership and the state – to point to the elements of myth making without in any way reducing the gravity of the events and their implications.

After noting the sharp emergence of human rights onto the agenda of dealings between China and the West following the Tiananmen killings, the chapter looks at the terms in which the story of the massacre was presented in much Western commentary of the time – terms with which, arguably, it continues to resonate. This is not, however, an attempt to reproduce a detailed account of events surrounding the killings – several such accounts are available.[2] The chapter then endeavours to situate both the leadership and the arms of the state and the students within the conflicts and the fragmentation of their political circumstances. This discussion draws on a range of commentaries on both the Tiananmen killings and China in the latter part of the 1980s more generally. Although certainly not as nuanced or as authoritative as the work of specialist historians, this discussion nevertheless allows consideration of the central issue of the chapter, that is, the extent to which efforts to undo systemic infliction of injury and to respond to abuse become preoccupied with reductionist Lockean constructions of the state and of the individual, thus overlooking the actual dynamics of the situations in question.

The Tiananmen Square massacre, following upon the heady months-long Beijing Spring, has for many in the West become at least a kind of touchstone and point of reference to contemporary China, standing alongside economic growth figures in an awkward patchwork of seemingly incommensurable indices. Initially it called powerfully upon an obdurate confusion with which atrocity, particularly when highly public, often seems to confront us. The images of tanks, the staccato of repeater rifles, the anguished voices on the mass media, particularly in the context of China's prominence in world affairs, engendered a double effect. A strong sense of the need to respond became coupled with an awareness of not knowing how to respond effectively. This frustration seemed to intensify the sense of indignation and blame.

The events of Tiananmen have pointed to a number of quandaries for Western responses to China. These are often couched in terms of a conflict between what are too easily characterised as pragmatics and principle (reflecting realism's division of politics and ethics). That is, in this context, the need for good state-to-state relations – maintaining reasonable patterns of communication, particularly with a major power, across a wide range of interaction, interdependence and tension – versus the importance of upholding, even symbolically, principles intermittently identified as fundamental to orderly relations within and among states. And yet the Tiananmen 'incident' caused such an intense reaction in part because relatively little emphasis had been given by the West to questions of human rights in China over the preceding decade. While not insignificant, human rights diplomacy in general during the last decade of the Cold War remained comparatively low-key. Economic growth figures, against the background of relative strategic ease with which China was viewed during the later Cold War years, had loomed large in many relationships at the state level and allowed the growth of considerable warmth in both national and community links. Moreover, modernisation policies within China had enabled an increasing exercise by certain sectors of the population of informal political and civil rights – ease of publication and circulation of a range of political views for example – creating a general impression of positive trends. There has been an implicit belief in some Western circles that through 'modernisation' China would become more like 'us'. Questions of *principle* were thus, in practice, left for the confusion and abnormality of a crisis, as for the rest of the time pragmatism seemed to be undertaking all tasks so well.

As well as formal statements of shock and protest, states (particularly Western states), organisations and international bodies such as the World Bank imposed international trade or financial sanctions following the killings. Some sanctions were tied specifically to the release of certain prisoners; some involved questioning, at least for the moment, the wisdom of sales to China of military or surveillance equipment; others were more simply statements of indignation. These actions drew some concessions and were an emphatic message to the Chinese government. But beyond this reasonable but highly generalised goal their aims and effects were unclear, and most sanctions were lifted by June 1991. Criticism by human rights groups and others, upholding the primacy of principle, of the speed with which Western states resumed full trade links with China may perhaps only have been matched by the feelings of frustration, confusion or aimlessness on the part of the many officials called upon to use general commodity trade to affect, suddenly, the orientations of the Chinese government. As with many debates about trade sanctions against not fully industrialised states engaged in gross public and attention-drawing human rights abuse, Tiananmen again stirred the murk of our complicated assumptions about the civilising effects of market disciplines and international trade.

The dominant public reaction of shock and uncertainty was gradually over-taken or at least matched by the belief that there was nothing to be done except continue business.

Over time, however, another issue became increasingly significant in the more public international activity about rights in China – a more classically geostrategic concern. The events in Tiananmen Square, occurring on the eve of the collapse of the Soviet Union and the end of the Cold War, could stand as the marker for a significant shift in the relationship between China and the United States, and more broadly of China's increasingly assertive international posture. In the two years after the killings, China was criticised in both the UN Human Rights Commission and the ILO. But continuing efforts by states within the UNHRC or by the United States (or the US Congress) to penalise China over human rights were largely unsuccessful. The issue became explicitly a test of strength and strategy between the remaining and the potential superpower. In this light, the killings, in China's own heartland and in full international view, could stand as an assertion by the government (or the faction that emerged vic-torious from the struggle played out behind the Beijing Spring) of its determi-nation to pursue its own agenda and its own definition of the proper state as ruthlessly as seemed necessary, in defiance of the convictions and conventions of the US and others. The assertion of principle and of 'rights' in this context becomes absorbed into the struggle for power and influence described by realism. The sense of frustration and impotence on the part of China's critics hardened and was rewritten as a version of the 'clash of civilisations'.

Since 1991 the Chinese Government appears to have maintained a double-track policy (or a strategy of 'attacking the few, and winning over, dividing and reforming the majority'); that is, signalling a carefully contained willingness to cooperate with selected (and significant) proposals, while adopting attack as the best form of defence. Thus, throughout the early 1990s the Chinese Govern-ment made clear its willingness to engage with the United States and other Western states on the symbolic ground of human rights. Efforts within the UNHRC to condemn China on the grounds of abuse seemed to operate essentially as a litmus of China's ability to wield influence and threat in its inter-national relationships. But the government also took some major steps of long-term significance – signing the International Covenant on Economic, Social and Cultural Rights in 1997 (and accepting the principle at least of Red Cross access to prisons in the same year) and the International Covenant on Civil and Politi-cal Rights (ICCPR) the following year. Shortly after signing the ICCPR, however, Beijing gave long prison sentences to activists who had taken the unprecedented step of establishing a new political party, the China Democracy Party, charging them with attempting to overthrow the government. China wishes to engage, cautiously, with notions and regimes of rights, but on its own terms and without challenging the control of the Communist Party.

China's official international position on rights draws on its role as a great power within the developing world and its desire for unchallengeable status as a global great power, as well as on the dynamics of the 'Asian Way' debate and selective quotation of its Marxist ancestry. While endorsing the importance of the idea of rights, Chinese spokespeople remark that the West has no copyright on its content. The rights given first priority in statements in international fora (e.g. the 1993 Vienna Conference) are those pertaining to the self-determination and sovereignty (both economic and political) of states – the elimination of colonialism and racism, and of abuses resulting from invasion and occupation or from underdevelopment. China here claims ground as spokesperson for developing states, 'which make up the overwhelming majority of the world population', and so proposes an alternative – quantitative – universality to the principles put forward by many Western powers (Liu Huaqiu, 1993: 1). It also implies the guilt of the West, as coloniser and imperialist. By contrast, Western efforts to promote rights are portrayed as selective and aimed at undermining the growing power of developing states, thus threatening their independence.

The concept of rights is thus placed firmly within the context of sovereignty. This is done not on a strictly utilitarian or even a Marxist basis but rather by virtue of the (somewhat Hobbesian) argument that only a strong state can both protect the Chinese people against the depredations of and exploitation by foreigners and provide subsistence (which is otherwise threatened by both natural disaster and social turmoil). Making reference both to historical materialism and to the argument concerning the necessary limitations imposed by different stages of development, official statements frequently provide a short history of rights in China. In common with the position of many other developing states and the traditions of the former Soviet *bloc*, the 'foremost human right' is subsistence. But the foundational achievement, upon which even subsistence depends, is national independence – in historical terms, ridding the country of the imperialists and 'alien powers' at whose hands China had suffered 'dismemberment, oppression and humiliation' (State Council, 1991: 4). This history enables a listing of pre-communist atrocities against Chinese people that establishes a kind of pre-emptive indignation in the face of whatever charge others may lay at the door of the Chinese State. It also stands as a contemporary assertion of the pre-eminence of the state in any weighing of the claimed rights of individuals or groups within China. (Constitutional guarantees likewise remind the reader that the interests of the state are primary.) In a more scholarly and classically Marxist reflection, Chen Xianda, (1992) writing in *Qiushi*, contrasts liberal concepts of rights as the abstract rights of 'the universalised capitalist' with the proletarian citizen's rights within the concrete life of society, which means simply the state: 'Thus the sovereignty of the state is the most important substance of human rights.'

But China's posture has also been shaped by the leadership's own reading of the collapse of the Soviet *bloc* and the end of the Cold War. For some, the country stands as the last bulwark of socialism, beset by forces working for 'peaceful evolution' (that is to say, subversion) on every side. Human rights universalism is seen as a direct attack on national sovereignty and an affront to the orthodox Marxist identification of citizenship rights as the only rights. Chen Xianda (1992) put this quite clearly:

> Those people who glibly argue that . . . 'human rights have no national boundaries' are in fact . . . subverting human rights . . . While they mouth the language of human rights, their hearts are bent on hegemony and their hands are wielding powerful weapons . . . The struggle of the proletariat for human rights is the struggle to establish the socialist system.

This suggests the broader international context within which discussion of human rights in China takes place. It was not altogether the atmosphere in which the Tiananmen killings occurred – indeed those killings and their after-math were rather the nominal source of the heightened suspicion and tension between China and a range of Western states. It is the context, however, in which much contemporary discussion of or reference to the massacre must now proceed.

The story

According to statements by the Chinese delegation to the UNHRC in 1990, the demonstrations were 'an anti-government rebellion aimed at overthrowing the government of China' which jeopardised the lives and well-being of the whole population. Western representations are often almost the precise opposite of this (hardly plausible) account of the state as national bulwark struggling to save the masses from an impending chaos wrought by demonstrating students. Many of the stories told about Tiananmen in the West revolve around the broad theme of the individual versus the state – the youthful idealist and heroic individual, 'the student martyrs of Tiananmen' (Johnson, 1990: xiii), staking everything on the desire for freedom and unfettered expression, crushed by the organised violence of the repressive and illegitimate state. Variations of this understanding of events have been put forward, particularly by the popular Western press, by some Western academic responses and by some Chinese participants in or supporters of the demonstration. This representation was captured visually and with great iconic power in the poignant television image of the youth holding up the flower to the gun of the tank, which all at once invoked traditions of heroism, sacrifice and peace in the face of aggression and force ('speaking truth to power').

There are subsidiary themes to this story, not necessarily occurring together but linked loosely by a strong current of indignation and disgust at the killings. One is a preoccupation with the evilness of the Chinese regime. Generally that evil is identified with the communism of the regime; it may additionally, more occasionally and faintly, refer to certain culturally Chinese traits or to the difference or threatening exoticness of this large and powerful Asian place. 'Last June in Beijing, the beast of communist totalitarianism suddenly stripped off its beguiling Oriental masquerade and showed itself, contemptuously naked, on the television screens of the world' (London, 1990: 246). The evilness of the regime is counterposed to the innocence of the demonstrators, 'the student martyrs of Tiananmen'.

The opposition between students and the regime becomes easily totalised into a confrontation between good and evil, or between fundamentally different and antinomic things. Businessmen and politicians now 'return to sit at the banquet of the murderers, and meanwhile, in the cellars of the secret police, with one bullet in the back of the neck, the youth, the intelligence, and the hope of China are being liquidated' (Leys, 1990: 157). 'June 4 is likely to prove only the first salvo in a long battle between ideas and bullets' (Hicks, 1990: xx). President Reagan commented at Oxford: 'You cannot massacre an idea.' The totalising of the opposition between the demonstrating students and the state, between good and evil, allows other forms of totalisation. Thus Simon Leys, for example, can write of 'the entire nation rallying round the Tiananmen demonstrators' (1990: 156), offering this not as an empirical observation but as the expression of a prior truth awaiting its moment of expression. The demonstrating students become the symbol of the Chinese people who, yearning for freedom, will one day, like 'the irrepressible surge of the tidal wave', sweep away the regime and the 'last remains of Chinese communism' (Leys, 1990: 156). 'For five glorious weeks the Chinese people showed where they stood and raised a Goddess of Democracy [identified as a replica of the Statue of Liberty] to show where they wanted to go. The final chapter has yet to be written' (McGurn, 1990: 244).

In this account, the Chinese people sometimes yearn not only for freedom or democracy but for a completely free market system. 'China's experience with partial economic changes and halfway reforms since 1979, culminating in the Tiananmen massacre and systemic recidivism, is an object lesson in the futility of taking the capitalist road without going all the way to advanced democratic capitalism' (Prybyla, 1990: 187). Because the Beijing Spring happened to coincide with the Bicentennial of the French Revolution, and because it was (not coincidentally) resonating with the excitement of the momentous changes in the Soviet Union and the Eastern *bloc*, the events in Tiananmen can also be absorbed into a larger picture, 'celebrated as a new watershed in revolutionary behaviour' (Johnson, 1990: vii) to the extent that they threaten to disappear altogether, except as a sign of something else.

The presentation of the confrontation as one between good and evil was echoed by official representations of the event within China. Those elements of the leadership which gathered the forces to crush the demonstrators referred to the protest as a counter-revolutionary rebellion, led by a small clique of 'beaters, looters, smashers and burners' (a reference to the violence of the Cultural Revolution) and backed by insidious forces in the West. They became the 'enemy'. Within Chinese constructions of rights, those who are deemed enemies of the state forfeit citizenship – since citizenship exists only by virtue of the state – and so are without rights. 'The People's Liberation Army . . . serves the people wholeheartedly. They are ruthless to the enemy, but kind to the people' (Chen Xitong, then Mayor of Beijing, in Yi Mu and Thompson, 1989: 75).

We have tended to romanticise Tiananmen in a way that we do not romanticise the extraordinarily high proportion of indigenous and black people in the prisons of many states, for example, or the sale of women into prostitution or abusive labour conditions. This is because Tiananmen echoes so pointedly an idealisation of themes running through our own political mythos. In the words of George Hicks: 'The West looks at China and sees not what it is but an Oriental mirror image of its own hopes and dreams' (1990: xvi). The events of the Beijing Spring are testimony to many things, including the aspirations for political change and more participatory political forms, however understood, among the urban Chinese population. In the same way, the consequent response of the government – the needless and irreparable moment of the armed killing the unarmed, the subsequent repression – demonstrates again the extent of the rigidity, stupidity and ultimately of the violence allowed or produced by certain political and social forms, communist or non-communist. The moral drama of this is not disputed. But many representations of Tiananmen construct from these potent elements a confirmation of the categories of person, state and rights embedded in the Lockean story of man, discussed earlier.

The students called for freedom of expression; for the removal, within this story, of the fetters of the oppressive state to reveal the autonomous, self-possessed individual. The individual confronts the state, which appears as other than 'human' and merely a form of vicious restraint. In some versions (as some of the statements quoted above suggest), the 'state' is all that stands between the people and advanced democratic capitalism, as if that complex form of economic, political and social life were waiting, embryo-like, within the Chinese people. The 'human' and the old emperor struggle for sovereignty. In an inversion of official Chinese statements, the emperor is 'an enemy occupying power' (London, 1990: 256). The natural subject protests the state, while the image of demonstrators, young, enthusiastic and ultimately tragic, in the heart of the political space of the state appears again as focal point of all rights. From the midst of the jumble and the contradictions of our political and economic institutions, Tiananmen can thus be held as a talisman for the ideals that 'advanced democratic capitalism' claims as its own, and at times at least cultivates, and against the dangers of overtly repressive political and economic control that it endeavours to reject. Tiananmen seems to attest that people have again found these ideals worth dying for.

The problem with this kind of representation is that it abstracts the Tiananmen massacre from its own social and political context and reality. It abstracts it, too, from our own grasp – from the dense and ambiguous (and sometimes brutally clear) world of human interactions – and places it in an idealised domain of almost pure moments. It is celebrated as tragedy and inspiration, but an inspiration that sheds little light on the painstaking, costly and uncertain efforts of working to change abusive institutional and social structures. This has a most practical consequence. By the time an army is crushing its own fellow-citizens with tanks in the streets there is nothing (short of the very mixed and politically and ethically fraught benefits of military intervention) that anyone or any entity can do, except express displeasure after the event. It is in the mundane webs of social practice, which either support or obstruct events such as Tiananmen, which lower or raise the threshold of acceptable violence, that practical action may sometimes be possible. To focus on the drama of the individual versus the state is to overlook the specific social, political and legal institutions that make up the state and in which the dividing line between state and person becomes unclear. But it might be in the messy realities which involve the state in various, sometimes contradictory, positions that efforts to strengthen participatory political forms, or render public institutions more accountable, may be possible.

The next two sections of this chapter, then, provide some discussion of the leadership and the general political context of China in the 1980s as well as of the student demonstrators. While necessarily brief, the function of the discussion is not to offer new insight on China but to allow events a significance, particularly in any consideration of questions of human rights, extending beyond the retelling of 'man' versus 'state'. There are numerous accounts of the Beijing Spring, the massacre and the intensified repression following it – many of them very full. This study does not attempt to reproduce or summarise them beyond some essential references.

The political context – the 'state'

For some commentators the Chinese state is evil and confrontation with the more politically conscious sectors of the Chinese population is therefore inevitable.[3] But as, for example, Lowell Dittmer's examination of events leading up to the killings suggests, 'the Tiananmen massacre was not inexorable. Rather, it was the outcome of a subtle interplay of developments whose complexity must be thoroughly examined' (1989: 3). Any focus on divisions within the leadership on how to handle the Beijing Spring, however, itself draws on the broader context of rapid change within China – in particular the climate of increasing economic expectation and uncertainty coupled with growing political openness and underlying dissension, within the leadership and the population, on the structure of the state and the nature and scope of political and economic reform.

China's leadership, certainly in the 1980s, was deeply divided. These divisions, however, were not solely a matter of generational cleavage and succession, or of the factionalism of court politics, although these elements were powerful enough. Rather, they were part of far-reaching transformations of political, social and economic life in China, and of fundamental struggles about how state power was constituted, and how it might be wielded. Thus the role of the Communist Party and of the people, the nature and basis of political legitimacy and the need to recreate or strengthen legitimacy for political rule within China, and the mechanisms by which political power in its broadest sense is exercised and communication or participation is made possible were and still are 'unresolved and festering questions' (Dittmer, 1989: 2).

China's poverty, the chaotic violence of the Cultural Revolution, and for some the desire to strengthen China's international security, power and prestige, led in late 1978 to the leadership committing the country to a process of 'modernisation'. Modernisation was envisaged as the route to an increasingly prosperous, orderly and secure state. An indication of the scope of these changes is perhaps clearest in the economic sphere, which has been central to the modernisation project and where the country was set on a path from a command economy towards increasing scope for market forces. Movement towards a market economy, however, involves not merely removing direct state controls but establishing a broad network of indirect controls for setting the rules of the game and making government policy possible – a workable taxation system or some system for raising revenues, for example, methods for redistribution, for the provision of welfare and for social investment, a reliable system of commercial and administrative law. But such processes of transformation are hugely complex, costly and need time; as well as movement towards the desired outcomes, they generate confusion, disruption and contradiction. Throughout the 1980s, China was a 'neither this nor that economy' (Raby, 1990: 1). Moreover, there is a 'fatal interconnectedness . . . between industrial reform and the political and social systems' (Kent, 1993: 79).

Ann Kent characterises the social and political changes that modernisation involved as necessitating a shift from the overwhelming preponderance of traditionally embedded *Gemeinschaft* practices to intermittent and fledgling reliance on more formal and juridical *Gesellschaft* practices, contributing to an 'increasing gap which the modernisation process opened up between state and society in China' (Kent, 1993: 79). This characterisation provides some indication of the nature and depth of the social and political revolutions underway in the 1980s and beyond. Legal reform – 'strengthening socialist law' – has been a crucial element of modernisation with the independence of the legal system from party cadres widely seen as critical to economic restructuring and combating corruption. But the introduction of a substantial body of new statutory law may have rendered more complex, without fundamentally altering, the more traditional elements of the structure and the orientation of Chinese law, often described as 'principally a system of punishments for ordering society' – of 'law from above' or 'rule by law' in contrast to the 'rule of law' (McCormick, 1990: 96). Traditional Chinese law draws also upon an extensive system of grassroots security and mediatory functions as well as adhering explicitly to policy directives from the Communist Party. 'The resultant condition of law has been conceived as a complex intertwining of the jural (formal) and the societal (informal) models of law' (Kent, 1993: 47).

In the mid-1980s, around the time of movement from the initial stage of agricultural reform to reform of the urban economy and more complex rural changes, the coalition of economic 'modernisers', from which Deng Xiaoping had drawn his support and which formed the basis of direction and stability within the leadership, disintegrated. For the remainder of the decade, two factions, the more orthodox communists and the relatively radical reformers, were increasingly bitterly divided over the nature and direction of reform. Much of the debate focused on loss of party control over economic and political directions – over the degree of predominance of centralised economic planning and over the means by which 'leadership' by the party should best be achieved. This debate was intensified by the fear not only of the direct loss of dominance by the party but of the potentially chaotic social and economic consequences of removing the command structure in an economy and society which lacked established alternative mechanisms of management. Opening production to market forces required removing the 'iron rice bowl' of employment and subsistence security, but this was to destroy the network which had assured that most people's basic needs were met without there being another means for meeting these needs in place. By the mid-1980s China was operating on two economic systems with two pricing systems – a fixed system, to protect supply of basic or essential commodities, and a market system. This situation gave tremendous scope to and in many circumstances necessitated corruption. (Efforts in 1998 to introduce full market pricing led to panic buying, and were abandoned.)

Whereas the conservatives argued for a continuation of the pattern of saturation leadership and more orthodox Leninism, the more aggressive reformers, including Hu Yaobang and Zhao Ziyang, argued for a revitalisation of the party through an increasing separation of party and administrative powers. Borrowing initially from European Marxist humanism, but later from the Singapore and Taiwan models of 'new authoritarianism' (or 'Leninist Confucianism'), the new legitimacy would be based on a meritocratic, streamlined and executive-style party – better educated, able to deliver on economic management, less enmeshed in the details of implementation, more open to the expertise of non-party intellectuals and advisers and more open to the scrutiny of other loyal but non-party bodies (particularly the national and provincial people's congresses). There was considerable emphasis on introducing rule-governed order, predictable, legally based and in principle accessible to all, into the political and economic domains. None of this, however, envisaged any real diminution of the party's overall dominance or 'leadership'. This pattern of political reform produced considerable tension, particularly between the levels of independence needed to make systems of scrutiny effective and constrain misuse of power and the dominant understandings of political leadership and 'harmony'. Commenting on legal reform in China, McCormick (1990: 96) proffers a frequently drawn interpretation of this tension:

> On the one hand, 'law from above' has patrimonial implications and therefore fails to adequately order society or steer the state. On the other hand, an accessible, autonomous legal system would threaten the autonomy of the state and the Party's leading role. Consequently, reforms to date are incomplete and contradictory.

This tension remains a significant feature of China's political system.

In effect, throughout the 1980s the legitimacy of the leadership and the Communist Party was based increasingly on successful economic management and people's increased buying power, plus increased personal and economic autonomy. In the early 1980s improving living standards and the prospect of on-going economic benefit maintained an optimistic atmosphere. But the urban reforms and the second stages of the rural reform proved highly destabilising. While many benefited from market reforms, millions lost employment or faced a suddenly insecure employment future – in an environment where social welfare, education and health care, as well as social identity, have been tied to employment. Spiralling inflation in the late 1980s fuelled intense anxiety and eroded real incomes in the state and collective sectors, especially in the cities:

> Were one to single out one single factor conditioning workers' support for communist regimes, it would be the expectation of protection from insecurity, inequality and uncertainty by a strong welfare state. Deng Xiaoping gambled on being able to compensate Chinese workers with greater prosperity in exchange for any erosion of security, equality and certainty. (Wang Shaoguang 1990, in Seymour, 1993: 41)

The prevailing tactic of tightening and loosening economic controls, the removal and reimposition of price controls for example, left many farmers and enterprises unexpectedly exposed. Moreover, this decade was marked by the

relatively sudden, and for the Chinese people the novel, emergence of significant disparity in income. This resulted in acute social envy, particularly among
those on fixed wages (the formerly privileged industrial workers in state enterprises and other state employees), so that even those who benefited from the economic policies suffered a sense of relative deprivation (Walder, 1996). The
ethical goals of socialism – equality, solidarity and security (Kornai, in Saich,
1992) – which had formed the moral universe for many Chinese, and were a
source of social consensus, were being dismantled.

The erosion of the social value structure became particularly sharply
focused around questions of corruption. Because the economy and the broader
allocation of benefits and privileges remained primarily patrimonial, success
or wealth was often perceived to reflect not skill, effort or luck but the
right connections and corruption. Moreover, the maintenance of party dominance at all levels of economic organisation, together with the double pricing
system, created the perfect conditions for corruption. By the late 1980s,
'Chinese society had become "on the take" where, without a good set of connections and an entrance through the "back door" it was very difficult to
partake of the benefits of economic reform . . . Abuse of public positions and
the privatisation of public function . . . reached extreme proportions' and was
highly visible (Saich, 1992: 50). The legal, political and administrative structures struggled to respond.

The process by which the party experimented with more flexible forms of
'leadership' and economic control, however, created conditions of increasing
economic uncertainty and division that were not underpinned by correspond-
ing changes in social welfare structures. It also both enabled and presupposed
an expansion of political toleration, or openness. In the period up to June 1989,
citizens enjoyed 'increased access . . . to greater freedoms of movement, of
speech, press, publication, association and assembly, and of the right to more
personal space' (Kent, 1993: 232). This situation constituted an almost complete reversal of the traditional communist division of and hierarchy between
subsistence and political rights (Kent, 1993). These freedoms facilitated a more
widespread political confidence and heightened critical awareness of the contending forces and potentials simmering within Chinese society. But increasing
political awareness served to make corruption or the manipulation of power
only more apparent. Addressing the changing politics of the factory, for
example, Andrew Walder points out that the consequence of greater openness
in the decision-making processes was 'to make cadre privilege and abuse of
power more transparent than before, and since this is open subversion of the
democratic process promised by the committees, it may make cadre privilege
appear to be even more illegitimate and intolerable than in the past' (Walder,
1996: 56).

At the same time, despite tentative movements towards rule-governed order and nominal constitutional guarantees, greater political openness and 'expanded civil rights of expression . . . were not anchored in any enabling legislation and were therefore vulnerable, as in the Maoist era, to arbitrary cancellation at the leaders' whim' (Kent, 1993: 232). Moreover, the abuses of power that were repeatedly coming to light and the evident gap between government rhetoric and practice – or the tensions between competing policy directions – remained largely unattended. To reverse these problems would have required embarking on a deeper or more extensive reform of the political structure, including a reorientation of the mechanisms through which the Communist Party exercised authority, a reconceptualisation of the party's role in society and most importantly the party's preparedness to let go of many of its direct levers of control while enabling the growth of alternative channels for the legitimate exercise of power – a difficult task. But greater political openness increased the expectation of and demand for reforms of just that magnitude. Intellectuals, encouraged to contribute to the revitalisation of Marxism-Leninism, became increasingly active through the decade, pressing not for an end to party dominance, but for various forms of genuine power sharing. The fragile results of the political reform process throughout the 1980s and the relative reliance of the continuing implementation of these reforms on patronage within the leadership rather than institutionalised guarantee became a source of increasing disillusionment and discontent amongst intellectuals. By 1989 the 'regime was confronting the beginnings of a "desertion of the intellectuals"' (Nathan, 1989: 24).

Within the leadership Deng maintained his own pre-eminent position and some semblance of unity between the competing factions by alternating support between the two groups, playing one off against the other. But this tactic actually underlined reliance on personal power and so weakened the process of institutionalising the political system that was part of the platform of 'modernisation' which Deng had championed. 'The lack of institutionalisation has meant that the fate of the reform programme has depended on the disposition at any given moment of influential individuals' (Saich, 1992: 12). The rapid swings between the loosening and the tightening of economic, political and cultural controls produced an atmosphere of uncertainty and a tendency to paralysis within administrative apparatuses. Perhaps most notably, the party failed to create any mechanism for succession, which remained trapped within the model of personalised power. The question of succession only sharpened factional tension, leading to the destruction of the careers of Deng's first two anointed successors, Hu Yaobang and Zhao Ziyang. Despite efforts to create a more rule-governed society, 'when the system came under stress, individual power relationships built up over decades proved to be more important than the rule of law or the formal functions people held' (Saich, 1992: 58). Fear of loss of control leading to chaos worked to obstruct and erode exactly those kinds of institutions that could enable predictable and potentially more accessible decision making and implementation.

In the early years of the People's Republic of China (PRC) the credibility and legitimacy of the Communist Party was based on its success in overcoming the chaotic, corrupt and impoverished conditions that had characterised much of the first half of its century. The unquestionable dogma and idealism that characterised the first decades was in part rooted in widespread experience of this success. Party rule provided an effective (if slowly stagnating) subsistence economy underpinned by what was in the economic domain a relatively egalitarian value structure. The painful political education that was a by-product of the Cultural Revolution, however, ate away at the practice of unquestioning faith. Over subsequent years the 'manipulation and mobilisation of the population to support the goals of the various factions increased the tendency towards a deep, bitter cynicism on the part of many' (Saich, 1992: 20) – a cynicism only compounded by the fact that Marxism remained a fundamental point of reference, if experienced as increasingly empty.

In short, economic modernisation produced the promise and, to a lesser but still considerable extent, the reality of prosperity. But it also removed the guarantee of subsistence, introduced an entirely new dimension of both expectation and anxiety, and undermined the dominant egalitarian social value structure. Corruption emerged as a particular source of contention and threat to the legitimacy of the party's rule, while the significantly freer political climate to some extent unmasked both the operation of economic corruption and the manipulation of political power. The more tolerant political environment thus intensified dissatisfaction at the lack of accountability. But it also encouraged people to think that change was desirable *and possible*, and that their own actions might bring it about (Kent, 1993; Shi, 1997). The Democracy Movement was not essentially an expression of despair, or of frustration at lack of rights. Rather, ordinary social and political life was caught in an intensifying contradiction between discontent and optimism, 'a revolution of rising expectations in the arena of civil and political rights, and of a combination of rising expectations and relative deprivation in the area of social and economic rights. The 1989 Democracy Movement was the ultimate point of collision between the old structures of Maoist rights and the new rights of the modernisation decade' (Kent, 1993: 167).

As Dittmer (1989) and others (most recently Nathan and Link (eds) (2001), *The Tiananmen Papers*) have detailed, both the leadership and the broader arms of the state were deeply split on how to respond to the demonstrators. This split reflected both tactical differences and the growing divergence of views on the nature of the state and the basis of its power and legitimacy – and a divergence in the ways power was operating within the state itself. The Democracy Movement was itself made possible by this *de facto* heterodoxy of the state. The violent suppression of the movement was in part the product of the factional battle which destroyed, for the time being, the pro-reform grouping and stripped Communist Party Secretary Zhao Ziyang of his power. Zhao himself clearly had some sympathy with the demonstrators – certainly his handling of the protests was consistently conciliatory. According to *The Tiananmen Papers*, 'if left to their own preferences, the three-man majority of the Politburo Standing Committee would have voted to persist in dialogue with the students instead of declaring martial law' (Nathan and Link, 2001: xviii). (The declaration of martial law on 20 May proved crucial to the final outcome: by sharpening the opposition between the 'party state' and the students and casting by the students as near-traitors, the declaration all but closed off any effective avenue of retreat to the demonstrators.) Indeed a united party leadership, whether more reformist or more orthodox, may well have avoided the destructive extremity of the final response. But perhaps more important than this was the extent of support throughout the party for the Democracy Movement and the rejection of the use of force against the students.

> [N]ewspaper and television stations, retired generals, university presidents, members of the National People's Congress and the democratic parties, and even the All-China Federation of Trade Unions – expressed public sympathy for the student demands for negotiation, or donated money to the student hunger strikers' while factory workers drove trucks to the square in solidarity. (Walder, 1996: 61)

The declaration of martial law in Beijing was met with widespread resistance and protests, an estimated 1 million people demonstrating in Beijing in support of the May hunger strike and later against the declaration of martial law.

Subsequently, the question of the use of force against unarmed civilians reportedly 'created a crisis of loyalty within the military' (Byrnes, 1990: 132). The crisis of legitimacy within the arms of the state themselves which had been gathering force, particularly in the latter half of the decade, was 'so severe that in the spring of 1989, it was unclear whether the army would respond to the political leadership' (Dittmer, 1989: 3). 'One of the PLA's elite units, the 38th, [near Beijing] initially demonstrated reluctance to participate in putting down the student demonstrations. The 38th's commander . . . was removed, along with a number of his subordinate leaders' (Byrnes, 1990: 137). According to Dittmer (1989), direct appeals to Deng or Yang Shangkun, or clear statements of opposition against the use of force to suppress the Democracy Movement were made by more than 150 top party cadres, China's two surviving marshals, the former minister of defence and the former chief of staff, seven generals, some 260 serving high-ranking military officers as well as twenty-five retired senior veterans and almost half of the Standing Committee of the National People's Congress.

None of this was sufficient to stop the killings. The decision to enforce martial law and use the PLA to clear Tiananmen Square was taken by a meeting of only three members of the five-member Politburo Standing Committee plus those 'retired' party elders whose support was crucial to a decision. It thus by-passed the institutionally designated channels of both party and state formally required for a direction of such gravity. While the relevant leaders issued clear instructions to troops not to fire on civilians, even in the face of violence (according to *The Tiananmen Papers*), and while it appears that the army may have lost self-control, the use of troops to respond to civil disturbances produced the result here that it frequently has had elsewhere. In the end, the system of political rule, plus the individuals involved, both allowed and produced the massacre. Neither faction of the leadership, the more reformist or the more orthodox, was able to negotiate a peaceful resolution with a large and vigorous, but not essentially antagonistic, demonstration. (It is worth noting that demonstrations in many other Chinese cities were dispersed without deaths.) But just as the final outcome was hardly inevitable, so the system of rule – the state – is not to be reduced to a merely repressive and homogenous layer. It is rather a complex, contradictory and to some extent changing set of institutions with a range – now further limited by the choice taken at Tiananmen – of different potential directions.

The students

Students initiated, led and acted as spokespersons for the demonstrations throughout urban China in 1989. Nevertheless, the participation of workers was a crucial element of the political activities. Earlier demonstrations by students (1986–87) had not attracted significant support from other sectors of society and had, at least partly as a result of this, been relatively easily contained. The possibility of a successful coalition between students and urban workers was a source of considerable anxiety to the party leadership, for not only did workers represent a potentially far more significant proportion of the population and a real reservoir of power, e.g. through coordinated strike action, but as in Poland the growth of independent and aggressive unions could challenge, ideologically and pragmatically, the supremacy of the 'workers' party'. Across the country during the Beijing Spring, 'close to thirty "illegal organisations" . . . made an effort to form an independent union or workers' association' representing workers' interests (Walder, 1996: 64). But the crucial debate about what leadership of the party should mean was – and remains – precisely a debate about the possibility of organisations genuinely independent of and sharing power with the party. Deng, here backing the conservative faction, viewed the frank assertion of independent political organisations as 'counter-revolutionary'. Perhaps as a result, during the killings and reprisals, it was workers (particularly the 'Dare to Die' corps) rather than students who bore the heaviest (although less internationally publicised) toll in terms of deaths and prison sentences.

But it was students who shaped the demonstrations and, as Jane Macartney (1990) points out, after 4 June it was the students who became 'figures of mythology'. The intense drama of the events of Tiananmen, the high aspirations of the Beijing Spring, the foreboding of the final days, the killings and the search for bodies, the arrests, public denunciations and efforts to escape, the sense of waste – all of these are the natural elements of public tragedy. The students' own rhetoric contributed significantly to the mythologising effect: 'On a day in June that should have belonged to a season of fresh flowers, my people, my countrymen, my classmates and my beloved comrades-in-arms fell' (Wu'er Kaixi, in Yi Mu and Thompson, 1989: 75). The student pledge in the Square included: 'I swear that I will devote my young life to protect Tiananmen and the Republic. I may be beheaded, my blood may flow, but the people's Square will not be lost. We are willing to use our young lives to fight to the very last person' (in Barme, 1990: 79).

For many Western observers the students stood as an unquestionable endorsement of the ideals which form part of our own broad family of modern political institutions and a vindication of the universality of our own contemporary assumptions about the necessary structure of political life. The students' slogans (in the earlier 1986–87 demonstrations as well as in 1989) of 'freedom and democracy' underscored this. But other observers of Chinese affairs (e.g. notably Geremie Barme, David Hinton and Jane Macartney, and in a milder form many others) have set out to demythologise this rather romanticised and arguably ethnocentric presentation of the students. The milder analyses (e.g. by Andrew Nathan and Marie-Claire Bergere) have argued that few, if any, of the students or pro-democracy intellectuals in China conceived of government in a form bearing much resemblance to that of Western liberalism. The more acerbic commentaries have in general focused on two factors: first, the immediate, concrete nature of the students' concerns coupled with their lack of intellectual or practical grasp of what their slogans of 'freedom' or 'democracy' might entail; and, second, the extent to which the students, far from being the interpolation of a natural subject or a universal man giving expression to natural desires for Lockean civil liberties, were profoundly part of the distinctly particular political context and vocabulary which they were criticising.

'Demythologising' the students' actions is important for this argument insofar as it promotes a more contextualised and grounded understanding of events. As already suggested, mythologising Tiananmen, whether by situating it within an explicitly Lockean paradigm or more simply by seeing it a version of the ancient story of youth and freshness crushed (for the time being at least) by calcified and corrupt old age, takes it out of reach as an effort to effect social change and as deserving of reflection on its own account. Instead events are locked into perhaps ultimately unreliable moral absolutes – planes where no ordinary mortal dares tread. However, in a move which the present argument does not intend to repeat, demythologising often sets out to reveal feet of clay or to uncover a tawdry or otherwise disappointing reality behind the 'illusion' of the myth. Thus the process of demythologising is frequently itself in search of the heroes it aims to unmask, but a search driven by disappointment, anger or cynicism. In such cases, the students are judged by the criteria of heroes, and so are found wanting.

Students in China were caught in a particularly exposed position in the pincer between rising material expectations and an increasingly unpredictable economic reality. On the university campuses, as elsewhere, economic growth was upheld by the leadership and by social commentators as, for all practical purposes, the primary goal of national and individual endeavour. Meanwhile Marxism remained the required point of intellectual reference while being evacuated of relevance. Extremely poor conditions on the campuses (which had been the focus of earlier demonstrations) intensified the 'incentive for students to seek improved conditions in life after graduation. They expected these improved conditions to come from the economic reforms' (Macartney, 1990: 5). However, the pace of economic reform was failing to meet rising expectations, and the shift to the market was proving a very mixed blessing for students. Prior to the mid-1980s and the urban economic reforms, university graduation had been an excellent guarantee of at least a modestly good job. Employment was allocated by the state, severely reducing or eliminating choice but ensuring a basic level of security. Broadly speaking, those attending the capital's leading universities either were, or had reasonable expectations of becoming, part of the nation's elite, with the prospect of a good job and party membership, with all its attendant privileges. However, as part of the urban reforms the system of job allocation was to be gradually wound back, to be replaced finally, in 1993, by a totally 'open' market. Compounding the insecurity of being close to the first generation of students to search for their own employment in a growing but highly unpredictable economy was the recognition that the right contacts and connections carry infinitely more weight than do academic results.

The urban reforms carried another bitter reality for students and intellectuals more generally. The get-rich mentality that was promoted with economic reform worked to undermine the social value accorded education, so that the status of intellectual work, only just recovering from being the 'stinking ninth category' of the Cultural Revolution, was again eroded. Moreover, employment was now an uncertain prospect, and the relative value of intellectuals' incomes, mostly derived from work in the state sector and fixed in a time of rapid inflation, was diminishing rapidly. By contrast, small entrepreneurs in particular were shooting ahead. 'Even the official media had begun to discuss a hot topic among students – that doctors and university graduates earned less than cab drivers and hairdressers, and that everyone earned less than private entrepreneurs' (Macartney, 1990: 6).

It is sometimes observed that the students themselves gave little content to the slogans they used, beyond that of expressing pervasive dissatisfaction with the conditions of their life. The movement's 'democratic prestige was, to a large extent, conferred on it by foreign observers and media, misled by the vocabulary used by the intellectual vanguard. Actually, the words "freedom" and "democracy" seem to have been fetish words; the young demonstrators were unable to give them any meaning other than their own immolation' (Bergere, 1992: 140). For some commentators the material concerns of deteriorating campus conditions and worsening economic prospects (and the social envy they generated) were the driving forces of the students' actions. According to Jane Macartney:

> Asked about their ideals, most [students] were hard pressed for an answer. 'Freedom, democracy,' students said during demonstrations in the winter of 1986–87. Pressed to elaborate, they complained of official corruption and high-level nepotism, poor food and uncomfortable dormitories. Were they talking about universal equality of opportunity or were they merely envious of those who held higher-paying jobs? (1990: 5)

It is important to keep drawing attention back to the concrete bases or dimensions of the students' concerns (although Macartney is here also pointing to a complex of envy and elitism), and not to presume the exile of material concerns from the loftier realms of political community. Perhaps, too, rather than suggesting that the students meant nothing by their slogans, these concrete concerns offer some insight into what the students actually did understand by 'democracy' – perhaps some version of greater fairness and the opportunity to air grievances. Certainly lack of access to university-level or local leaders was a persistent frustration (see, e.g. Nathan and Liull, 2001: 16). While Macartney's observation asserts that at the heart of the students' apparently universalist rhetoric was a preoccupation with their own circumstances, it also implies that concern with concrete life conditions may be a poor basis for political action or incipient democratic commitment – a highly questionable belief which the students themselves may have shared.

> Their living conditions were abominable . . . The food was inedible, the lighting inadequate . . . yet the students could not concentrate their complaints on such pragmatic, concrete personal problems because this would expose them to the criticism of being selfish. They had to escalate their demands to more abstract, lofty, and essentially idealistic themes. In Chinese political culture, the ultimate sin is selfishness. (Pye, 1990: 165)

Moreover despite such criticisms of the students' motives, their concerns clearly resonated with enough of the hopes, anxieties and experiences of significant sectors of the urban population that the demonstrations attracted widespread support. Allocation of housing, for example, was an intensely sensitive issue among urban dwellers. This sensitivity reflected people's dissatisfaction over material conditions and an underlying uncertainty about the extent to which they could trust, or participate in, those mechanisms that significantly patterned the conditions of their lives. Moreover, as indicated earlier, changing material conditions were themselves a fundamental part of a much broader revolution in the economic, social and political constitution of Chinese society, and these changes were given added meaning in this context of transformation. A sense of unfairness regarding housing and employment can act as a focus for and a nexus of dissatisfaction and aspiration of many kinds. The students' concerns were concrete – as were those of many of the workers – but they were not *merely* concrete.[4]

Various commentators have emphasised the extent to which the students, far from giving expression to a Western ideal of universal man, were operating from within the terms of the same political outlook as the was the leadership. Jane Macartney argues that the students sought not an alternative to but rather the approval and reassurance of the party leadership. 'The students felt they had been left out . . . The establishment had rejected them. They had not rejected the establishment. Rather they simply wanted a dialogue with it. Thus the repeated cry for the government to recognise their movement' (1990: 15). But dialogue could be regarded as fundamental to any demand for more participatory politics (as well as strategically necessary to the survival of the students). Moreover, the students could be allowed to stand more squarely in Confucian and Chinese Leninist traditions of dissent. For without reducing the complexities and contradictions of modern Chinese life to its Confucian or Leninist (or Maoist) histories, these traditions remain powerful active veins of meaning.

Within Confucian society, loyal dissent, where the bureaucrat-scholar petitions the emperor to correct errors of government, was an institutionalised function of the intellectual elite. '[I]t was the duty of the literati . . . to speak out as the conscience of the government . . . intellectuals served simultaneously as ideological spokesmen, servants of the state, and moral critics of the ruler' (Kent, 1993: 137). It was not their task to point the way to fundamentally alternative sources or forms of power. Rather than seeing themselves in essential conflict with the state, during the 1980s many Chinese intellectuals adopted relatively traditional postures towards government. They called for party reform

> that would bring people of quality to power, whom they, as intellectuals, could serve as advisers. Very few of them were actually concerned with the problem of

creating new institutions or modifying the structure of the state . . . all problems, including those of economic modernisation and political reform, could be solved by good leaders and honest administrators. (Bergere, 1992: 136)[5]

Leninist patterns of rule in China were to some extent the modern bearers of the tradition of loyal opposition. Despite the serious challenges offered during the Cultural Revolution and by the worker-led movements (such as the Democracy Wall Movement) that grew out of the experiences of those years, the aim of dissent post-1949 was repeatedly the refinement of the party leadership. Thus, for example, the purpose of the hunger strikes during the Beijing Spring was to underscore the patriotic nature of the student movement. 'The message was that the students valued the welfare of the state above their own lives. It was thoroughly in the tradition of Qu Yuan, who lived in the fourth century BC, and who committed suicide to show his loyalty to the ruler who failed to heed his advice' (Nathan, 1989: 24). More pragmatically, the opposite of patriotism under these conditions was the crime of counter-revolution – a danger realised in the declaration of martial law.

The reform process, however, carried a double potential for this relationship between the leadership and the intelligentsia. While the leadership, in its efforts to revitalise the party, sporadically promoted (and then repressed) 'new ideas', this process of reform by renewal was unreliable; moreover, in the tumult of modernisation, privatisation and get-rich schemes, the role and standing of scholars were again wavering. Students thus had a special reason to feel that they were being excluded from playing their anticipated role in life. According to this understanding, the students' protests were an appeal to the leadership to recognise the role of students and intellectuals as patriotic interlocutors on the social good – a natural part of an elite meritocracy but also a broader, more pluralist or complex, base for state decision making. Demands for freedom, democracy and rights were not associated by the students with particular kinds of political structural reforms or with a clear vision of a fundamentally alternative political community or with egalitarianism. Understood in this context, the lack of structural alternatives and the elitism of the students were weaknesses for the movement; but this does not mean that the protesters' demands were politically empty. Rather, the students were appealing to and, according to their own understanding, operating within particular traditions of political virtue: 'the persistence of a Confucian moral regulating the reciprocal rights and duties of the governors and the governed in the common interest [must be] recognised. It was, in fact, in the name of virtue that the honest critics, the generous students and the indignant population arose' (Bergere, 1992: 141).

Dialogue with the leadership and an end to corruption (leadership by bad men) were thus both key student demands. According to Wu'erkaixi, a prominent student leader, 'our purpose was to make the government listen to us and talk to us. That was our only real demand' (quoted in Macartney, 1990: 12–13). Both demands were part of the leadership's own policy slogans (with 'dialogue' being associated with Zhao Ziyang and the reformist faction). But the now ascendant conservative faction within the leadership, while committing itself to talking with the students, approached the exchanges as opportunities 'to feel the public pulse' without listening to the students' concerns. Meanwhile, perhaps unsurprisingly in the confused developments of April–May, the student leadership's approach to dialogue was angry and rigid. Key figures among the students demanded a dialogue, though it would have little room for manoeuvre and little potential to be anything other than a public parading of success or failure, with live television coverage, the presence of foreign and local journalists and preparedness on the part of the premier and others to commit themselves to on-the-spot policy decisions. The hour-long meeting that resulted stood as a confrontation between the entrenched arrogance of Premier Li Peng and the presumptive arrogance of Wu'erkaixi. Perhaps crucial to the outcome of the exchanges, however, was the students' demands for independent student associations, which confronted the regime's inability, further hardened during the crisis, to loosen its grip on power. On a broader level, the public meeting between Li Peng and Wu'erkaixi is indicative of a crucial lack of political mechanisms for articulating and negotiating conflict.

In pointing to the presence of Confucian rather than liberal models of political dissent, it is also worth noting that Confucianism is by no means a homogenous source of reference, even for this particular confrontation. Liu Xiaobo, for example, one of the older intellectuals prominent in the Beijing Spring and one of those who negotiated the students' final retreat from the Square with the commander of the tank unit, was himself highly critical of the elements of 'Confucian personality' in the students' actions, while demonstrating elements of that tradition himself. Liu 'felt that calls by Chinese intellectuals over the years to achieve freedom always had a plaintive tone to them . . . [He was] highly critical of the students who had petitioned Premier Li Peng . . . by kneeling on the steps of the Great Hall of the People' (Barme, 1990: 71). This was an example of 'the merely moral dimension of pressuring the government . . . the traditional "petitioning the throne through death"' (Barme, 1990: 71). Liu advocated instead practical methods for 'social advancement' but also emphasised the crucial importance of a highly self-critical form of inner rectitude. Liu took part in the second hunger strike. For Liu, the hunger strike could serve as 'social advancement' because it was a form of purification and 'repentance' (Barme, 1990: 70).

The more romantic Western presentations of the students reflect too something of the students' own vision of themselves. Barme (1990; see also Barme, Hinton, Gordon *et al.* 1995) in particular has drawn attention to the importance to the final outcome of the preoccupation with the 'revolutionary' – the heightened emotion of the bloody sacrifice for the preservation of the true way – over a willingness to face the confused field of the everyday as the principal dimension of political change.

> The revolutionary tradition of the past century has shrouded death for a cause in a romantic garb. It is a tradition in which 'romanticism and revolutionary impulse fused in a cult of action' . . . The suicidal student pledge contained the lines: '. . . I may be beheaded, my blood may flow, but the people's Square will not be lost'. The cult worked for the soldiers as well. The troops in the martial law invading force took an oath . . . which read in part: '. . . If I can wake up the people with my blood, then willing I am to let my blood run dry.' (Barme, 1990: 79, 80)

Perhaps a more telling form of continuity between the student demonstrators and the party leadership, however, concerns the lack of practical democracy in the students' own dealings. The demonstrations grew out of an increasing demand among the urban population for more accountable and participatory political forms – a demand that was not cast essentially in opposition to the state or the Communist Party (indeed many pillars of the state supported it) but which nevertheless required fundamental renegotiation of the structures of political legitimacy. The students gave voice to this shifting climate, but in its full contradictions and desire for change rather than as the articulation of a clear way ahead. They were not able to give content in their own organisation to the drive for a more participatory politics. This is the sense in which the students' demands were not empty but self-contradictory. A repeated failure to discuss key decisions (or to vote on them), the secrecy, elitism and strongly hierarchical character of the organisation, an emphasis on a repressive interpretation of 'unity', and purges were what marked the student movement. This is suggestive of the dynamics of political immaturity, compounded by panic, and the nature of the students' own prior political experience, but also the students' own position as the pool from which a later generation of the Party elite could emerge. '"In the struggle for democracy we can sacrifice a few smaller aspects of democracy," said Wu'erkaixi, asked in late May whether the student movement reflected democratic processes in its own organisation' (Macartney, 1990: 16). According to Macartney, the student leaders 'saw themselves as inheritors of the mantle of communist rule . . . there was little attempt to foster participation by the main student body. The leaders took control, seemingly assuming that their emergence in the front line . . . was enough' (Macartney, 1990: 16; see also Barme *et al.*, 1995.) Driven by insecurity and a fear of losing privilege as well as by the desire to broaden participation and to contribute politically themselves, the students captured the contradictory desires and commitments that perhaps often characterise periods of intense social and political change.

It is worth touching briefly on the broader discussion of democracy, particularly among intellectuals, in the debates around political revitalisation of the

1980s. This debate would have contributed significantly to most students' grasp of 'democracy'. But it was itself only part of the broader pattern of changing political demands, expectations and assertions around the issue of participation within the population – a second dimension is noted briefly below. As Andrew Nathan has pointed out, within the context of debate among intellectuals 'democracy' was understood as 'something much more and much greater than an improvised and unstable and flawed compromise among competing forces that can never be satisfied' (Nathan, 1991: 33) and much greater than 'institutionalised uncertainty' (1990: 199). The notion sits firmly if tacitly within a traditional emphasis on natural harmony and the Maoist belief in society as a radical unity. 'Democracy' here denotes that which is modern, 'scientific' and successful. In its strongest form it is an idealist notion: conceived of less as a fabric of institutional structures and expectations enabling participation, restraining concentration of power and mediating conflict than as a sophisticated expression of a highly evolved but ideal political unity.

In the Chinese context, this approach has three ramifications. First, questions of structure have tended to be understood as the province of expression or form – significant, but secondary to what could be regarded as questions of political 'essence'. Particularly for debates at the time, '[w]hen Chinese democrats speak of democracy as scientific . . . they mean that democracy is the only ontologically correct political system, the only kind of system that is compatible with the nature of the universe. Institutional questions are secondary, because democracy carries the inevitability and the perfection of science' (Nathan, 1991: 34).

Second, bearing in mind the leadership's desire to retain control, conceiving of democracy as the expression of an ideal unity does not enable the emergence of independent power bases or assist in the task of mediating among them once they have emerged. It is in keeping with this that one of the striking features of the progress of the demonstrations was the apparent lack of mechanisms available for mediating a peaceful resolution.

The third ramification, in practice, is that while democracy may be regarded as inevitable, many Chinese scholars have been highly pessimistic about its arrival in the near future. The 'masses' are understood to be backward and feudal, and the arrival of the necessary 'scientific' spirit depends on 'a reconstruction of the Chinese people's cultural-psychological structure' (Su Xiaokang, in Nathan, 1990: 196). Commenting on the party's official verdict on the Cultural Revolution and the Mao era, Nathan has noted: 'In placing the responsibility for authoritarianism on Chinese national character, both the party and the democratic intellectuals transferred much of the onus for an acknowledged catastrophe from the shoulders of those who wrought it to the backs of those who suffered it' (1990: 196–7).

Thus, while encompassing more open and accountable channels of government and more extensive sources of policy debate and advice, the predominant notion of democratic practice within intellectual circles was *not* broadly participatory (in contrast, for example, to the earlier, much smaller, Democracy Wall Movement) but rather something 'that could only be practised by an educated elite' (Kent, 1993: 148). It could be understood as a form of communication (which may produce a greater sharing of power) to enable the centre to guide and respond more sensitively and effectively to the needs of the people. As James Seymour has pointed out, 'the number of Chinese reformers and dissidents concerned with empowering the majority is very small', while 'the idea of placing political power in the hands of farmers strikes most Chinese intellectuals as ludicrous' (Seymour, 1993: 46; see also Kelly 1990). This deep 'ambivalence among the intellectuals about democracy' (Nathan, 1991: 32) has much in common with the notion of a more or less authoritarian meritocracy. Such mistrust of the *demos* may be the result of the low emphasis on structures and mechanisms – that is, on structures at all levels of political life through which people can channel interests, concerns, and grievances, and which enable people to experience and themselves shape more participatory political forms.

Nevertheless, there remains scope for real difference within this broad model. For many reformist intellectuals, democratic practice 'centred on a system in which the communist party continued to be dominant but was checked by competitive elections and a free press in order to keep it honest and close to the people . . . [and regulated by] laws and established procedures'; on the other hand, for many in the leadership, democracy was to be managed from the top down – 'an instrument of mobilisation whose function is to strengthen the links of citizens to the state' (Nathan, 1989: 21, 18). These ideas patterned the intellectual context informing the student movement.

Sitting next to these elitist constructions of democracy were the dynamics of people's actual participation in politics in China. The picture of political activity is hugely mixed (changing markedly from locality to locality) and far from clear. The widespread participation in and support for the 1989 Democracy Movement indicates a population that is far from quiescent. But occasions for such visible involvement in questions of national politics are rare, while the crushing of the demonstrations enforced withdrawal from questions concerning the fundamental legitimacy of the state. Tianjin Shi's 1997 account of engagement in local politics in Beijing in the late 1980s (that is, in exactly those matters of housing, local corruption, local elections, and so on), however, shows an active, feisty population, prepared to pursue its concerns through people's congresses, trades unions, the bureaucracy and other political organisations. Moreover, '[c]ompared to citizens of other countries, Beijing citizens have a penchant for acts that require initiative, entail risk, and generate conflict' (O'Brien, 1999: 161).

In practice, the elitism of the student movement impeded its ability to consolidate the support from workers and the general population that distinguished this movement from earlier student protests. While enthusiastically accepting this support, the students made clear their separation and distance from the workers. 'Other social groups were more or less rigorously excluded by the student leaders (Nathan, 1991: 32). Organisational links were not made, key equipment such as the broadcasting facilities were not shared (Macartney, 1990). This may have been partly tactical: the students were endeavouring to communicate with the leadership, not to threaten. Yet it may have been among the newly formed workers' organisations that the more concrete and more radical political proposals, and the more practical bases for participatory politics, were taking shape. If the student movement was open to criticism for contradictory or unclear notions of democracy, the same could not be said about Gongzilian (the Beijing Workers' Autonomous Union).

> It wanted to take over the task of representing workers at the national level . . . [to] exercise 'supervision' over decisions made by the Communist Party that affected workers . . . to establish within all enterprises union branches endowed with the right to negotiate with management . . . [and] to pursue their interests within the framework of plant level negotiation. (Walder, 1996: 67, 68)

Perhaps the most powerful criticism of the student movement's lack of practical democracy comes from within the ranks of the demonstrators themselves. The Hunger Strike Proclamation of 2 June, written by Liu Xiaobo and the other three June hunger strikers, and critically addressing the students reads in part:

> [The students'] theory is democracy, but in dealing with concrete problems, they have been undemocratic. [Efforts to democratise in China have been characterised by] talk about ends but a neglect of means and processes. We are of the opinion that the true realisation of political democracy requires the democratisation of the process, means and structure [of politics]. For this reason we appeal to the Chinese . . . to turn a democracy movement which has concentrated solely on intellectual awakening into a movement of practicality, to start with small and realistic matters. We appeal to the students to engage in self-evaluation which will take as its core the reorganisation of the student body on Tiananmen Square itself.

The struggle facing the students was to turn 'the question of democracy from a test of courage in some fantasy world of moral absolutes into a practical problem of the immediate present' (Richard Nations, in Barme, 1990: 68). This may also be the challenge confronting anyone endeavouring to respond to the events of Tiananmen, or working with broader questions of systemically abusive political and social relationships in China.

The final decision by the regime to crush the demonstrations was an expression of the leadership's profound failure to respond to or to manage, within the terms of its own legitimacy, the popular expression of independent political aspiration and will, and the rapid pace of political change – it was a failure of dialogue or communication. It was also a failure of the political system to manage conflict – to have mechanisms available for dealing across the political spectrum and mediating difference. (Indeed, at a tactical level, it was an expression of the state's failure to shift unarmed people from the central Square without deaths.) After some years of efforts to reconstitute the bases of the party's authority, the killings demonstrated the extent of the leadership's fear that it was ultimately unable to maintain stability and direction without the use of deadly force against its own population. Nevertheless the demonstrations occurred and gathered such strength over the months because, at least until the declaration of martial law, this outcome was not inevitable, even if it was according to an old script. The demands of the demonstrators were in themselves hardly revolutionary but were part of the prevailing context of officially acknowledged and sponsored, although highly ambivalent, discussion. The demonstrations, however, occurred at (and precipitated) a juncture of intense factional struggle within the leadership, and their emergence also indicated the potential for autonomous political organisations outside the network of party power: they threatened enough elements within the leadership with a model of participation that was not ultimately orchestrated from above, despite the fact that the students themselves may have been deeply uncomfortable with and untutored in such models. Thus the killings and later reprisals 'entailed a further loss of legitimacy for the government, and the transfer of moral power to the people, whose expression of legitimate grievances in a non-violent form required a response more adequate than short-term violence' (Kent, 1993: 235).

Responses

At one significant level, the repression of the 1989 demonstrations offers a classic example of the abuse of rights as conceptualised within a Lockean framework. As discussed in chapter 2, this framework provides a means of asserting that the ultimate basis of political authority rests in the people of a state, not the monarch. Although far from being the expression of a simple opposition between people and state, the protests were part of an on-going renegotiation of the relationships between the leadership and significant sectors of the population: they were an assertion of the power of these sectors of the population and of the legitimacy and independence of this power, not as conferred by the monarch but as generated by broader political realities.

At the same time, the events of Tiananmen, potent and full of significance on their own account, come to appear as, and in a sense are reduced to, an enactment and confirmation of one constitutive moment in our own political mythos – man against the state – an image in which both players are given an essentialised iconic quality. In that sense the Beijing massacre reminds us of how selectively we give our attention to violence towards people – a selectivity not wholly explained by the presence of television cameras or the strategies of international ideological or strategic competition. We can identify with young, educated, urban Chinese who call for freedom and democracy in ways in which we do not identify with marginalised blacks, malnourished Africans or Tibetans agitating for freedom to implement value systems we find difficult to comprehend.

As already noted, in its strongest form the Lockean story situates rights in the relationship between the individual and the state – in the public sphere at the heart of the state. The individual is already politically formed, essentially independently of the state; the state, once it abandons the role of facilitator, is merely repressive of the natural formation of the individuals who make up the people. In regard to Tiananmen, this reductionist view encourages a demonisation of the state and either sanctification of the students or bitter disappointment if they fail to live up to their appointed role as spontaneous democrats. It assumes that the students, as everyman, are natural representatives of the 'people'; that they are 'renaissance men' (Macartney, 1990) expressive of an imagined wholeness of Chinese society rather than a contradictory mixture of aspiration, idealism, aggrieved elitism and inexperience. This model suggests that if the repression by the state were simply removed, the natural condition of democracy would emerge. And it gives prominence to a universalised, but also a narrow and abstract, definition of 'the political', while tending to discount the seemingly less noble preoccupation over increasing economic insecurity, unsatisfactory housing and unreliable institutional mechanisms of many kinds.

But the circumstances of Tiananmen do not fit this representation. It remains of crucial significance that the protests are not reducible to a fundamental antithesis between the 'butchers of Beijing' and the 'student martyrs of Tiananmen'. They were part of a far more complex and interdependent relationship. We recognise this complexity often enough when discussing political or economic developments in China; less so when the topic is more specifically human rights, which is often left to a seemingly awkward and antinomical domain identified not as 'politics' but as 'principle'. Yet in recognising some of the complexities of the relationship, we acknowledge the broader field within which the pursuit of human rights must take place. To understand rights abuse as pre-eminently defined by the clash of natural man with the state-as-tank shapes the way it seems possible to pursue rights. When we respond to the Beijing massacre essentially by demonising the state, the focus of work on human rights becomes primarily one of negating the state – achieving condemnation becomes the overriding and apparently sufficient aim. This is a narrow aim, if sometimes an essential tactic. It is an aim which feeds the Chinese Government's claim that the struggle for rights is the struggle for national sovereignty and security and one that slides into the self-aggrandising agenda of competing states – a situation which cannot be relied upon to assist in working towards environments of mutual respect.

Similarly, when we imagine the students as natural universal subjects we give little weight to those processes by which fundamental attitudes and practices bearing on rights (such as attitudes towards participation) take shape. To understand rights as the natural expression of natural man in the political domain fixes attention on the world of notional essences and primordial conflicts – towards the moment of crisis and away from ingrained patterns of injury embedded in institutional and social practices, overlooking the extent to which the two can be entwined. It is in this context that the proclaimed universality of rights becomes abstract generality. As both Western and Chinese commentators have pointed out, it may have been precisely the abstract generality of the approach of much of the Democracy Movement that was its greatest weakness. The students demonstrating in Tiananmen called for freedom. Within the contractarian mythos 'freedom' implies the absence of constraints, particularly those identified with the state, and assumes the shape of human community to lie available, defined by its 'otherness' to the state. But what may be dangerously lacking in the political structure and traditions which produced Tiananmen is not 'freedom' in this sense, but the complex and difficult institutional mechanisms and habits of mind by which power is circulated, discussion is given place, conflict mediated and violence reflected upon and restrained. What is needed is not the removal of constraints, but the construction of different practices which both enable and constrain action. To engage in these practices involves working with the complex tissue of 'the state'. In this sense, some of our dominant models of rights, of civil liberties as 'negative' rights in Cranston's use of the term, limit efforts to promote human rights in China.

Within contemporary China, human rights questions have been broadly debated since the early 1980s. Chinese scholars have attributed this concern to the need 'for a basis upon which historic reflection upon certain crimes of the "cultural revolution" which everyone from common citizens through to high officials were forced to suffer could be undertaken. [Issues included] political persecution, deprivation of personal freedom . . . torture', and arbitrary arrest and execution – the loss even of 'the basic right to exist' (Li Lin and Zhu Xiaoqing, 1992: 375–6). Following the Beijing massacre, there was what one Chinese commentator called a 'craze' for human rights in China. Scholarly writing on rights has been an effort to elaborate 'socialist' rights – in this context, essentially the search for more accountable patterns of rule which do not challenge the overwhelming pre-eminence of the Communist Party. The reform of social institutions is fundamental to this search. Whereas the focus of much Western commentary on human rights in China is political expression, for many Chinese the integrity of the justice system and abuse of power by the police are more pressing concerns (see, e.g. Cullen and Fu, 1998: 128). Some Chinese officials will privately (and despairingly) point to police violence as one of the most persistent instances of rights abuse across the country. This represents a failure on the part of the state to define and control its own functions sufficiently to enable it to fulfil its own policy intentions. The scale of this kind of failure suggests profound problems in the political system, particularly in the justice system, as well as simply a lack of resources.

Talk of a tentative separation of powers between the Communist Party and the state and between political and administrative functions – widely seen as essential to political structural reform and, consequently, to effective civil rights practice – was largely put aside during the decade following the massacre. Nevertheless, in practice, and in a trend that began in the mid-1980s, structures of government at the municipal and county levels have become slowly more accountable, and bodies such as the National People's Congress are now more assertive, even if their power remains essentially on loan from the party's upper echelons (Tanner, 1998). Moreover, the growing incidence of corruption involving misuse of official position – one of the key areas of concern for the 1989 Democracy Movement – is seen by the government to be such a severe threat to its authority and its capacity to govern that it appears to be driving a slowly increasing independence of legal process from political power, as well as greater delineation of political and administrative functions (Hao, 1999). The Communist Party 'has become increasingly reliant on legalised modes of social, economic and political control' while still clinging to its position as unassailable vanguard and ultimate authority (Cullen and Fu, 1998: 131). The tension is sharp and the picture remains complex and ambiguous.

Official and predominant views of rights within China fix them unquestionably within the state, as rights of the citizen. The abstract universalism of the rights of 'man' is criticised, as it is here, and rights are argued to be grounded in the specific realities and relationships of concrete political communities. The realities in question, however, are understood to be defined by the state, or, more precisely, by the leading party organs, or in times of crisis by a few leading party figures. The idea of the universality of rights may be retained in this picture as a function of historical progress towards the universalisation of the proletariat (much as Donnelly, for example, proposes the universality of rights to be a consequence of modernisation). Ultimately it is the events of Tiananmen Square, not merely as notional possibility but as concrete reality, that point to the weakness of this position. It is a position which seeks to put aside the critical dimension of the notion of human rights – a dimension which challenges prevailing definitions of legitimate violence and the political dimensions of suffering – and which makes of the state a boundary where all questions must cease. The official defence of the Beijing massacre is that it was undertaken to protect the rights of the overwhelming majority of the Chinese people. But if a narrow, fixed construction of the state defines the extent of rights, by what processes is citizenship negotiated, power circulated, the limitations of action debated and established, and the on-going and often conflicting practices which make up the state constituted? This question need not lead back to the claims of man in nature outside of and prior to the state but to the concrete problems of conducting relationships across and within social and political institutions of all kinds.

The argument between human rights as rights of the universal subject and citizenship rights is often circular. The universal subject is itself part of an effort to conceptualise the rights-ordered community and the state. As discussed in chapter 3, the criticism of the ontological essentialism of this figure of man often works, explicitly or implicitly, as an assertion of the essentialism of the state, however conceived. It could be suggested that each side of the argument offers a necessary critique of the other in much the same way that E. H. Carr ultimately links idealism as antidote as well as antithesis to realism. This may be taken as a dialectic from which synthesis might emerge (not an understanding pursued here) or more simply and pragmatically as an assertion that the two broad positions are historically interwoven with and shaped by each other and other debates around the modern state.

Paul Hirst, upholding citizenship rights in his discussion of socialist legality, mounts his critique of universalist rights through a rejection of everything other than the action of institutions. 'All the proclaimed "civil rights" in the world are nothing beside the organisation of institutions; civil liberties are a codeword for certain effects of the control of institutions' (Hirst, 1985: 55). This point is relevant to the 'quiet revolution' in institution building in China, driven by the complexities of governing a huge state. '"[T]he principal builders of China's chief organ of socialist democracy" [i.e. the National People's Congress] are not liberal reformers but bureaucrats who spent much of their careers at the epicentre of classic totalitarianism' (O'Brien, 1999: 164). Yet while significant, this process remains tenuous. For its part, the contractarian promotion of universal rights points to the failure of positive notions of rights to allow conceptual space outside the already given dynamic of state institutions, from which legitimate claims to participation or protection can be asserted. 'Rights are put to use, claimed, exercised only when they are threatened or denied . . . In fact, the special function of human rights virtually requires that they be claimed precisely when they are unenforceable by ordinary legal or political means' (Donnelly, 1989: 11, 13). Both Hirst and Donnelly have something valuable to say here about the process of political change in China – neither point need be collapsed into an essentialised figure of the human or a reified state.

This commentary on the Tiananmen killings has endeavoured to draw attention to how complex events and relationships – events and relationships that generated extreme abuse – have been, for many, rewritten and mythologised as man versus state. This recounting provides some basis for reflecting on the power and the limitations of placing that confrontation of man and state at the heart of much understanding of, and action around, rights. One of the gravest limitations of the dominant understanding of rights and rights promotion is its focus on the heroic, on the point of opposition with the state and therefore on an essentially punitive approach to encouraging rights observance. When rights are left to be part only of 'principle' as grand gesture, or of a test of supremacy between competing state identities, how can we move beyond statements of indignation? When we focus only on the moment of brutal opposition between state and people we forget the broader story, yet it is in this broader context that efforts to construct rights practices may more often be possible. It is important to respond as strongly as possible to events such as the Tiananmen massacre, at the least in order to mark the intolerable. But it is the 'normal' times, before and after Tiananmen, working with the actual political and social institutions which structure people's lived reality, that might allow the greatest scope for the long-term work of encouraging the growth of social practices and institutional structures that restrain abuse and enable respect of rights.

There are many areas of systemically imposed injury and abuse in China, some openly acknowledged by the government (such as female infanticide, and the sale of women) some cautiously and informally acknowledged by certain but not all government institutions (such as excessive police violence and violent conditions in prisons and other state institutions), some highly politically sensitive (such as labour reform). Working with such areas (when it is possible at all) is laborious, slow and potentially highly confrontational. It is not an 'answer' to human rights abuse – its results can be unclear, and it offers no straight path to systemic change. In particular, under current conditions in China such work does not directly deal with the regime's effort to ultimately monopolise power. As Tiananmen made clear, however, the regime is not a monolith. But working with areas of abuse does open the potential for cooperative efforts to shift entrenched harm and to change people's lives. And it also feeds into the complex institutional dynamic that is producing the state and the social practices in which questions of power and identity are significantly shaped. The 'state', in this slower work, becomes more ambiguous, even if its upper echelons retain access to overwhelming force. It may at different junctures be enemy, ally or neutral. It is almost certainly divided against itself. And the line separating state and individual is not always clear.

Such an approach also steps aside from the certainty that the 'West' has a ready-made answer to the concrete problems of abuse or some specially reliable insight into the extraordinary complexities of political change. With definite exceptions, many references to the influence of Confucianism, for example, on the student demonstrators' behaviour do not regard it as a source of viable political action. Instead, Confucianism appears as a kind of arcane shadow-boxing, in implicit comparison to our own supposedly more 'real' preoccupations. Yet many of those Chinese associated with the Beijing Spring (such as Liu Xiaobo) are not notably Western liberals. Nor are they authoritarian neo-Confucianists in the style of Lee Kwan Yew *et al*. Within the context of working towards political forms that give voice to and constrain injury and marginalisation, the question for Western promoters of human rights in China might be what 'freedom', 'democracy' and 'rights' mean, in concrete as well as aspirational terms, for people and communities from China's mix of traditions and idioms.

NOTES

1   As Andrew Nathan has warned: 'Considering the national scope of the 1989 movement, we generalize about its meaning at risk. There were not scores of localities where demonstrations occurred, there were hundreds' (1991: 31, 32).

2   For example, Okensberg, Sullivan and Lambert (1990); Yi Mu and Thompson (1989); Nathan and Link (2001).

3   A view Deng Xiaoping, ironically, shared, with the categories reversed. 'The storm was bound to come sooner or later. This was determined by the macro climate of the world and the micro climate of our country. Its inevitable arrival was independent of man's will' (June, 1989, in Dittmer, 1989: 3).

4   'Why do a lot of workers agree with democracy and freedom? In the factory the director is a dictator, what one man says goes. If you view the state from the angle of the factory, it's about the same, one man rule . . . we want rule by laws, not by men . . . In the work units, it's personal rule' (Anonymous factory worker, in Walder, 1996: 59).

5   See also Nathan (1989).

5

East Timor

EAST TIMOR WAS forcibly incorporated into Indonesia in 1975 and managed, through a confluence of circumstances that was at once remarkable and yet another example of a suppressed people snapping back like bent but unbroken twigs (to use Isaiah Berlin's phrase), to become independent almost twenty-five years later. Now the territory, poised on the edge of statehood, is undergoing transition, but also flux and confusion. At the time of writing the United Nations Transitional Authority for East Timor (UNTAET) is effectively the Government of East Timor, with elections for a constituent assembly to determine a constitution expected in August 2001.

The following discussion looks in broad terms at the immediate background to Indonesia's violent process of incorporation and the pattern of abuse that characterised it, and touches briefly some of the issues facing the new state. It does not focus on East Timor's political struggles or the development of its contemporary political forms. As told here, the story of East Timor's occupation underlines what in conceptual terms is a very simple point, if difficult to grasp in practice: that is, the significance of approaching questions of rights and abuse not only through convictions about what must be done, or the dealings of international diplomacy, but through attentiveness to and engagement with the social practices, circumstances and perceptions of the people directly involved in the situation. This is the work of listening to the parties and the people involved and creating conditions where they can be more clearly heard.

Directions taken in the period leading up to the invasion of East Timor were shaped within a preponderantly realist understanding of international possibilities. The polarisation of pragmatics and principle – a polarisation that shapes much study of international relations as well as much rights talk – was a distinct feature of this approach. To emphasise human rights promotion as grounded in exchange with the actual patterns of social practice involved casts a different light on the apparent self-evidence of that polarisation, as the story of East Timor suggests. Now the territory is administered by the liberal internationalism of the UN, an orientation that can be expected to outlive the passing of UNTAET. It is perhaps too early to write a considered account of UNTAET's term of office (although analyses are emerging), while the work of the range of UN agencies and other international organisations upon which East Timor will be to a significant extent dependent will become clearer only over time. Nevertheless, the story of East Timor's occupation offers a warning of the dangers of inattentiveness to those now, directly and indirectly, shaping the new state.

East Timor occupies half of a small island at the outlying western rim of the Indonesian archipelago. For Indonesia, it was its most recent and twenty-seventh province, incorporated in 1975. For many others, it was a small nation awaiting self-determination, a *de jure* colony of Portugal, illegally and violently occupied by its powerful neighbour. Caught in what proved to be a long, draining conflict over its status, East Timor was also enmired in deeply ingrained patterns of abuse – 'a tense, tightly controlled territory . . . where arbitrary detention and torture are routine and where basic freedoms of expression, association and assembly are non-existent' (Human Rights Watch, 1994: 21). East Timor was one of those questions seemingly cast up and left stranded by the receding tide of colonisation, decolonisation and twentieth-century state building. As has happened with other sites of protracted conflict, the pattern of events in East Timor became a burden to nearly all of those directly involved, with the crucial exception of the interests benefiting from the monopolies that gripped much of the territory's economy. Nevertheless, it was a burden that for the key parties in Jakarta weighed less than the task of unravelling it.

While under Indonesian occupation, the case of East Timor had a more conventional geopolitical dimension than either of the other two case studies considered here. As will be discussed later, international acquiescence in Indonesia's invasion had much to do with the politics of the Cold War. The end of the Cold War then undermined the currency of Indonesia's status as bastion of anti-communism and eased the strategic pressures which could still demand overriding tacit support from many states for official Indonesian positions. At the same time the US was seeking to establish new channels to define its role as a remaining superpower, including (for much of the 1990s) active promotion of a range of liberal democratic and free-market values and postures. For the US, on-going violence in East Timor was an embarrassment which shadowed the standing of one of its leading regional allies. The Santa Cruz massacre in late 1991, in particular, made an international spectacle of the brutality of which Indonesia's management was capable.

International attention to East Timor, however, was not given substance by the commitment of any major players to a resolution of the dilemma other, perhaps, than slow burial. Its problems were not seen to threaten others and it was packaged as a tragedy – another sad account of the cruelty of geopolitics. The UN at least served as a forum for keeping somewhat alive the issue of self-determination. Most states did not recognise Indonesia's claim to *de jure* sovereignty over the territory. Because the process of decolonisation from Portugal, begun shakily in 1974, was overturned by Indonesia's invasion the following year, East Timor was widely regarded internationally as a case of interrupted decolonisation, thus offending norms the fulfilment of which has been one of the major achievements of the UN. The UN facilitated meetings between representatives of Indonesia and Portugal and among East Timor's political groupings. The European Union, spurred on by Portugal and Ireland, also adopted an increasingly activist position in the late 1990s. But East Timor remained largely isolated from interaction with the outside world. Despite UN resolutions, it made sense to call East Timor 'one of the world's great secrets' and to register the sharp disproportion between the scale of deaths in the territory as a consequence of Indonesian annexation – estimated as proportionately comparable to Cambodia under Pol Pot – and the largely ambiguous and restrained international reaction (Pilger, 1994: 1).

Public discussion of occupied East Timor in Western states often cast it as a simple issue. The fact of the suffering of the East Timorese was simple. The 'answer' to the 'question' of East Timor was independent statehood, and indeed Indonesia's violence probably left no other answer available. Effective self-determination, however, and effective international understanding of and response to East Timor's evolving circumstances may be anything but simple. Answers to questions around how to build a reasonably peaceful political order that East Timor's circumstances pose for its own population and leadership, and for others, may be fundamental to how we understand political community.

The history

This brief retelling, drawn from secondary sources and from sometimes conflicting accounts, cannot do justice either to the complex events leading up to Indonesia's incorporation of East Timor or to the varying interpretations of those events.[1] Moreover, the changed conditions in East Timor and Indonesia may, over time, allow a more complex history to emerge. This section will briefly discuss Timor's colonial period and aspects of the positions of the Portuguese, the United States, and the Australian and Indonesian Governments leading up to the annexation.

East Timor's principal 'difference' from Indonesia lies in its colonial history – its approximately 450 years of Portuguese influence and control, in contrast to Dutch colonisation of other territory in and around the archipelago. Given the highly heterogeneous nature of Indonesia, with approximately 13,000 islands and hundreds of different ethnic and cultural groups, other forms of difference, of which there are many, find their weight within this overarching context. The East Timorese are ethnically diverse. They speak a number of distinct languages, the most common of which is Tetum. But while ethnically and culturally distinct from Javanese Indonesians, they nevertheless share many similarities with Indonesians in the western half of Timor or in nearby islands, except for the effects of the Portuguese presence, including some intermarriage over many generations. The East Timorese have had a largely subsistence lifestyle, in contrast to the cultivated court and the 'feudal' cosmologies of the Javanese, but again similar to that of many other Outer Island Indonesians. Contemporary East Timorese identify as largely Catholic, in contrast to the religiously mixed but predominantly Muslim Indonesians. This Catholicism reflects in part the bequest of Portuguese colonialism, but more potently stands as a rejection of an Indonesian identity.

It is sometimes suggested that the period of Portuguese rule was one of benign neglect. The neglect is indisputable – little effort at development or the provision of services was made until the 1950s. By 1973 the illiteracy rate of the East Timorese was estimated at 93 per cent, and infant mortality in the 1950s (1960s' and 1970s' figures seem unavailable) was around 50 per cent. Since the East Timorese were used as 'free' labour for the coffee and copra plantations, 'benign' is perhaps a more questionable description. 'Forced labour under the whip goes on from dawn to dusk, and the Portuguese colonists . . . live with the same mixture of civility and brutality as they had 350 years ago' (1947 account, quoted in Schwarz, 1994: 199). There were numerous small wars in the colony during Portuguese occupation, some clan and regional feuding, some rebellions against colonial rule, or a combination, with the most recent occurring in 1959. Often local in scope, they were put down, at times with considerable loss of life. It was following a long period of unrest (1894–1913) that the Portuguese in the east and the Dutch in the west decided to settle their colonial borders, creating East and West Timor in 1913. Although there had been two indigenous 'spheres' in the eastern and the western parts of the island, the defining boundaries of East Timor were thus, as is common to much of Asia and Africa, a product of colonial administrative bartering.

In contrast to the later Indonesian presence, however, Portugal did not maintain a large garrison in the territory. With some significant points of exception (the addition of Catholicism to local animist practices, the co-opting of local power structures, taxation of certain activities), Portugal left the social and cultural structures of the East Timorese relatively intact. In part, this is to say that as a coloniser Portugal did not try to 'modernise' or 'develop' East Timor, or to undertake the level of economic activity that in many other colonies hammered out, painfully and destructively to traditional society, the elements of a proto-state. Coffee was a productive cash crop, but in this case the highly dispersed pattern of indigenous social and political life and the self-supporting native economy were suited well enough to the purposes of the colonisers.

Portuguese administration returned to East Timor after being displaced by the Japanese during the Second World War. The Lisbon Government was an authoritarian regime, and the character of its colonial administration reflected this. Portugal had been neutral during the war and was outside the ambit of the reconstruction programmes for the devastated victors or vanquished. Portugal was also one of the poorest countries in post-war Europe – 'the South of the North' – and so clung to the economic potential of its colonial territories, particularly those in Africa, and to the dreams of imperial greatness they symbolised. East Timor itself, however, offered little economic benefit. The half-island had been devastated by the battle between occupying forces during the war (with 40,000 East Timorese dead and extensive destruction of agriculture and infrastructure) but, officially hidden from view by its status as part of Portuguese neutrality, received no post-war reconstruction assistance. Portugal joined the United Nations in 1955 but, despite international pressure, resisted efforts to lock it into UN-sponsored processes of decolonisation until 1974.

The Dutch, like the Portuguese in East Timor, returned to reclaim their colony of Indonesia after the war. But the Indonesian independence movement had gained momentum and organisation during the Japanese occupation. Two days after the Japanese surrender in 1945, leaders of the nationalist movement proclaimed independence. After four years of battling for control over the colony, the Dutch were forced to relinquish their grip, allowing the agglomeration of disparate islands, united to some extent by the patterns of colonial administration, to emerge as an independent Indonesia. During the struggle the independence movement, after considering whether to include East Timor within its ambit, instead focused on ousting the Dutch and, in accordance with emerging norms of decolonisation, on uniting and asserting the independence of those areas that had been held under Dutch control (the 'successor state' principle). For a time the Dutch retook and held the outer islands of the archipelago and successfully managed 'a federation of puppet states' there (Reeve, 1996: 151). Some areas of the archipelago made it clear that they preferred Dutch rule to the new leadership, dominated by Javanese. While the Dutch were eventually expelled, for the emerging Indonesian leadership this puppet-state experience profoundly compromised any consideration of a federal arrangement – as one mechanism for managing questions of regional diversity and local autonomy – emerging in the archipelago (Reeve 1996: 151). Survival of and resistance to Dutch colonisers and Japanese invaders, and the final fight for independence against the Dutch forces, became the basis of a powerful legacy and symbolism of respect, even reverence, for the Indonesian nation and nationalism. Mirroring this reverence, however, and growing from the same roots, was a deep unease about the fragility of the Indonesian State and the loyalty of the outer islands.

By contrast, within the decentralised society of East Timor there was no organised independence movement. Any sign of political activism was quickly repressed by the Portuguese authorities. In the end progress towards decolonisation of East Timor was the result neither of internal nor of international pressure. It was rather the consequence of Portugal's inability to sustain, economically or politically, that form of government of which its 'colonial follies' were an expression. A coup by left-wing groupings in the military, dissatisfied with the draining and unwinnable wars of independence in Portugal's principal African colonies, toppled the Caetano dictatorship in April 1974, and there quickly followed a further shift of power to the left within the Portuguese military and government. The new socialist leadership in Lisbon wished to rid 'Portugal of its former colonial liabilities as soon as possible' (Dunn, 1983: 83). But the coup that for East Timor opened the door so abruptly to independence from the colonial power also plunged that power into an on-going political crisis. The administration whose task it was to implement the slow and complex business of decolonisation, preoccupied with internal crisis and events in its African colonies, had little attention to spare for the circumstances of this distant, small and seemingly quiescent community with a population seen as illiterate, underdeveloped and politically inactive.

Nevertheless, the rhetoric of the new left-wing government in Lisbon was one of self-determination. The Timorese were to elect an assembly to determine the future status of the territory. In accordance with UN norms, there were three options – full independence, some form of association with Portugal or integration with Indonesia (or another independent state). The decision was to be the responsibility of the Timorese. 'It is part of our policy that the wishes of the population will be respected', said the minister responsible for East Timor (quoted in Dunn, 1983: 82). However, two approaches to decolonisation were becoming evident in Lisbon, reflecting shifts in factional dominance. The first emphasised gradual devolution of power; the second, an ascendant position, associated with the younger officers and the Government of Costa Gomes, wanted radical decolonisation as rapidly as possible. Doctrinal enthusiasm combined with administrative inattentiveness, a lack of resources and the desire to avoid the costly open-ended process of participating in the reshaping of East Timor's political life to dictate Lisbon's approach to their colony's direction.

On Timor itself, three main political parties emerged: Apodeti, UDT and Fretilin. Apodeti, by far the smallest group, was strategically significant as it received significant backing from Indonesia and the hierarchy of the Catholic Church in Timor. Apodeti sought eventual integration with Indonesia, after a transitional period of some years during which the people of the two regions could 'become acquainted with each other on the basis of freedom' (Aditjondro, 1994: 2). UDT was a centrist party that began by favouring loose federation with Portugal, but also canvassed gradual transition to independence and finally proposed full autonomy within Indonesia, followed by an act of free choice. It was supported by tribal heads and the small urban bureaucracy. Fretilin, drawing on a mix of Catholic radicalism and Marxism, favoured full independence, also after a period of transitional government. Fretilin developed a significant profile within rural Timor, largely through mounting literacy programmes and conveying its political ideas through the local language and culture, thereby generating 'a new language of independence' (Taylor, 1995: 36). Increasingly, the young radicals leading Fretilin came to see themselves as the 'sole representative of the Timorese people', leading them to 'denigrate negotiations with other parties' (Taylor, 1995: 39). It is perhaps hardly surprising, given the centuries of colonial rule, that independent statehood was seen by Fretilin not as a complex, negotiable and historical form of political structure, but rather as an absolute moral good and a natural expression of ethnic community, with Fretilin itself as the sole interpreter of this good. In the words of the young Jose Ramos-Horta, then a leading figure in Fretilin:

> Independence is a fundamental right of every nation in the world. So the position of Fretilin is quite clear – Independence or Death! Nobody should ask a slave if he wants to be free or not. After 500 years of colonialism, oppression and exploitation of the people, we don't accept any interference from foreign powers in our internal affairs. . . . Independence . . . is not to be negotiated between the people of East Timor and the dominating power or other vested interests . . . The people . . . always wanted independence. But only due to the war superiority of the enemy, all their efforts of resistance failed. (Aarons and Domm, 1992: 11)

In Lisbon the Timorese political parties were assumed to have shallow roots and were given little weight. Meanwhile, Lisbon's own position appeared elusive. In late 1974, Santos, the Portuguese minister responsible, held discussions with the Indonesian and Australian Governments, and in Timor. 'Santos managed to leave both the Indonesians and Australians with the impression that Portugal favoured Timor's integration with Indonesia, but told the Timorese that Timor would continue its ties with Lisbon and ruled out integration' (Viviani, 1976: 204). Whatever the reasons for this outcome, it engendered the suspicion in Jakarta (and Canberra) that Portuguese commitment to the processes of decolonisation could not be relied upon, 'that Portugal could precipitately offload Timor, and would not take pains to avoid playing the interested parties off against each other' (Viviani, 1976: 204). In Dili, the Portuguese officers running affairs on the ground were responding to the gathering pace of local events with little reference to Lisbon. Thus within Timor 'the roles played by conflicting Portuguese expatriate factions, principally in the civil administration and the army, were of more importance than any far distant metropolitan attitude' (Viviani, 1976: 198). While the governor may have supported integration with Indonesia, the colonels actively promoted Fretilin.

In January 1975, UDT, at that stage supporting eventual independence, entered a coalition with its rival Fretilin. The overwhelming weight of opinion within the popularly supported parties favoured independence. In March the local Portuguese administration, after talks with the Timorese parties, arrived at a plan of a three-year devolution of authority to a Timorese government. Visiting Australian delegations at this time noted their belief that full independence would be the choice of the majority of the Timorese (Dunn 1983; Taylor 1995). However, the coalition between the leading parties collapsed, reflecting the differences between them but also pressure and disinformation from the Indonesians. In June Portugal held a meeting in Macau to bring together parties interested in the decolonisation of the territory (including Indonesian representatives as 'observers'). But, in a crucial move, Fretilin refused to attend the meeting, making an authoritative outcome impossible. Identifying itself as the 'true voice' of the Timorese and distrustful of UDT, Fretilin would not negotiate with those East Timorese favouring different platforms.

Meanwhile, in Lisbon the leadership were unconvinced that East Timor's complete independence was feasible. Nor was it in favour of long-term association with this economically dependent and logistically taxing territory. According to an Indonesian account of a meeting between President Costa Gomes of Portugal and Indonesia's General Murtopo, 'there were not three options [facing Timor] but two: joining Indonesia or independence under the Portuguese umbrella. Full independence was described by [Gomes] as "unrealistic". Even Timor remaining with Portugal did not accord with the policy of his state' (in Dunn 1983: 84). In effect, by mid-1975 Lisbon was inclined to believe that there was only one 'option' for Timor.

Thus Lisbon's 'position' on East Timor was that the East Timorese must be able to choose their own direction and, at the same time, that the only 'real' option was integration with Indonesia. To establish this as a coherent possibility rather than refuse to face inconvenient realities would have required encouraging, over a considerable period of time, the growth of relations of trust between the various Timorese groups and the Indonesians. It would have required efforts towards a more consensual politics within Timor, and developing a working, but not overbearing, relationship with the mundane realities of village politics. Most of all, it would have involved taking the East Timorese seriously. None of these endeavours would have guaranteed integration. But Lisbon was unwilling and perhaps unable to play any long-term role in a transition process. At the same time, in Dili, elements of the Portuguese administration were encouraging the quite different aspirations of Fretilin.

The Portuguese Government wanted 'to respect the wishes of the people' of East Timor, but the people were characterised as politically illiterate. Respecting their wishes did not count as respecting the wishes of people taken to be serious interlocutors. Distinctions could be drawn here between a community's ability to manage its own resources and community life and its preparedness for the quite specific tasks of governing a modern state and choosing in a reasonably informed way the form of sovereignty the community, on balance, desired. The questions of self-determination faced by the East Timorese at the time involved the interrelationship of all three elements, but centuries of Portuguese rule had left the Timorese with few tools with which to engage the latter two. Gaining sufficient of these tools would have required some time and international effort. Lack of the specific arts of modern government, however, can too easily be equated with a lack of political life (as the discussion of Aboriginal Australia makes clear). This equation allowed the relative unfamiliarity of the East Timorese with the institutions of the modern state to be read, in Lisbon and other capitals, as a blank sheet upon which the determinations of others could simply be written.

Lisbon's judgement that full independence for its colony was 'atrociously unrealistic' drew also on doubts about East Timor's ability, as a potential micro-state with few economic resources and a population unskilled in modern commerce and industry, to pay its own way in the world or to defend its own strategic interests. It would not have been the first micro-state to have been in this (indeed vulnerable) position, but Portugal, struggling with its own economic crisis, was unwilling to face the prospect of an economically dependent state with moral claims on its former coloniser. Again, Lisbon was scarcely alone in these concerns. Australian Prime Minister Gough Whitlam commented to Indonesia's President Suharto in November 1974: 'An independent East Timor would be an unviable state, and a potential threat to the area' (Taylor, 1995: 28).

Geostrategic and security concerns were a dominant factor shaping Timor's options. Indonesia is by far the most populous state in Southeast Asia. Within the region, encouraging the stability of Indonesia was a significant priority for all those who had been affected by the earlier, more turbulent, foreign policy of their largest neighbour. There was concern, too, that a radical or potentially argumentative micro-state perched at the tip of the Indonesian archipelago would be open to manipulation by interests outside the region, whether Soviet, Chinese or American (Viviani 1976: 205). In the broader context of the Cold War, the US, recently withdrawn from Vietnam, still harboured anxieties about communist power in Southeast Asia, while a number of regional states struggled with, or had recent memories of, communist-backed insurgencies. The complex patchwork of East Asian states appeared vulnerable, or worse, in the global patterns of the Cold War. The island of Timor is situated at a strategic point on a crucial deepsea shipping lane – the only lane in the area capable of providing safe access through the region to US submarines. Within Timor, the leading party was a nationalist, anti-colonialist and broadly socialist spectrum which contained, and was perhaps in 1975 increasingly dominated by, Marxist elements – moreover one which took a posture of non-negotiable idealism.

Within the prevailing preoccupations of the Cold War, dominated by the strategic trajectories of the superpowers, and not too burdened by the local concerns of small players, this registered as cause for serious alarm.

Fretilin was characterised, in the powerful dynamics of 'us and them', simply as Marxist. But for policy makers in Washington and other capitals perhaps as important as Fretilin's possible political inclinations was the insignificance of this tiny, distant, supposedly immature population, powerless by all the criteria of international hubris. Timor was seen as a potential Cuba, perched perhaps malevolently or simply chaotically on a major strategic sealane. Whatever the composition of Fretilin, for many governments it was an unknown and unpredictable quantity thrown into an already tense equation – and therefore essentially undesirable. In its unwillingness to negotiate with other parties to the situation, Fretilin itself contributed to this characterisation. Instability was itself seen as a permanent asset to, and an object of infiltration by, the 'other side'. Mopping up sites of unpredictability was thus a standing goal in the Cold War polarities that underpinned American foreign policy. And the staunchly anti-communist Suharto Government was a bulwark against such instability.

The Indonesian Government's position was more complex. Since the struggle for independence in the 1940s, Indonesian governments had been preoccupied with keeping the state, and its highly diverse population, together. The archipelago did not form a 'natural' or pre-colonial unity or a traditional state. Nevertheless, the region's history under colonialism was often anachronistically cast as a struggle with disunity, with disunity blamed for the vulnerability of the kingdoms of the central islands to a small European power (Reeve, 1996). During the independence struggle, the archipelago and the independence parties were deeply split and factionalised. In the following decade 'several regions rebelled against the unitary state of Indonesia and the dominance of Java . . . [These] rebellions were strong enough to raise the possibility that the country might fall apart . . . [and] were finally defeated by the use of force' (Reeve, 1996: 135). The intense instability of the last years of Sukarno's 'Guided Democracy' culminated in 1965 in an incident interpreted as a communist coup attempt. This sparked, or was used to mount, a counter-coup in the wake of which hundreds of thousands of Indonesians – Marxists, sympathisers and others – were massacred in waves of violence across the country. It was this counter-coup which brought the regime of Suharto, a general in the Indonesian army, to power. A profound and ruthlessly enforced anti-communism was seared into the Indonesian polity. In the same move, the army was entrenched in its role as essential to the survival of the state, primarily against threats from within, the common thread holding the disparate parts of the state together. It was against this complex knot of intense but fragile national pride, a driving fear of national disintegration and the consequences of chaos, and violent anti-communism that the problems posed by East Timor's changing status were considered.

It is not surprising, then, that references within Indonesia to self-determination for the East Timorese were often focused not on the East Timorese but on the Indonesian State, and evoked the kind of nationalism for which the nation state as transcendent idea or organic whole comes to be imagined as the *self* that determines. Thus appeals were made before and especially after the annexation to a putative Indonesian unity preceding the division imposed by colonisers and justifying this belated reunion. An Indonesian parliamentarian for example, speaking in 1974, called for Indonesia to 'Work out a special policy on East Timor so that finally the area will once again return to Indonesian control' (in Taylor, 1995: 25). The East Timorese themselves evinced little sense of sharing a 'common destiny' with the Indonesians.

In 1974, there was a range of opinion on Timor within the Indonesian Government. One strand, of which the then Indonesian Foreign Minister Adam Malik was the leading proponent, drew in a way quite different from that of the anonymous parliamentarian quoted above on the traditions and goals of Indonesia's own anti-colonialist struggle against the Dutch. In his famous letter to Fretilin leader Jose Ramos-Horta in June 1974, Malik stated that 'the independence of every country is the right of every nation, with no exception for the people in Timor . . . that whoever will govern in Timor . . . after independence can be assured that the Government of Indonesia will always strive to maintain good relations, friendship and cooperation for the benefit of both countries' (Ramos-Horta, 1987: 43). Malik later stepped back from this position. The apparent unreliability of the Portuguese and what was understood to be the increasing Marxist dominance of Fretilin may have made Malik's position difficult to sustain within Jakarta.

The second strand of opinion was promoted by the Indonesian intelligence service BAKIN and powerful elements within the military. BAKIN, focused on Indonesian strategic and domestic security concerns, was alarmed at the possibility of an unpredictable and potentially rogue micro-state within the archipelago. BAKIN had a long-standing commitment to the consolidation of territory within the archipelago to deny a beach-head to any forces potentially subversive of Indonesia's unity. For BAKIN, three potent concerns intersected in Timor. The anti-communism, of which they and the military stood as guarantors (where communism was seen as the catch-all domestic threat to Indonesia's unity and sovereignty), interlocked with their commitment to the broader strategic dynamics of the Cold War. At the same time, the prospect of Timor standing outside the Indonesian State touched off anxieties about the unravelling of this mosaic of disparate islands.

Moreover, debate over Timor was occurring in a context of political crisis for Jakarta, marked by intense semi-public struggles within the leadership and serious rioting. According to Benedict Anderson, 'the "team" which had helped bring Suharto to power and to consolidate his initial dominance was falling apart' (1995: 141). The sense of crisis, the sudden change of personnel and the competition for position and favour, not least within BAKIN, encouraged adventurism. In an important distinction, those favouring integration themselves divided into supporters of a policy of gradual persuasion and supporters of what was believed would be a short, sharp and decisive military intervention. And weaving through these debates was the cautious position, apparently adopted by President Suharto, of waiting to see what developments might bring.

President Suharto and other key figures in the Indonesian Government put considerable effort into testing the opinion of governments internationally on acceptable solutions to the problem of East Timor. The Indonesians needed to establish what the limits of acceptable behaviour were; in particular, what would be the cost of a military operation in terms of their regional and international standing and bargaining power, aid and crucial exchanges. Indonesia consulted the United States, and Soviet opinion was also made plain. Jakarta talked, naturally, with Portugal, with governments in the region, including Australia, Timor's other nearest neighbour, the ASEAN states, Japan and India, and with the European Community. All these governments supported, either mildly or with vigour, international principles of self-determination. But, with the notable exception of the small island state of Singapore, for varying reasons none of them placed much significance in practice on enabling a solution to emerge from the East Timorese themselves, in consultation with the other party principals, such as Portugal, Indonesia and the United Nations. The cost of committing resources to the open-ended and hence unpredictable processes of transition – that is, the cost of engaging in the process of self-determination – plus global and regional strategic preoccupations were the dominant concerns.

Within East Timor Jakarta attempted heavy-handedly to pressure the East Timorese into embracing the benefits of integration through sabre-rattling propaganda broadcasts into the territory and by active support for the otherwise marginal Apodeti. It exacerbated tensions and suspicions between the two major parties, Fretilin and UDT, endeavoured to bribe support within UDT, and caricatured all those not supporting integration as communists. Reports in early 1975 of Indonesian troop movements along the Timorese border suggested preparedness to take Timor by force and spurred both Fretilin and UDT to call for independence. In August 1975, UDT – fearing that Fretilin was planning to take over the decolonisation process, and with the encouragement of Jakarta – staged a coup. While the Portuguese governor came out in support of UDT, Fretilin managed access to the Portuguese armoury. In a crucial move, the Portuguese army presence withdrew during the ensuing battle for the capital, not only abjuring a policing function but effectively clearing the way for

Indonesian intervention. Confusion and violence ensued. Fretilin defeated UDT but the conflict cost around 3,000 lives and involved torture on both sides. UDT supporters fled to West Timor, where they were manipulated for propaganda purposes, trained for military action and used as a cover for increasingly active Indonesian covert military action within East Timor. Within the Indonesian Government, President Suharto now supported those favouring direct intervention. Internationally, Jakarta claimed that the chaotic developments in its neighbour were leading to destabilisation, while Indonesian news agencies carried to the world unfounded stories of PRC and Vietnamese veterans training Fretilin troops. In November, Fretilin declared Timorese independence.

Despite Indonesia's significant involvement in encouraging conflict within East Timor, that conflict cannot be reduced to Indonesian instigation. Nor, however, was Indonesian invasion the only feasible response to the circumstances. Presumably knowing the likely response, Jakarta approached the Portuguese to either intervene or to condone Indonesian intervention. Portugal, unwilling to accept either of these options, attempted unsuccessfully to organise an international peacekeeping force. Half-hearted efforts to organise negotiation among all parties collapsed in mutual suspicion. Meanwhile, UDT and Apodeti called for integration with Indonesia. 'The Indonesian propaganda campaign reached new heights . . . and Indonesian ships blockaded East Timor while Fretilin struggled to consolidate and improve its military position and make a beginning of civil administration' (Viviani, 1976: 216). Fighting, involving the significant but unacknowledged presence of Indonesian troops, intensified. Fretilin appealed unsuccessfully for international support. After final tacit approval from US President Ford, Indonesia invaded Timor in December 1975.

After the violence of Indonesia's invasion, occupation of and departure from East Timor, the option of 'integration' with Indonesia amounts to near-heresy to most non-Indonesians. But prior to the Indonesian invasion, integration may not have seemed in principle any less promising than the legally ambiguous but politically constructive incorporation of the formerly Portuguese Goa by India. It would certainly have appeared no less unworkable or strange as a form of decolonisation than the questionable, but internationally legitimised, incorporation of Irian Jaya. Intermediate arrangements, with Indonesia managing external powers and East Timor having domestic independence, canvassed by Indonesian Foreign Minister Malik and Fretilin in 1974, were a potentially workable option but would have taken time and the gradual development of trust. To those in geographically or culturally distant capitals considering 'what to do' with East Timor, the shift from an alien European administration, particularly one with a long history of fascist dictatorship, to a neighbouring, ethnically less dissimilar, Asian administration which had itself engaged in a successful self-determination struggle could seem both in the rational interests of all parties and to almost pass as decolonisation. More importantly, if the Timorese had accepted integration with Indonesia, it would have been decolonisation.

But there was no effort to recognise the East Timorese as real participants in the process of determining their own community directions. 'Participants' is used here, rather than calling for the Timorese to be accepted as sole sovereigns of their future, because the international dynamics within which the Timorese were operating (and the dynamics which established 'self-determination' as a formal option in the first place) involved the interests and vulnerabilities of a range of parties – interests which also needed to be negotiated if a viable arrangement were to be achieved.

What is notable in the events leading up to Indonesia's invasion is not that principles of decolonisation and self-determination were ranked a poor second to the contemporary strategic preoccupations of a number of states. One does not have to be a realist to accept that security, however defined at the time, is a powerful concern. It is striking, rather, that no government's actions indicated acknowledgement that the wishes of the East Timorese were a significant *practical* factor in the dynamics of the situation. This is a statement about how power is understood, not about post-war international principles *per se* – although these principles emerged not from some supposedly ethereal moral universe but came most immediately out of the hard experiences of the First and Second World Wars. But despite the experience of 'the power of the allegedly powerless' afforded by these and other conflagrations, the gamble was taken that because the East Timorese were marginal players they were without power, or were no real players at all (Carroll, in Pettman, 1991: 60).

Thus the failure to engage with the East Timorese was not primarily a 'moral' failure, where the moral is regarded as essentially 'elsewhere', far from the requirements of political life. It was rather a failure of the most practical kind to deal with, to spend the time to understand or communicate with, the concrete life situations of the people at the core of the matter. As a result, and in the name of 'pragmatics', the spectrum of possible outcomes was in effect never effectively weighed by any of the governments involved in discussing the fate of the East Timorese. Thus the possibility that the East Timorese would refuse to accept integration with Indonesia if it were forced upon them, or that they may be capable of obstructing the wishes of all the more 'weighty' powers around them, was slipped, along with the counsels of self-determination, into the box of 'principle', and so ignored. It proved a very costly error.

This 'overlooking' of the East Timorese produced persistently contradictory policies upheld by governments seemingly unprepared to face even the possibility of a serious conflict between self-determination and integration. As was the case with Portugal, key decisions seem to have been made and attitudes formed in a haze of ambiguity. Official statements indicate a kind of wishful thinking that geopolitical concerns and obligations to support aspirations for self-determination would happily coincide. The Australian Government's position on East Timor is instructive here. The approach was to hope for no inconvenience – for all the desired outcomes: regional stability, reassurance to Indonesia, decolonisation, and self-determination for the East Timorese, to fall effortlessly together. Prime Minister Whitlam made it clear to the Indonesian president that he supported East Timor's integration with Indonesia. The Australian Government has often been criticised for placing first priority on the relationship with Indonesia and for its emphasis on regional security. But a workable resolution to East Timor's status would have to have been acceptable to Indonesia. A good relationship with a significant and near neighbour is a staple of international relations. And regional security is a necessary context in which to consider the potential implications of each one of the region's shifting elements. These priorities in themselves were not problematic (although there is considerable room for debate over the character of a 'good relationship' and regional security). All of these priorities would have been consistent with quite different policy orientations regarding East Timor.

The official Australian position was problematic because, in ignoring the potential conflict between two of its goals (self-determination and integration), it dealt itself an impossibly narrow hand of options, it failed to acknowledge frankly what its position was and, as a result, it did not properly assess the potential consequences of that position. The whole policy turned for its success upon integration with Indonesia being voluntary (or at least grudgingly accepted). A voluntary union *would* have been an internationally acceptable form of self-determination, would have served the interests of stability and also the well-being of the bilateral relationship. But despite the fact that this was a vital hinge in the whole enterprise, little weight was given to the possible consequences of the East Timorese not accepting, or even resisting, integration. Such an approach was therefore incapable of evaluating likely outcomes to courses of action, or of generating alternative strategies to protect its own key goals if events unfolded other than as expected. The goal of such a policy, consciously or not, becomes to get away with what you can; this opens the door to being captured by events. Despite calls to Jakarta not to use force, forcible integration operated as either an implicitly acceptable option (as with the United States' 'big wink' to Jakarta) in direct contradiction to what was being explicitly stated, or it became a form of self-deception – an eventuality secretly grasped without being fully acknowledged or properly assessed. However, the outcome of forced integration, welcomed in by the back door, served *none* of Australia's goals – not stability in the region, not decolonisation and certainly not the promotion of the bilateral relationship. Australia's course of action was the outcome not of an inevitable tension between pragmatics and principle, as it was portrayed by some significant actors at the time, but of poor management.

No doubt, all of the many governments with which Jakarta discussed East Timor would have preferred a non-violent integration of the half-island with its neighbour. Some surely imagined a replay of the almost entirely non-violent integration of the Portuguese colony of Goa with India a decade earlier – another case where the norms of the successor state were dispensed with. Some decision makers were undoubtedly reassured by the belief of the Indonesian army that it would all be over quickly, with no or few casualties. In not engaging with the East Timorese, but designating them as a determinable blank sheet or empty agency, participants in these events entered upon a path of unpredictable cost.

The effort to understand and learn from Indonesia's violent incorporation of East Timor has been bedevilled by the polarisation of debate. The emphasis of much of the international legal argument around the invasion has been to find Indonesia the 'guilty party'. And Indonesia is, of course, guilty, but it is a guilt in which many governments that later became accusers were complicit. Many governments were faced with the option of directly or indirectly assisting East Timor's decolonisation process. They were faced, that is, with spending the resources – of time, effort, money, patience, engagement – that the prevention or resolution of particular patterns of abuse may routinely require, but they did not take that direction. Instead, the Indonesian invasion of East Timor was allowed to sweep out of sight what was the cause of an incipient headache for a number of states. Changing geostrategic balances have allowed what were once put aside as unfortunate necessities, badly handled on the ground, to be weighed differently. It is not surprising that in the gatherings of states' representatives, Indonesia resisted condemnation – and may continue to resist condemnation of the original incorporation – so vehemently.

East Timor in Indonesia: the human rights situation

The Indonesian military originally considered that the operation to forcibly annex East Timor would be quick and relatively painless. Perhaps this reflected a genuine belief that they would be welcomed by sufficient numbers of East Timorese, or that the Timorese were too politically passive to resist the annexation so obstinately, or too militarily inexperienced to pose any serious problems to Indonesia's superior numbers and equipment. Encounters with the fighting wing of Fretilin preceding the full invasion led to a re-evaluation of this assessment, however (Kingsbury. 2000). And whatever the feelings across East Timor prior to the invasion, the death and torture of many people carries its own powerful logic. The advance of Indonesian troops was marked by widespread slaughter. East Timor was indeed annexed by Indonesia but, almost twenty-five years after the original invasion, the campaign to integrate the territory had essentially failed. Major counter-insurgency operations to destroy resistance forces were phased out in 1978, but organised insurgency was never quashed. Civilian unrest was met by violent military response but resistance of various kinds was common. Over 20,000 troops were routinely stationed in East Timor to maintain 'stability', somewhat under 1,000 of which were East Timorese.

Some patterns of rights abuse in East Timor were consistent with problems elsewhere in the archipelago and, more broadly, with the problems of poor areas in rapidly developing post-colonial economies. Beyond this, however, the contested status of East Timor was the 'key to understanding the human rights violations that take place there' (Human Rights Watch, 1994: 21). It is widely estimated that 60,000 East Timorese were killed in the first year of Indonesia's 'pacification' programme, which included mass executions of villagers, women, the elderly and children. To wipe out Fretilin's mountain bases, in 1978 Indonesia launched a counter-insurgency programme of 'total encirclement and annihilation', using fragmentation bombing, strafing, chemical weapons and napalm, supported by ground troops. To eradicate Fretilin's support in the villages, the army adopted a strategy of mass relocation of the population of largely subsistence farmers. About half the population was transplanted to more visible 'designated hamlets' away from the better farming land. Food production collapsed. These two operations, and the agricultural devastation that followed, led to a quick escalation of the death toll: 'thousands simply died of hunger' (Ramos-Horta, 1987: 2). Relief organisations were not allowed in. Summary executions continued throughout the 1980s and 1990s, the worst of them the massacre of an estimated 1,000 people at Creras. It is thought that over 200,000 Timorese died as a result of the Indonesian occupation, out of a population in 1974 of 700,000. Approximately 15,000 Indonesian soldiers were killed there.

In principle, Jakarta pursued a two-track carrot-and-stick policy in East Timor – encouraging economic growth, improving infrastructure and services and pumping in aid money while maintaining tight security. The Indonesian Government did endeavour to develop its most recent province. Per capita income rose from US$40 in 1974 to US$90 in 1990. During the 1990s (according to Indonesian figures) economic growth in the territory was approximately 10 per cent per annum, higher than elsewhere in Indonesia. Education became more available and illiteracy was reduced from 93 per cent in 1974 to 53 per cent in 1990. By 1998 schools had been built across two-thirds of East Timor's populated areas. Hospitals, mobile clinics and public health infrastructure were provided. Although higher than for nearly all other areas of Indonesia, infant mortality rates dropped; general infrastructure and services were improved. Much of the infrastructure, of course, was necessary to sustain military operations, while the direction of the economic development suited Javanese and military business interests. According to Lansell Taudevin (2000: 109), despite the destruction of an estimated 70 per cent of East Timor's built environment by the departing Indonesian troops in 1999, more remaining infrastructure remains in place than there had been during the Portuguese era. Excluding security operations, the annual costs of government and services were in the range of US$100 million (Taudevin, 2000), a higher figure per capita than any other province. A major development programme was initiated in 1998.

However, the campaign to integrate the territory with Indonesia was in practice dominated by 'the security approach' of the Indonesian military. Immensely powerful in the fabric of political, social and economic life throughout Indonesia, the security forces, as guarantors and icons of national unity, took a free hand in this recalcitrant province. Despite the activities of local governors, management of the territory was essentially a military operation which, despite actual economic growth and massive infusion of aid, was characterised more by punitive brutality and repression than by efforts to win trust. 'The armed forces, and in particular the military intelligence services, have ruled East Timor since 1976 almost as an institutional fiefdom, accountable neither to the law nor to the political apparatus in Jakarta' (Schwarz, 1994: 197).

The army's operations exhibited the kind of careless savagery that can mark occupation by a rival ethnic force. Unarmed Timorese boys and men were used as human shields when moving through guerilla territory. Torture, killings, arbitrary cruelty used as a 'warning', and rape appear to have become routine practices of soldiers. As Monsignor Belo noted to the Indonesian Bishop's Conference, 'the military, perhaps because of the anger in their hearts, do not seem to have a sense of humanity in them' (in CCJDP, 1993: 15). Nevertheless, various reports suggest that the army generally believed it was providing a good to East Timor, bringing the benefits of Indonesia and the nation to the territory and protecting Indonesia from fissiparous pressures (see e.g. Crouch, 2000). The army and the intelligence services, rather than the police and the judiciary, dominated the legal and policing mechanisms, rendering them in effect unaccountable.

The security approach had a particular economic twist. For example, indicative of the level of control believed necessary to manage the population, until 1989 the Timorese were required to have a travel permit for movement within the territory. But the relocation of villages had necessitated travel to arable and seasonal land. The need for travel permits helped keep local agriculture depressed, which in turn contributed to unemployment, so that basic foodstuffs had to be imported at high cost. This increased the territory's dependence on financial support from Jakarta. Through patterns characteristic of Indonesia but more pronounced in East Timor, the army dominated the territory's economic activity. One conglomerate in particular, intimately associated with army interests, maintained a monopoly on the export of coffee, which accounted for approximately 90 per cent of all East Timor's exports, and so artificially depressed the incomes of numerous local producers. As the team of Indonesian academics sent by some leading Indonesian financial bodies to investigate the causes of Timor's poor performance delicately pointed out, Jakarta 'repaid its moral debt for the financial support that . . . [a company associated with the general who directed the invasion] had given during the war of integration by awarding large concessions to this company . . . [enabling it] to monopolise the economic and trade network in East Timor' (Gadjah Mada Research Centre, 1991: 47). The monopoly system dominated all dimensions of the East Timorese economy, including rural employment, to the systematic disadvantage of the indigenous people. Corruption was deeply entrenched. Thus the carrot of economic development, apparently offered by the central government with one hand, was whittled away by other hands. The territory was the army's prize.

The Indonesian administration system undermined traditional village authority structures. 'The war of integration drastically changed the social hierarchy in East Timor, while the establishment of a new administrative system has given rise to problems in the pattern of decision making and in the way development is conceived, particularly with regard to the aspirations of the local community' (Gadjah Mada, 1991: 45). Moreover, '[m]ost key positions in the provincial government are occupied by newcomers who . . . have not obtained even a basic understanding of the social and cultural life of the East Timorese' (Gadjah Mada, 1991: 4). Local political control, as well as service delivery, was overwhelmingly dominated by non-Timorese as well as by the monopolised trading interests. This meant that there was a lack of any authority accepted throughout the community as legitimate.

During the 1980s, the Timorese resistance movement, led by Xanana Gusmao, changed emphasis from a guerilla campaign to civilian resistance. Believing that armed Timorese opposition to the Indonesian army had been contained, in 1989 Jakarta moderated the intensity of the security approach. There was some relaxation of travel restrictions, for local people and for those travelling in and out of the territory. Opposition increasingly took the form of civil protests, identification with the Portuguese elements of their culture being one avenue for the expression of local resentment. The most internationally explosive indication of the failure to successfully integrate East Timor or to pacify resistance – the 1991 Santa Cruz massacre – erupted from the civilian resistance. Young East Timorese, testing the limits of the post-1989 policy of 'moderation' and sharply disappointed at the cancellation of a planned visit of Portuguese parliamentarians to their former colony – ironically intended as a display of the success of integration – held a funeral march commemorating the death of a pro-independence youth. After a scuffle Indonesian troops opened fire on the marchers as they approached the Santa Cruz cemetery. Troops followed and bayoneted many of those wounded and seeking refuge within the cemetery walls, leading to about 240 deaths. In Jakarta, the Armed Forces Commander Sutrisno defended the army's actions: 'Delinquents like these agitators have to be shot and we will shoot them' (in Schwarz, 1994: 213).

Within East Timor, the massacre further 'radicalised a new generation of East Timorese' (Human Rights Watch, 1994: 22). Those marching and killed had grown up after Indonesian annexation and were the beneficiaries of Jakarta's two-track policy, with access to better education and some of the fruits of economic growth in the territory. The very public killings also intensified pressure on Jakarta. Internationally, the Santa Cruz massacre reinvigorated discussion of East Timor within the United Nations and led to Indonesia being censured in the Human Rights Commission, with the United States, a staunch ally of Indonesia, joining the censure motion. Within Indonesia itself, the 1975 invasion had always been portrayed – and accepted – as an operation welcome to the overwhelming number of the East Timorese. Fretilin (which continued to spearhead the resistance) was painted as an extreme communist faction aided by the imperialist Portuguese. The relative closure of the colony to the outside world assisted the maintenance of this position among most Indonesians, up to the highest levels. The troops stationed in the territory were bearers of the benefits of Indonesian nationhood, and protectors against civil war and communist insurgents. East Timor was not the only restive province, and East Timorese acceptance of their place within Indonesia remained for Jakarta an unquestionable basis of policy. Indeed, the original decision to invite Portuguese parliamentarians to view the territory indicates the extent to which not only the general population but significant elements within the leadership were out of touch with feelings in Timor. The 1991 killings, however, cast doubt on the prevailing account of the liberated and integrated East Timorese.

In an unprecedented step, and largely in response to international pressure, a National Investigating Commission into the killings was established. The commission's final report presented the massacre as an isolated incident, without acknowledging the history of abuse and intimidation in East Timor; the soldiers' sentences were lenient. But, in a rare departure from the norm in Indonesia, the commission rejected substantial elements of the military's initial account and criticised army procedures and behaviour: 'the trial testimonies paint a picture of a sloppy, ill-prepared, ill-informed, poorly disciplined and poorly led army, with some soldiers reacting spontaneously to the stabbing of their colleagues and others apparently panicking amid sounds of shooting at the cemetery' (Asia Watch, in Schwarz, 1994: 216). One Indonesian cabinet minister, commenting anonymously on the killings, accepted that 'the Dili incident was an accident . . . but it was the kind of accident a drunk driver gets into' (in Schwarz, 1994: 221). The massacre strengthened criticism of the armed forces' operational style and of their extraordinary pre-eminence within political and social life. And it made patently clear that the 'theory of "through economic development we win the hearts and minds of the East Timorese" has not worked so far' (Saldhana 1994: 370).

One consequence of the easing, in 1989, of travel restrictions between East Timor and the rest of Indonesia was the emergence of both planned and spontaneous transmigration. After 1989 Jakarta encouraged migration of mainly Muslim Indonesians into urban and rural East Timor as part of its endeavour to remould the territory politically and economically. This resulted in resentment and conflict, and reduced opportunities for both rural and urban Timorese. Land rendered idle by the coralling of Timorese farmers was awarded to migrants from Java and Bali, with no compensation being granted to the original land-owners, 'under the pretext of teaching the East Timorese better farming techniques' (Aditjondro 1994: 34). In urban areas, approximately half the population of Dili consisted of migrants, and urban enterprise was increasingly dominated by non-Timorese.

Clashes between the Timorese and the migrants, sometimes escalating into rioting, became commonplace in the 1990s. This tension expressed itself in religious terms, as an opposition between the mainly Muslim migrants and the largely Catholic Timorese. Religious affiliation provided one of the few ways open to the East Timorese to assert their community identity as distinct from that of Indonesians. Church activities became the only way of associating in public, while the Church was (until the late 1990s) the only organisation within Indonesia to speak on behalf of the Timorese community with the authorities and to criticise military excesses. As a result, and due also to the requirement that all Indonesian citizens had a religious affiliation, the number of Catholics in East Timor rose dramatically from 31 per cent of the population before 1974 to approximately 90 per cent in 1992. At the same time, however, the number of non-Catholics also grew, mainly as a result of transmigration. Within Indonesia, violence between religious affiliations was frequently read as being essentially anti-Muslim.

In 1994 the Indonesian scholar George Aditjondro identified what he called the culture of violence and intimidation in East Timor as the most serious indirect consequence of the invasion and military occupation of the half-island. This was not solely the violence of the Indonesian military towards the East Timorese. In this case violence and repression as cultural norms reproduced indiscriminately their own patterns of secrecy, suspicion and reprisal. 'What is meant here is the emergence of an appalling habit among East Timorese of spying on their compatriots, trying to solve the conflicts between them by making – often false – reports about the activities of their rivals to the security forces' (Aditjindro, 1994: 12). The army played to its own advantage on clan, regional and ideological conflict among the Timorese, and resentments remaining from the period of civil war. Moreover, Indonesian rule had undermined local community leadership and dispersed traditional authority. In the absence of authoritative community constraints, such conflict festered. Increasingly throughout the 1990s, the military harnessed it, employing groups of East Timorese youths in shadowy 'ninja' gangs – half engaged in criminal or semi-legal activites, half in terrorising civilian resistance movements. Beyond this, however, having no reliable system of justice, and its community and church authorities hamstrung, in the pervasive climate of brutality violence became a readily available way of managing conflict.

Jakarta officially countered criticisms of abuse in East Timor by arguing that they merely reflected the prioritisation of civil rights in the already prosperous and politically stable West. Official Indonesian statements on human rights upheld the argument that in developing countries human resource development must form the primary focus of human rights, as the human being was both principal agent and ultimate beneficiary of such development (Alatas, 1993: 11). Indonesia could not afford to allow its restless youth to dictate conditions in the streets – the first and most pressing task was to ensure stability (a pre-condition for rights, or development) and to meet the local people's basic living needs, neglected under colonialism. Conditions in East Timor provide a vivid illustration of the failure of that argument and the danger of separating economic from political categories of rights.

After two decades of economic growth, what was the outcome of develop-ment for the East Timorese? The answer is more complex than that given here, but (to focus on some key points) the Indonesians implemented a monopoly trading system with a heavy dependence on imports from the central islands and serious indigenous unemployment. A substantial proportion of the huge annual subsidy that kept the province afloat was corruptly siphoned off; as much again was used in answering a need that was itself an artificial product of the military occupation. Per capita income was not indicative of the distri-bution of income, productive capacity or economic power. Most assets were controlled by a few people, of whom a very small number were East Timorese. Development was 'largely oriented towards growth and the desire for quick results . . . [in order to] legitimise integration with Indonesia' (Saldhana, 1994: 93). Improved education was a genuine benefit for the East Timorese but as access to employment was undermined by discriminatory development it contributed little to effective social participation.

The economic growth strategies implemented indicate little comprehension of the actual conditions, whether cultural, historical or even material, of the East Timorese. Thus the displacement of East Timorese rice farmers by the Indonesian military was followed and compounded by the assumption that the East Timorese did not in fact farm rice. This provided the rationale both for maintaining at high levels the (expensive) import of rice from elsewhere and the migration of Javanese rice farmers to the most fertile areas of the territory, intensifying local unemployment. The expansion of industrial and commercial activity was controlled by monopolies, leaving local people as price takers in an often artificial market. Indigenous people became marginalised onlookers in the 'development' of their economy. This repeated the 'overlooking' of the East Timorese that was used to make sense of the original decision to invade. Economic development that does not enable people to exercise some control over the fundamental material realities of their lives does not enhance their 'economic' rights.

The divorce between abstracted categories of economic and political rights upon which official Indonesian arguments rely is so familiar to liberal thought as to be scarcely questioned, even if the reversal of priority may seem shocking. But the experience of East Timor suggests that both categories of rights directly address people's ability to shape the direction of their lives and that the dynamics of economic development are densely interwoven with those political and social power structures which generate or tolerate the systemic infliction of intimidation and violence. What may be the fundamental, if partial and elusive, level of self-determination, that is, people's ability to exercise some reasonable level of control over and creativity within their own collective and individual lives – to be able to take part in a non-violent way in the 'conversations' that structure their interlocking political communities – was rendered largely impossible in East Timor, to the cost of all parties concerned.

Incorporation reversed

Indonesia and less directly the international community were thus faced with the problem, and the cost, of East Timor. As the Gadjah Mada team gently pointed out: 'With . . . integration, the Indonesian government considered the problem of the decolonisation of East Timor to be resolved. However, for the people of East Timor it would appear that this is not so' (1991: 5). The standard options of decolonisation remained frozen on the table – independence, integration with another independent state and free association with another independent state, in principle determined through an act of free choice such as a vote. At the same time, developments within East Timor contributed to and were shaped by the difficulties seaming Indonesian political life. East Timor was a problem that would not simply go away also in part because it was embedded within questions of political direction simmering throughout Indonesia.[2]

The anti-settler riots in East Timor during the mid-1990s prompted calls in the mainstream Indonesian media for the government to rethink its East Timor policies. Within Indonesia's policy community, impatience at the cost of East Timor grew – in terms of the expenditure on resources, of damage to Indonesia's international standing, of the deaths of soldiers in counter-insurgency operations and of the pressures on Indonesia's complex political architecture. Moreover, despite Foreign Minister Alatas's off-hand description of East Timor as a pebble in Indonesia's shoe, it was a cost with a potential for unpredictable escalation. Rather than understanding East Timor in terms of secession, many Indonesians saw conflict there as essentially a manifestation of problems running throughout the archipelago. 'What people in Bandung, West Java feel as government high-handedness may appear the same to people in East Timor. Hence to stop high-handedness against people in East Timor should also mean its abolition in other parts of Indonesia' (*Indonesian Observer*, in Schwarz, 1994: 229). But there was also resentment at the ingratitude of the East Timorese, who were being subsidised at rates above those enjoyed by most other poor Indonesian provinces – being offered milk and responding with poison, in the words of Muslim leader Amien Rais (quoted in Crouch, 2000: 153).

An overriding concern with national unity drove Indonesia's approach both to the decolonisation of East Timor and to the management of the territory. But rather than assuaging Indonesian anxieties about national unity, the acquisition of East Timor fuelled even greater uncertainty. 'The failure to pacify Timorese unrest has engendered in the army real doubts about the strength of Indonesian national unity and kindled fears that democracy could lead to the unravelling of the Indonesian archipelago' (Schwarz, 1994: 197). Resistance in East Timor threatened to carry demonstration effects for West Irian and Aceh, stirring the recurrent hostility to the Javanese centre. It also heightened sectarian religious tensions. The management of East Timor underscored the powerful position of the military in Indonesian society while at the same time throwing into doubt their credibility. The army was (and, despite curtailments and reforms, remains) enmeshed in almost all spheres of power within Indonesian political and economic life, from national monopolies to the most parochial activities. It was a role that drew increasing, if muted, scrutiny and criticism within Indonesia during the 1990s. As Schwarz asked (1994: 197), was 'the military's "security approach" solving political problems, or merely postponing them'?

Critical voices within Indonesia approached East Timor in terms of a reduced role for and greater accountability of the military, increased indigenisation of the public service, policing and judicial functions independent of the military, and even greater autonomy for the province. But many in the military were alarmed by this combination of a reduced role, greater accountability and experiments in pluralism. Anxiety about both the threat of disintegration and the risks that might have to be taken to respond to it in turn carried back into broader Indonesian political life. President Suharto, meanwhile, was unsympathetic to changes to a policy so closely associated with his own leadership. Within the frozen frame of the ageing Suharto's leadership, simply holding on to the territory, 'postponing' indefinitely any changes that might threaten to pull at the thread of the state or challenge the military became its own rationale.

The politics of postponement that overwhelmed Indonesia under the final years of Suharto was shattered by the Asian financial crisis in late 1997. Indonesian growth rates plummeting to negative figures from 6–8 per cent per annum, undermining the legitimacy of a presidency that had already stretched the limits of acceptance to breaking point. Following widespread rioting, Suharto was forced to resign in May 1998 and was replaced by his deputy B. J. Habibie. Habibie, seeking to address the country's desperate economic and polit- ical circumstances, and conscious of Indonesia's increased dependence on the goodwill of international financial institutions, initiated a range of cautious liberalising reforms. Probably partly in order to remove a persistent obstacle in Indonesia's relations with donor states, but partly because of a belief in the need for changed management of East Timor, Habibie proposed demilitarisation and autonomy within Indonesia for the territory in return for international recognition of Indonesian sovereignty. But the proposal did not satisfy the standing requirement for decolonisation that there be an 'act of free choice', generally understood as a vote. Xanana Gusmao, the widely respected leader of the East Timorese resistance forces, held in jail by the Indonesians since the early 1990s, rejected the proposal. But the issue was now on the table.

The Portuguese and Australian Governments pressed for some form of an act of self-determination. Unexpectedly, in January 1999, Habibie agreed. The East Timorese were to have a UN-supervised ballot to vote for or against wide- ranging autonomy, but it was made clear that rejection would lead to reversal of the incorporation – in effect, to independence. The ballot was to be held within seven months. Gusmao, the UN and others, had envisaged some years of transition for the Timorese – a withdrawal of the military, a more enlightened management of the territory, a UN-monitored process of decolonisation – in effect, the slow process that had been snatched from them in 1975. But Habibie held to the short time-frame. Years of transition would be costly, could be divi- sive, and the window of opportunity for a vote might pass. The UN proposed a peacekeeping force for the territory. But the Indonesian Government, under new arrangements, decided that the Indonesian police were to be responsible for ensuring security leading up to the ballot. Otherwise the status quo was to be maintained – the military were to remain.

The military had lost many men in East Timor. Many Indonesians believed that they had made great sacrifices to save the East Timorese from communism and civil war and to save Indonesia from a communist beachhead. 'Indone- sianisation' was seen as a long-term benefit for the East Timorese – even if indi- viduals, East Timorese and others, had to suffer for its realisation – and the military were its guardians. The belief was widespread that without the army East Timor would 'again' disintegrate into civil war. Moreover, high-ranking military interests had major financial assets in East Timor. The military leadership did not want to lose the province, but did not openly oppose the 'act of popular consultation' proposed by Habibie. It seems likely that key elements of the military leadership saw the referendum 'as an opportunity to settle the East Timor issue once and for all by making sure that the vote would be in favour of continued integration with Indonesia' (Crouch, 2000, 160).

Mimicking in cruder form the broader management of East Timor, the military again used a carrot-and-stick approach to ensure a vote for integration. The 'stick' was the militias. East Timor already had a constellation of paramilitary forces. These were made up of local civilians formally employed by the military and armed for operations against the Fretilin guerillas, plus the 'ninja' groups that had been formed in the mid-1990s to intimidate those engaged in civilian resistance movements. As agitation for independence had intensified in the 1990s, the ninja groups, under direction of military intelligence, had likewise grown. By late 1998 there were militia groups operating across East Timor. Leading military figures coordinated and re-formed the militias for their new task and oversaw their operations. Altogether, the militia could call on an estimated 6,000–9,000 members (Crouch, 2000). New members were press-ganged into support. In the period leading up to the vote, the militias terrorised individuals, families and whole villages known to support independence, slaughtering and injuring with machetes and guns. To escape the violence many people fled into the hills, driven by what was probably a concerted effort to disrupt voter registration. The terror campaign can also be understood as an effort to incite or give the appearance of a civil war that would again 'prove' to the outside world the inherent uncontrollability of the Timorese and the need for a full-scale Indonesian military presence.

The 'carrot' was organised via the military's manipulation of food and medical supplies, with the army attempting to monopolise supplies and eke them out in return for a pledge of a pro-integration vote. The East Timorese were again cast as children, this time in cynical recognition of their vulnerability: 'winning over the people of East Timor . . . [is] not difficult . . . They will follow whoever gives them food and medicine' (from an alleged military communication, quoted in Crouch, 2000: 164). The unarmed UN presence, able to protest but not intervene in the militia violence, assisted the penetration of the country by NGOs delivering food aid to the Timorese, so undermining the military's apparent attempts to control supplies. The UN presence was thus deeply resented by the military and itself became subject to efforts at intimidation.

These strategies failed, however, and the referendum on 30 August saw both a 98 per cent voter turnout and an overwhelming 78.5 per cent vote for independence. The size of the loss, at almost four to one, seemed to stun many in Jakarta, who had been led to believe that the vote would support integration. After a brief calm, the violence that had marked 1999 now culminated in an explosion of destructive activity. This violent rampage has been documented by an Indonesian Commission of Investigation report (KPP HAM), in a report compiled by James Dunn (2001) as well as by other accounts. It was not 'the spontaneous response of those who favoured integration' (Dunn, 2001: 1). Indeed, many East Timorese who genuinely supported autonomy within Indonesia did not support and were not linked with the militias, whose hierarchies seem to have been tied predominantly to the military. As it became clear that the vote was indeed going against integration, it seems militia leaders and military officers in East Timor, as an act of revenge, but also perhaps believing that violence may yet achieve their goal of integration, planned sweeping counter-measures. Whether or not the full extent of the rampage was directly intended by senior military figures – and this is something which a court or tribunal may be able to clarify – it was the outcome of the campaign of intimidation, destruction and terror which they had instigated (Crouch, 2000; Dunn, 2001). The violence included executions, the mass-murder of many hundreds of unarmed people, torture and rape, the forced deportation across the border into Indonesian West Timor of many thousands of people, as well the dislocation of three-quarters of the population, and the destruction of an estimated 70 per cent of East Timor's infrastructure and built environment. Many of the towns and villages were left in ruins and people's lives shattered. The Indonesian leadership, under intense international pressure and itself seemingly shocked at the extent of the violence, accepted an international peacekeeping force which arrived on 20 September.

The killings and the devastation have meant a savage and threatening conclusion to Indonesian rule. Militias remain potentially dangerous across the border in West Timor. While now embarked on its own process of political and economic reform, Indonesia continues in a state of crisis. It may now be Indonesia that is the fragile and unpredictable neighbour – and it will remain in the interests and the convictions of some there, not least the militia leaders who have fled to Jakarta, to act to undermine the newly emerging state. Within Indonesia, responses to East Timor are profoundly unsettled – while the Commission of Investigation into Human Rights Violations has produced a damning report on abuse and, at least as importantly, has called for investigations of operations in East Timor going back to 1975, one of the most prominent militia leaders is fêted as a patriot. Within East Timor, in an atmosphere of some hope, but also uncertainty, destruction, social dislocation and trauma, the East Timorese are now facing in an extreme form the problems common to decolonisation and state building.

Self-determination

UNTAET is managing both the rebuilding of East Timor and its initial transition to statehood. It is a peace-building enterprise concerned in broad terms with the

creation of structures capable of institutionalising peace. Peace building represents an extraordinary set of social and political experiments, made across
cultures, by a chaotic mix of international, national and non-governmental
agencies with competing agendas. Over the past decade, the international community has been increasingly engaged in the tasks of peace building, and has
struggled to come to grips with the complexity of the task. East Timor is the most
recent and by far the most extensive peace building mission undertaken by the
UN. In this case, and for the first time, the UN (or UNTAET) *is* the transitional
state, responsible for all aspects of governance.

The brief comments that follow are not an assessment of UNTAET's work.
They are rather a reflection on what the international community might learn
from the story, as it has been briefly told here, of East Timor's recent history.
There are three interlocking points to emphasise. The first concerns the participation of the East Timorese in the building of their state; the second, the
problem of the emergence of reasonably peaceful political orders after long-term
violence; and the third, which runs through the other two, is the theme of
dialogue.

East Timor will be significantly dependent on the international community
for the foreseeable future. At present, this dependence is expressed through the
presence of UNTAET, but the role of the World Bank, the International Mone-
tary Fund (IMF) and other agencies, as well as individual states and NGOs, will
be more long term. International peace building is a liberal endeavour. In
general, and certainly in East Timor's case, it involves the effort to reconstruct
the state as a liberal market democracy. This is in part because liberal models of
representative democracy and market capitalism are widely assumed to be con-
ducive to the management of conflict and so to peace (the 'democratic peace'
argument). Liberal democracy enshrines notions of rights, and respect for rights
reasonably enough appears as the antidote to the systematic infliction of injury
embedded in the conflicts and crises to which peace building is a response. But,
perhaps as important, the international administrators staffing peace-building
missions, facing situations of great complexity and tight time-frames, must
draw on the managerial models with which they are familiar. Leading figures in
East Timor themselves use the language of liberal market democratisation, so at
the level of rhetoric at least there is no conflict.

To date, the large-scale international peace-building efforts have focused on
the creation of national politico-legal structures, such as constitutions and
party and electoral systems, on development projects and the lineaments of economic governance. Elections and IMF-approved economic models have been the
cornerstones of the projects. Relatively little attention has been paid either to
the grassroots dynamics of these political and economic models, or to other
dimensions of governance – in particular, to whether and how practical
alternatives to violence, as a means of managing conflict, may be evolving. Yet

experience to date in peace-building efforts indicates that the development of such alternatives, at all levels of political life, are fundamental to the rebuilding of sustainable political and economic orders.

The history of East Timor underlines the cost, in terms of human suffering and of pragmatic politics, of not engaging the apparently powerless as participants in shaping their own future. This lesson reiterates what peace building and development programmes elsewhere have indicated. But participation is extraordinarily demanding, both as an ethic and an administrative discipline. The joint-statement on planning released by the UN and the World Bank in late 1999 recognises the importance of local participation in development and rebuilding programmes – community empowerment is one of eight sectors addressed. (The others are macro-economic management, the civil service, agriculture, the judiciary, health, education and infrastructure.) Moreover the UN and the World Bank involved the Timorese, both exiles and those who had remained in Timor, in the formation of the plan. The plan identifies village councils as an accessible and accountable site for local governance. It is not clear, however, that these village councils actually feed into decision making in the other seven sectors – that is, the sectors which form the practical business of governance (Bleiker and McGibbon, forthcoming).

The IMF (2000) has also produced its blueprint on 'Establishing the Foundations of Sound Macroeconomic Management' in the new state, and has asserted the importance of indigenous participation at all stages of the process of forming East Timor's economic agenda. At the same time, however, these recommendations for East Timor echo the IMF's many other structural adjustment programmes and reflect the neo-liberal economic orientations of its leading donors. In keeping with its traditional outlook, the programme is austere – one of its more controversial aspects may prove to be the size, scope and pay scales envisaged for the civil service. The IMF wants a small public sector on low pay scales, and foresees further cuts in salaries. The East Timorese, with the influence the social justice traditions of the Catholic Church and Fretilin, may see it differently. Nor does East Timor have the strong private sector institutions that assist the operation of neo-liberalism. Following comparable pay cuts in Mozambique, its civil servants needed additional income, leading to a rise in corruption, while the well-qualified found work in international agencies on international salaries, draining skills from government (Hanlon, 2001), and teachers left in droves, undermining education programmes.

Programmes of rapid economic liberalisation in El Salvador, Nicaragua and Mozambique have had disastrous effects on peace building. 'The restructuring process is pursuing the objective of developing a market economy at the cost of a serious deterioration in standards of living, resulting in pauperization and a concomitant resurgence of violence' (David, 1999: 35). Roland Paris's 1997 survey of eight peace-building missions during the 1990s noted that World Bank and IMF policies 'have continued to place the principal burden of adjustment on the poorest and most vulnerable groups in developing societies, which is a recipe for political instability', particularly in societies already seamed by conflict (1997: 77). Moreover, strong free-market policies rewarding competition in a society that lacks a real safety net, and where pressing questions hang over the most basic forms of ownership of resources, are likely to feed into powerful political antagonisms. Many people in East Timor have been stripped of everything by the rampaging militias, while others, due to luck but also sometimes to political associations, have been spared. And does ownership of a particular piece of land rest with those who were recognised as owners by traditional – Portuguese or Indonesian – authorities? Given the co-existence of some traditional and Portuguese systems, people with a legitimate claim to any such competing titles may be claiming the return of their resource. In such cases, the benefits of unrestrained market competition can mesh with unexpected social faultlines.

While the IMF emphasises consultation, it is an organisation of immense power; and, without IMF approval, East Timor is unlikely to receive on-going assistance from the World Bank, or any other bank. The danger in all these instances is of a form of 'participation' that, whether because of perceived time constraints or the dynamics of power at play, does not really extend beyond the giving of consent. But to be effective, participation must also encompass the goals and parameters of the exchange. Not only the outcomes but the processes by which such directions are taken have potential for profound impact on the emerging shape of East Timor's political and economic life:

> Unless the Timorese community has a sense of ownership over the social, political and economic rebuilding of their society, tensions will remain high and the influx of foreign funds will only heighten existing problems. The greatest dangers emerge from the possible external imposition of a rebuilding process that neither involves local participation nor achieves national reconciliation. (Bleiker and McGibbon, forthcoming)

Political structures have been emerging more gradually – until independence UNTAET remains the sovereign authority. UNTAET is planning to choose a government from the constituent assembly, and will pass what decision-making scope it sees fit to that government, while retaining ultimate responsibility. While transitions are by nature awkward, questions remain concerning the space allowed for Timorese participation in debates on the shape of the government. Deep divisions mark Timorese society. After all, 20 per cent of adults voted to accept autonomy within Indonesia; among them are some of the more powerful and wealthy Timorese. Some pro-integrationists are already arguing that (despite the Indonesian Parliament's acceptance of the divorce, in October 1999) the vote was simply a rejection of one particular model of integration – other models might yet be found accepted (see e.g. Araujo: 2000). Nor do those united by the desire for independence from Indonesia necessarily agree on other fundamental matters.

In this context UNTAET favours a government of national unity rather than one formed by a single winning party. Again, on the basis of past peace-building experiences, there is a strong argument for this. While established democracies may have a low propensity for war, *democratising* states ('those that have recently undergone regime change in a democratic direction') are highly war prone (Mansfield and Snyder, in David, 1999: 43). Competitive elections in a fragmented state can intensify fragmentation while the formal marks of Western electoral systems are no guarantees of democracy. But if arrangements at the national level are not matched by work towards a participative ethos in East Timor that can at the same time manage conflict, government could again simply degenerate into dictatorship. The challenge and the great difficulty for the East Timorese, and for the international community working with them, is to develop institutional and social contexts at all levels of society within which the people can work against the 'deafness', violence and ingrained marginalisation which have enclosed their lives.

Impending statehood and the withdrawal of the Indonesian military will not simply wipe clean the legacy of that history of conflict, violence and marginalisation. Part of this legacy are the eroded traditional structures of authority, an erosion matched not by the development of legitimate non-traditional mechanisms but by increasing reliance on violence as a means of achieving group and individual objectives. Many Timorese had expected that independence would bring a better life. While in time that hope may well prove justified, East Timor is now one of the poorest countries in the world. The desperation and frustration that flow from 80 per cent unemployment and widespread devastation only compound those pressures to violence. The need to recreate a reasonably peaceful political and social life at all levels and to re-learn non-violent ways of handling disagreement and constructing difference is of fundamental significance, paralleling and intermeshing with the importance of widely shared access to economic growth and livelihood.

The East Timorese face, in a very raw form, fundamental questions about how to build political life. These are questions raised by what was widely seen as an 'alien' occupation that reshaped major dimensions of social, political and economic life. But they are also posed by the reality of division and the systemic infliction, and experience, of suffering. After long periods of conflict the fracture lines of enmity can often be complex, confused and highly personalised. As Xanana Gusmao, the highly respected former leader of the anti-integration forces, has commented:

The waves of wounds to the Timorese people are the consequences of both internal and external conflicts. They come from our thorny civil war, and from the problems of our early years in the mountains and the related acts of revenge, as well as those inflicted by the Indonesian military and those Timorese serving the integration process. (Gusmao, 2000: ix)

How now do returned militia members, guerilla fighters and their opponents and victims find ways of living together? How is justice to be sought, recognised and respected, and is there a limit to its pursuit? How do you mark and give voice to your suffering or to that of others, particularly when there is no suggestion of remorse or when the application of justice to the perpetrators is out of reach? Denied such an exchange, how do we not shut the perpetrator – or the victim – out of the category of 'human', or from 'the referential world of self and other' (Williams, in Brown, 1995: 96)?

It may be that, in broad terms, how people see the injuries of history dealt with at national and local levels affects deeply their acceptance of and commitment to mechanisms of justice, order and governance. The manner in which the extreme abuse of the past is dealt with becomes, in the words of Raoul Alfonsin, Argentina's first elected president after the military regime, the primary instrument for forming the 'collective moral conscience' at an attitudinal but also an institutional level (in Huyse, 1998: 276). It is thus not only the past but the foundations and legitimacy of political and social relations in the future that are at stake in the complex intermeshing questions of justice and reconciliation. Xanana Gusmao speaks of the need to forgive and rebuild, as do some other leading Timorese figures. In effect, the fragile nature of the Indonesian state means that the chances of prosecuting Indonesian senior military officers and militia leaders who have taken high-profile 'refuge' in Jakarta are uncertain, at least in the medium term. The embryonic legal system is struggling with the prosecutions of some of the returned militia members, and a South African-style Truth and Reconciliation Commission is under discussion, although key witnesses remain beyond its jurisdiction in Indonesia.

Justice may prove elusive, and while not questioning the value of pursuing it, as the hundreds of stories of the more local acts of violence come closer to the ground, justice may not always be preserved from ambivalence and revenge. Nor may it prove a sufficient answer to trauma and loss. But how to forgive and rebuild? Certainly, while both reconciliation and justice must be pursued at the formal level of the state, through overarching mechanisms such as the developing legal system and a Truth and Reconciliation Commission of some nature, the underpinning realities of the locality and the village, where 'civic' life has often been transformed by fear, enmity and trauma seem likely to be at least as important. The quandary of reconciliation and the need to deal with the obdurate realities of anger, loss, pain and injustice lie at the level of 'everyday life' – of the basic social and political institutions which shape people's lives – as much as they reside in the more formal dimensions of the state. The slow and difficult task of dialogue is hardly an answer to the questions posed by injury and suffering, nor can others provide answers for the East Timorese; but dialogue offers at least a way of working with these questions, from which answers – the different answers that will be needed for different aspects of people's collective existence – may emerge.

The Indonesian departure from East Timor and the arrival of the UNTAET mission was sparked by a sequence of unpredictable international shifts; but it was also the result of a struggle over twenty-five years, inside but also outside East Timor, for fundamental change in the governance of the territory, whether that was achieved through independence from or by a transformation of Indonesia. This struggle could be characterised, accurately, as a demand for self-determination. Self-determination is a fundamental reference point of the post-Second World War order of states. It offers a potent language, and perhaps the only available language, for the East Timorese to register the suffering of their circumstances and articulate a demand for redress. But although sometimes claimed as a self-evident moral truth, self-determination is an ambiguous principle and a multivalent reality. Far from signifying absolute sovereignty, it is rather a complex process of transaction, occurring in the context (in this case) not only of a traumatised and fractured community but of the relentless demands of international political and economic exchange. Like the notion of 'human rights', its practical ethical value depends on how it is used and what it makes possible in particular circumstances and histories.

In international politics the language of self-determination is generally that of independent statehood, but this is not because being a state in practice best expresses, or necessarily expresses at all, a potential for communities to manage their affairs to some reasonable extent. Self-determination struggles have often been the effort by a collectivity to ensure that it will not in the future be subjected to the same violence and exploitative disregard to which it was subjected in the past. But, as in East Timor's case, while the achievement of statehood is no guarantee of effective self-determination, nor are other routes to an acquisition of some measure of control over community life and to freedom from the systemic infliction of gross humiliation and destruction readily available. East Timor is in the process of achieving statehood, but more fundamental questions of self-determination remain.

The violent incorporation of East Timor and its subsequent 'burial' made sense in part because it could draw on a polarisation between ethics and the realities of power. That polarisation, touched on in chapter 2, is a fundamental 'common sense' weaving through the ways in which it is possible to think about international politics. It is evident in approaches to East Timor from both a predominantly idealist and a predominantly realist perspective, but it was the assertion of pragmatics over principle that carried the most powerful and deleterious effects in this case. The *de facto* acceptance of a forced annexation over a more strenuous support for the principles of decolonisation – principles to which East Timor had indisputable legal access – was done in the name of pragmatic good sense. What turned out to be a protracted violent and costly conflict was justified in terms of the prudence and practical grasp of power that realism advises. Principles of self-determination were, in effect, treated as somewhat 'lawyerly' regulations – desirable, but to be put aside when necessary – rather than as part of an effort to deal with the complex interplays of power by which communities, whether they are weak or strong in terms of quantifiable strategic resources, are persistently bound to one another.

'Pragmatism' operated here as its opposite – a narrow and reified self-interest, shorn of the need to take much account of the reality on the ground, which in this case included the reality of the 'powerless' actors in the drama. This reflects directly the evacuated concept of 'power' – power to impose – that characterises much strong realism (and, in a different way, idealism). It is this narrow and abstract conception of power that so completely divorces principle and pragmatics, placing one in a world of ideal essences and the other in a repetitious and solipsistic cycle of calculations. The value of listening, however, flows not from principle enshrined in an ideal world but from the need to be attentive to the factors that go to make up a concrete situation and to their dynamic potential. The East Timorese were not heard in part because of the deafness made possible by realism; it is important, now, that the support lent by liberal internationalism does not have equally damaging effects. The brutality of the Indonesian military presence has gone – and this is a hopeful thing – but people's need to be able to shape their own collective lives and to give voice to and work against the systemic infliction of violence and the imposition of suffering remains.

NOTES

1   For example, Dunn (1983), Taylor (1995), and Viviani (1976) are three detailed accounts.
2   That is, those debates around Indonesia becoming the kind of place that, in Goenewan Mohamad's words, 'even the powerless can love' (1994: 106).

6

The status of Indigenous Australians

T HERE ARE A number of avenues through which the 'place' of Indigenous people in Australia can be approached. One fundamental arena
of struggle has been over land rights. The approach to rights taken
here, however, starts from an account of suffering and sets out to trace the
political roots of that suffering. One of the clearest forms of suffering to mark
Aboriginal lives in Australia is entrenched and widespread ill-health. Thus,
across the Indigenous community, the story is one of premature death, often
from diseases associated with poverty, poor environmental health and mental
distress, a high death rate for infants and small children, and appallingly high
rates of suicide, violence and substance abuse.

As will become clear, patterns of ill-health lock into the struggles around
land rights. At a concrete level, however, almost all Indigenous Australians,
including those who live beyond the immediate scope of land rights, are affected
by high levels of disease. Questions of Aboriginal health often have a curious
status. The linkage between Aboriginal ill-health and what could be called,
rather neutrally, Indigenous disadvantage in Australia is taken for granted – for
example, in the use of mortality rates as a standard statistical measure indicative of broader life conditions. However, in this case the causal linkage between
specifically political orders and patterns of disease can seem frayed. There are
no powerful political forces fighting improvements in health, as there are for
progress on land rights. On the contrary, since the 1960s at least, the Australian
Government has, as well as other relevant bodies, been expressing increasing
concern, investigating and writing reports and budgeting monies in response
to Aboriginal ill-health. The challenge then is to make clear the political
dimensions of Indigenous ill-health, not just in the past but in contemporary
political life – in effect, to clarify the linkage between health and land rights,
while recognising their specificities.

Unlike the other case studies, this one examines a situation of persistent
systemic infliction of abuse in the context of a wealthy, liberal democratic state

which enjoys extensive rule of law and which has a reasonably active record of human rights promotion internationally. Meanwhile, in the conditions in which most Aboriginal Australians live their lives, their 'life chances' – understood as access to health, education and employment – are comparable to those of people in a poor Third World economy; for many Aborigines participation in decision making concerning basic control over their own lives and environment has, at least until the mid-1980s, been at a lower level than that routinely available in many highly authoritarian societies, and the extent of the violence both generated within and endured by the Aboriginal community, including at the hands of the police, is comparable to that of countries with little tradition of the rule of law. Moreover, these conditions are not such as can be put securely into the 'otherworld' of the distant past and attributed to the excesses of a frontier mentality.

The extent of on-going Indigenous suffering can be approached as an incomplete application of liberal values, practices and processes – a failure in this problematic instance to apply the procedures and values more or less in play in most other zones of contemporary Australian society. But it can also be approached as a *product* of those procedures, practices and values. These two approaches are in complex tension with each other. The way we weigh patterns of politically generated suffering, so that generations of Aboriginal ill-health and early death, often from violence, seem so *extraordinarily* less grave than the killings in Tiananmen Square, is itself in part informed by a Lockean language of self-possessed individuality, political community and injury. That large-scale human rights abuse is not something that happens only 'somewhere else' – perpetrated by other peoples or at other times, or in societies with authoritarian political structures or poverty-stricken economies, underdeveloped legal systems or immature 'civil societies' – is a simple point that can nevertheless prove extraordinarily difficult to grasp in practice.

This case study thus considers some of the limitations of those dominant understandings of rights that mark both international rights promotion and the constitution of the liberal state. How we understand and pursue principles of participation, dialogue and negotiation is a particular focus of this chapter. This is a matter at the core of the approach to rights pursued here as participation, dialogue and negotiation are also, more broadly, fundamental to liberal norms of state legitimacy. Exploring the question of what participation has meant and might mean for Indigenous Australians in the context of Australian political community underlines the narrow parameters within which participation has been envisaged and in practice offered to Indigenous peoples. More positively, such a discussion is also a reminder of the dynamic and evolving nature of participation as a principle – a dynamism that will need to be engaged if the pattern of systemically imposed injury borne by this sector of the Australian population is to be addressed.

Approaching health as a matter of human rights can be contentious – certainly more contentious than the subjects of the other two case studies, which can be easily bundled under the category of civil and political rights abuse. There can be some polite disbelief as to the gravity of ill-health as properly an issue of rights, despite the international focus on Indigenous rights, despite declared rights to 'the highest attainable standard of physical and mental health' referred to in the UN Covenant on Economic, Social and Cultural Rights, and despite many states' legal or political commitments to their citizens' health entitlements. Or, worse, the matter can appear simply uninteresting. In contrast to the internationally broadcast acts of violence in Tiananmen or the relentless war of attrition in East Timor, the ill-health characteristic of indigenous communities has not been a focus of searching international attention. While accepting the natural impact of dramatic and tragic events, it is worth noting that the deformation of Indigenous peoples' lives and their appalling levels of disadvantage, expressed directly in their high rates of premature death, goes comparatively unnoticed in international rights talk.

Health is an issue that falls self-evidently into the 'social and economic', or 'second-generation', component of the standard, if misleading, international divisions of human rights. It has been argued in earlier chapters that rights are always essentially political in that they are concerned with the production of the social, economic, legal, cultural and political categories and mechanisms – the structures of power, broadly understood – that shape people's participation within the communities that they inhabit and constitute. In this sense the right to an attainable health standard is not solely a matter of the distribution of material goods and services, although improved distribution should generally result from the recognition of such a right and, crucially, contribute to people's capacity to exercise it. More fundamentally, the right to (attainable) health is a question of the production of the capabilities and the practices by which over generations people participate in, and constitute, community. The persistent lack of adequate nutrition, for example, excludes people from effective political and social participation and, within the broader context of a well nourished environment, indicates their marginalisation in the first place. Health entitlements are important not only because health is important but because collective patterns of ill-health can both demonstrate political marginalisation in operation and themselves act to marginalise people. To look at Aboriginal health, then, is to question certain constructions of political community in Australia which have arguably worked to systemically marginalise and deform constituencies within the Australian population.

Aboriginal disadvantage is sufficiently acute to be noted by various international and domestic Australian registers as an abuse of rights. Bodies such as Amnesty International, the World Council of Churches and the US State Department regularly comment on patterns of systemically imposed discrimination.

Most notably, UN committees and treaty monitoring bodies have been increasingly expressing their concern with aspects of Indigenous life conditions, with the UN Committee on the Elimination of Racial Discrimination (land rights and sentencing regimes), the UN Human Rights Commission and the Committee Against Torture (sentencing regimes and incarceration practices) registering disapproval during 2000. The Australian Government's response (as of 2001) has been to downgrade its cooperation with UN human rights bodies.

Within Australia, Indigenous disadvantage is sometimes assumed to be largely self-inflicted or, perhaps more commonly, rooted in a cultural context that is profoundly out of step with modern life or in an ancient history of dispossession. Thus, in 1999, the federal government rejected the proposal that an official apology be made to the Aboriginal Australians as part of a process of reconciliation and instead offered an expression of regret that they had 'suffered injustices under the practices of past generations' (Prime Minister Howard, Australian Parliament, 26 August). But, as will become clear, these perceptions are deeply misleading.

At the same time, however, various dimensions of Indigenous disenfranchisement are being documented with increasing urgency, power and detail – by the Royal Commission into Aboriginal Deaths in Custody (RCIADIC), the Aboriginal and Torres Strait Islander Social Justice Commission, the Human Rights Commission, among many other official, scholarly and personal accounts of life conditions. Landmark high court judgments recognised the existence of Indigenous land rights (Mabo, 1992) and upheld the principle of negotiation to manage joint rights to land held by Indigenous and non-indigenous parties (Wik, 1996). In 1991, the Labour Government set up the Council for Aboriginal Reconciliation to explore and promote reconciliation between Aboriginal and settler societies. The Council's report in 2000 was, however, rejected by the Liberal-National Government. As noted above, the government (in particular the prime minister) also declined to apologise to Aboriginal people 'for the errors and misdeeds of earlier generations' – an Indigenous demand and recommendation emerging from both the Human Rights Commission's report (*Bringing Them Home*) and the Council for Aboriginal Reconciliation (Howard, Parliament, 26 August 1999). (However, all state, i.e. provincial, governments as well as many leading political and social bodies and, through marches and displays, large numbers of people, have apologised.)

The reports, the numerous court cases brought by Aboriginal people on contentious political and social matters (such as land rights), the controversy generated over the prime minister's refusal to 'say sorry' and over continuing deaths of Aboriginal people in custody have generated an unprecedented level of attention to the realities of Aboriginal Australia. As the historian Rosalind Kidd noted: 'Only recently has the irrefutable evidence that Australia was not peacefully settled impacted on our consciousness', although the violent realities of settlement were 'common knowledge in the nineteenth century' (2000: 4). This tentative and fraught awakening, in conjunction with the Mabo and Wik decisions, represents a breakthrough in political life in Australia the dimensions and significance of which cannot yet be judged. In terms of concrete gains for the lives of Indigenous people, however, there has been little progress. The number of Indigenous deaths in custody has risen since delivery in 1991 of the report investigating the jail and prison death rate over the preceding decade. Incarceration rates of Aboriginal people (approximately twenty-one times that of non-Aboriginal people) have likewise increased. Despite real progress on land rights, land reserved for Aboriginal use continues to be alienated for the benefit of mining and other interests. And health standards remain abysmal.

There is a further problem with understanding disease as an abuse of rights in cases such as this. As the Aboriginal activist Noel Pearson has commented in relation to substance abuse:

> [T]he symptom theory [that addiction is a symptom of underlying political problems] absolves people from their personal responsibility to confront and deal with addiction. Worse, it leaves communities to think that nothing can be done to confront substance abuse because its purported causes: dispossession, racism, trauma and poverty, are beyond reach of social resolution at present. (2000: 10–11)

This raises the question, one which sears through many rights issues, not only those domains classified as economic and social, of how we understand 'will', 'autonomy' and 'responsibility'. I cannot answer this question, but only respond in a limited and interim way to Noel Pearson's warning. Various kinds of factors are relevant to health, including genetic susceptibilities not even touched on here. These factors interact but do not necessarily overrule each other. Local Indigenous community efforts to deal with particular health problems have been significant and are a fundamental practical dimension of the approach supported here. A sense of individual or local responsibility can be a powerful and empowering imperative – we have and we need different modes of address when grappling with complex social, personal and political problems. But marked, collective, and longstanding patterns of disease among a particular group in an otherwise comparatively healthy society call for analyses and responses that go beyond a consideration of individual responsibility. Indeed, lack of individual responsibility has been for some time a ground on which white Australians have dismissed the problems of Aboriginal society. It is surely essential for Aborigines to consider their individual and collective responsibility for health choices. But it is equally essential for settler Australians to consider our own collective, intergenerational responsibilities for the conditions of Aboriginal lives, and to reflect also on the kind of political engagements we wish to carry forward.

The chapter briefly establishes the current conditions of Aboriginal health in Australia. While discussing the broad causes of ill-health, it examines the construction of the 'Aboriginal problem', an apparent conundrum which has dominated government and popular approaches to Aboriginal welfare and according to which the 'chronic destitution' (Kidd, 1997: xix) of much of the Aboriginal population is seen as a mysterious state of affairs that is less an ordinary consequence of actions taken regarding Indigenous people than a reflection of Aboriginality itself. The discussion looks briefly at federal government measures since the late 1970s to improve Indigenous health and considers why these measures have in large part failed. It explores the continuing impact of what the Australian anthropologist W. E. H. Stanner in 1968 called the 'great Australian silence' – a consistent 'overlooking' of Indigenous people that could be understood as the inability to recognise them as participants in the construction of political community.

The 'silence' concerning Indigenous people is not peculiar to Australia. It has arguably been characteristic of the response to Indigenous people generated by colonialism and the globalisation of the nation state in the modern era. In this sense, the circumstances of Aboriginal people are not only an Australian domestic phenomenon but are interwoven with the history and constitution of the international state system. It is not surprising that Aboriginal efforts to overturn discrimination at home have increasingly drawn on Indigenous struggles elsewhere and on available international mechanisms and institutions, particularly UN mechanisms. The signing of the Convention on the Elimination of Racial Discrimination (CERD) and its enactment in Australian domestic legislation in 1975 in the form of the Racial Discrimination Act, the 1967 referendum on the status of Aborigines and the Mabo decision on native title (touched on later in the chapter) are notable examples of the contemporary interplay of domestic and international norms and pressures upon which Aboriginal people have been able to call. The UN plays an important role here, offering different forms of scrutiny, different coalitions, different frameworks of comparison from those generated domestically. The UN has been part of the long negotiation between Indigenous and non-indigenous peoples over questions of self-determination – quite naturally, as the questions posed by the life conditions of Indigenous peoples are also international questions.

The Australian Government has at times played an active role promoting human rights in the international arena. Indeed, in the late 1940s and the 1950s Australia was one of the founding parties arguing for and engaged in the drafting of the Universal Declaration and key elements of the UN rights architecture. It was at this time that, for example, the forced removal of mixed-race children from Indigenous parents, by authorities throughout the country, was at its height. This draws discussion back to the question not of hypocrisy but of how we grasp the principles and institutions that we hold aloft. It is a reminder of the need for conversations across societies on patterns of suffering.

This chapter addresses a pattern of ill-health; it is not about Aboriginal people *per se*, in their diversity and survival; it is about a history of profoundly injurious political interactions. Aboriginal lives are not themselves reducible to these interactions. Nor is it suggesting that patterns of ill-health are *only* a political matter – whatever may be the underlying causes of disease and dysfunctional lives, once engaged they have their own physiological, psychological and social dynamics.

Aboriginal health in Australia – current conditions

According to the most recent (1996) census data, the Aboriginal and Torres Strait Islander population accounts for approximately 2.1 per cent of the total Australian population. Indigenous people are distributed relatively evenly throughout remote, rural, small town and city environments although most live outside cities and major towns. The Aboriginal population is younger overall than the national population. This is because birth rates are higher but also because life expectancy for Aboriginal people at birth is twenty years lower than among non-indigenous people, meaning an average life expectancy of 56.9 years for men and 61.7 for women. 'As at 1993, Aboriginal and Torres Strait Islander life expectancy was lower than those for most countries of the world with the exception of some central African countries and India. There has been little improvement in the last 10 years' (*AIHWJ*, 1997: 9). Moreover, the gap between Australian Indigenous and settler health indices has now significantly outstripped those Indicated by comparable health statistics for New Zealand, Canadian and United States native and settler populations.

Aboriginal infant mortality was for a long time the leading, and perhaps the only, issue in Aboriginal health to capture the attention of the general public. It first became an issue of national concern in the 1960s, when researchers recorded rates among Northern Territory Aborigines of almost twenty times that for settler Australians. By the mid-1980s, infant mortality rates had dropped to approximately four times that for other Australians. A decade later, Aboriginal infants are more than twice as likely as other Australian babies to die at the time of birth and three times more likely to die in early childhood, generally from diseases that have all-but virtually disappeared from white mortality statistics. Many commentators do not expect further improvements using current methods of prenatal and natal health care, for reasons that are discussed later.

Infant mortality, however, is not the area of most marked difference between Indigenous and settler death rates. It is rather the 'exceptionally high death rates' for young adults and the middle-aged, which are 'up to ten times those of other Australians . . . [and] largely account for the very low expectation of life experienced by Aborigines throughout the country. It is this indicator, more than any other, which clearly summarises the extent of Aboriginal health disadvantages' (Thompson, 1991: 239). Moreover, the gap in mortality rates is not being progressively whittled away, as the broader history of health and health services in Australia might lead us to expect. According to the data available, in some regions death rates for Indigenous people between 20 and 40 years of age have increased, with 1990s' rates in some areas being almost 1.5 times those estimated for 1955 to 1964. In some respects, Aboriginal health is worsening (e.g. Hunter, 1999).

The direct causes of death are as notable as the gulf between the average life expectancies of Indigenous and other Australians. The leading causes of death, as of Indigenous ill-health, are the so-called 'life-style' diseases. This stands in sharp contrast to the patterns of mortality and morbidity that characterise the 'Third World' countries – India, Central Africa – with which Aboriginal life expectancy is, as above, commonly compared (Hunter, 1993: 270). Diseases of the circulatory system (heart attacks and strokes) are the most common causes of death. These lead the mortality figures in the settler community also, but there they predominate among the older age groups. A New South Wales study indicated that between the notably young ages of 25 and 44, the relative risk for Aboriginals of ischaemic heart disease was approximately forty times greater than that faced by the total state population (Reid and Trompf, 1991: 330–1). Death by injury, violence and poisoning (road accidents, murder, suicide and substance abuse) is the second leading cause of death. Diseases of the respiratory system (asthma, emphysema and pneumonia), cancer, and nutritional and metabolic disorders (diabetes) are in rank order the next most common factors in morbidity. For Indigenous children, infectious and parasitic diseases – regarded as entirely preventable – are the leading causes of death. Primary causes of death are consistently related to poor diet and social conditions; they affect a higher proportion of the Aboriginal than the non-Aboriginal population, and many Indigenous people suffer while young from diseases that, in the general community, are associated with old age.

Mortality can be seen within the context of patterns of ill-health. Malnutrition remains endemic. Communicable diseases (respiratory tract and middle-ear infections, diarrhoea, trachoma, hepatitis B, tuberculosis and, to a much lesser extent but still present, leprosy) continue to be important factors in Aboriginal ill-health, although they are no longer a primary cause of death for adults. Substance abuse, particularly alcoholism and petrol sniffing, are major contributors to ill-health and provide the context of much death by violence and injury. What is notable here is the incidence of conditions that are both a consequence and (like malnutrition) a cause of poverty, the associated prevalence of diseases resulting from poor environmental health, and the rates of death and injury from violence and substance abuse.

The immediate and uncontentious explanations of these patterns are a combination of endemic poverty and, in many outback communities, the simple lack of public services, such as sewage disposal, functional sanitation facilities and water, routinely made available throughout the broader Australian population by local and state governments. Personal and communal poverty, widespread throughout the urban and rural Aboriginal communities, are tied to high unemployment rates and low levels of education. The 1996 census records an unemployment rate of 23 per cent for Indigenous people (compared to 9 per cent for the general population), but if 'work for dole' schemes are included, Aboriginal unemployment stands at 34 per cent. As a result '[a]lmost four in ten Indigenous households were estimated to have either insufficient income to meet basic needs (even before taking housing into account) or not enough income to afford adequate housing' (Australian Bureau of Statistics, 1997: 3). The incidence of mental illness and of intracommunal violence is high. Alcoholism has become entrenched. Removal from traditional sources of food, lack both of nutritional knowledge and of cultural patterns regarding non-indigenous food sources plus the high cost of and poor access to fresh food in outback areas also contribute to poor diet, leading to malnutrition, high blood pressure, diabetes and heart disease. According to the 2000 House of Representatives Standing Committee report, anaemia in children and malnutrition are becoming more common (HRSC, 2000: 82).

Substandard conditions are among the most salient features of rural Aboriginals' lives. 'Nothing ever quite conveys the shock of coming face to face with the living conditions in some of these [rural Aboriginal] communities, the fact that we're still in Australia and not, as [then Senator] Richardson is to say later, some war-ravaged African nation' (Tingle, 1994: 3). Aboriginal living conditions 'are generally characterised by overcrowding, inadequate water and washing facilities, poor sanitation and sewage disposal, limited food storage and sub-optimal food preparation facilities' (Thompson, 1989:187). In 1996–97, 12,000 Indigenous Australians were estimated to be homeless. A visiting Parliamentary Sub-Committee on Human Rights described the living conditions of some Northern Territory communities as 'appalling' and awash in 'an ocean of sewage' in the wet season (*Age*, 1994: 2). A 1992 survey by the Aboriginal and Torres Strait Islander Commission (ATSIC) found that, of the 838 rural communities and homelands surveyed, water in 306 was unfit for human consumption, affecting 14,510 people, while over 30,000 people had been affected by water restrictions over the past year, mostly due to equipment breakdown. 'About four per cent of the 80,080 Indigenous people covered in the survey had no sewage disposal system and nearly eleven per cent had no electricity supply' (ABS, 1997: 18).

Such conditions fundamentally affect every dimension of health care and well-being. They are not only the direct cause of much illness but undermine the provision of infrastructure for more complex health interventions. So, for example, although Aborigines in north Queensland (where a significant number of rural Aboriginal communities are located) make up 45–50 per cent of patients treated in kidney units, taking dialysis machines to Aboriginal communities which lack clean water, sanitation and effective sewage is of debatable value. '[T]he built and physical environments both reflect and exacerbate the poverty and ill-health of Aboriginal communities. They promote a cycle of discrimination, neglect and sickness' (Reid and Trompf, 1991: xvii). A decade later, the need for improved housing and infrastructure is still registered as pressing (e.g. HRSC, 2000).

What are the reasons for this – in the context of present-day Australia – is a truly extraordinary picture: extraordinary in the extent of ill-health and degraded environmental health, in the contrast with non-indigenous Australian health standards, and in the fact that this situation has persisted despite apparently repeated efforts to address it? This chapter discusses a number of answers to this question. But the place to start is the history of the relentless dispossession of Indigenous people, from their land, their traditional social structures, their economy and their place – a place for which they could be makers of and participants in political community. It is a history that the Australian High Court described as 'a legacy of unutterable shame' for contemporary Australia (RCIADIC, 1991, Vol. 2: 3). As Neil Thompson, a prolific commentator on black mortality, has noted:

> Not only is the currently markedly lower health status of Aborigines deeply rooted in their substantial social inequality, but many aspects of Aboriginal health also demand a clear understanding of the cultural context of health . . . The social inequality of Aborigines [is] directly related to their dispossession, [and] is characterised by poverty and powerlessness. (Thompson 1989: 182)

The record of colonialism and dispossession is an account of not only the nineteenth but the twentieth century, continuing in certain places and respects until at least the 1980s. It is beyond the scope of this chapter to detail that history. Suffice to say, and as Kidd's study of the 'management' of Aborigines in Queensland (1997; see also Kidd, 2000) makes abundantly clear, there has been nothing mysterious about 'the processes by which dispossession is transformed into disease' (Reid and Trompf, 1991: xv). A nomadic hunting people was forced into fixed settlements without adequate waste disposal or housing, in groupings which did not respect tribal, clan or language affiliations, away from sources of food and economic resources and so into forced dependence on government or mission 'charity', with literally starvation rations, and little education or medical attention. In a fairly typical government communication, the medical superintendent of an Aboriginal reserve in the 1930s, noting the very high death rate from malnutrition and infection among children and the elderly, wondered whether it was 'worth trying to save them' by the provision of standard nutritional supplements (in Kidd, 1997: 101). Families were separated 'for their own good', in many cases native languages were disallowed, and almost every aspect of people's private and public lives was controlled. In Queensland, until 1986 for those Aborigines in state settlements, individual earnings, incomes and often bank accounts were mandatorily managed by state bureaucrats – in contravention of labour legislation – to the great benefit of state coffers. These circumstances have led quite simply and directly to the chronic poverty and disease patterns which afflict much of the Aboriginal population. '[G]overnments *made themselves* responsible' for Aboriginal people, punishing those who sought to run their own lives. 'And we know the results of this century of government controls: an appalling deficit on every social indicator' (Kidd, 2000: 6). What is remarkable here is the incidence not of disease, but of survival.

The Human Right and Equal Opportunity Commission (HREOC's) report into the provision of water and sanitation services to Indigenous communities draws one example of the underlying link between the dispossession of Indigenous people and their present lack of access to or control over services:

> The conflict between European settlement and Australia's Indigenous people was not only a clash of cultures but a basic competition for land and resources. One of the most important resources was water. The opening up of Australia for 'settlement' and 'economic development' saw the beginning of a conflict over water which continues today. Aborigines were dispossessed and reduced to remnant pockets of population on the outskirts of European settlement. Aboriginal resistance was crushed by whites seeking river frontage and isolated water-holes. Today the same people are drawn into protracted negotiations to gain living area . . . adjacent to water supplies or to improve water supply and sanitation in remote communities. (HREOC, 1994: 6)

However, from this broader history of destruction, two other responses to the question of Aboriginal health emerge, and it is with these that much of the following discussion is concerned. The first response is in terms of what are understood as welfare rights and the second in terms of rights as a process of mutual recognition or participation in political life. These two responses are interwoven, but they are also in some respects contrary to each other. The first focuses on the provision of services which all Australians, with some provisos and conditions, can claim as positive entitlements of membership of the Australian community. This response understands rights as bundles of entitlements to particular welfare goods that go, in this case, to make up public health.

In practice, this remedy is cast as the extension of given services from the settler to the Indigenous community, from those who have to those who do not have. Ideally, these services should be extended in a culturally sensitive manner and with all duty of care. In practice, the extension of services to Aboriginal communities degenerates into 'welfarism', where those who 'have not' become passive recipients constituted as incapable and incompetent, and those who 'have' as overburdened (HRSC, 2000; Pearson, 2000). As the welfare system is more generally wound back, the tensions in this approach become even more tightly strung. Access to entitlement becomes 'charity' in a degenerate sense of the word, the services become a fixed commodity and the transaction itself fixed and one way, serving to widen the gap between recipients and others. Welfare becomes 'income provisioning for people dispossessed from the real economy' (Pearson, 2000: 7).[1]

The degeneration of 'welfare rights' to 'welfarism' is not inevitable. Although some areas of general welfare remain highly susceptible to 'welfarism', across much of the non-indigenous population welfare retains a sense of reciprocity. It is a process of modest redistribution to which one contributes and from which one draws, which allows also for those unable to contribute at all. The claim for public services is not a request for charity, but for due recognition as a citizen. The claiming, however, occurs within and is made possible by a broad construction of the state and of citizenship that is not entirely fixed but is certainly not open-ended. Claiming entitlements is calling upon an exchange the parameters of which are already in place. Its function is not to renegotiate or reflect upon political relationships but to exercise more fully already established norms and trajectories (although the mix of actual entitlements may be renegotiated). The construction of citizenship in operation here is one that, through the history of formalising norms of equality and fairness as well as of sovereignty, has assumed and required key thresholds of uniformity – what James Tully (1995) calls the 'empire of uniformity'. Homogenising ideals of citizenship had been overtly imposed upon Aborigines under earlier policies of assimilation: 'the legislative acceptance of Aborigines as citizens was long contingent on behaviours which demanded a denial or suppression of identification as an Aborigine' (Hunter, 1993: 257).

There are numerous accounts of the requirements Indigenous people had to fulfil to attain state (provincial) 'citizenship' or to have removed some of the legislative restrictions governing Aboriginal life that were in force until, in some areas, the early 1980s. Up until the early 1960s a Queensland Murri,[2] for example, may be required to sign a declaration at the local police station stating that he or she would no longer associate with Aborigines. In West Australia an Aboriginal applicant for provincial 'citizenship' had 'to furnish . . . two recent references from reputable citizens certifying his good habits and industrious habits. The magistrate had to be satisfied as to the fact and duration of adoption by the applicant of "the manner and habits of civilised life"' (Hunter, 1993: 257–8). Good health was a further indicator of 'civilised life', as was eschewing the company of other Indigenous people, and a specific requirement of citizenship. 'Should [the applicant] subsequently contract any of the diseases described [communicable diseases] . . . or fail to adopt the manner and habits of civilised life, the Certificate [of citizenship] could be suspended indefinitely or cancelled' (Hunter, 1993: 258). Such requirements have been legislatively overturned, but they were arguably articulating much more powerful and historically embedded norms of political community as well as habits of administration. One is a member of the Australian community, just like everybody else, and can therefore claim access to certain entitlements, just like everybody else. This theme of 'equity' demanding uniformity has now been picked up by significant right-wing political trends.

The implicit price of access to 'ordinary' levels of welfare – education, housing, health, infrastructure – has been assimilation, if now resting on a less brutal body of requirements. This orientation seemingly remains a, and perhaps the, dominant functional approach despite the enunciation of goals of self-determination for Indigenous people, 'reconciliation' or even simply multiculturalism. Self-determination, reconciliation and multiculturalism can and have proved to be very difficult to grasp, particularly if the goal is one of administering an already complex service network. But part of the anger and confusion in sectors of the bureaucracy and the settler population concerning the failure of welfare delivery seems to be directed at the 'failure' of Indigenous people to be 'just like everyone else'.

But, like various groups within contemporary Australian society, Indigenous people are not 'just like everyone else'. Moreover, the problems they face are often systemic and structural, not individual. Even more potently, the structures and institutions from which they may claim entitlements emerged and were elaborated to the exclusion of Indigenous people and indeed on the basis of their dispossession. 'As a small minority with little economic, industrial or political power, Indigenous peoples and our interests are already easy to overlook but our marginalisation is not just a problem of numbers – it lies at the heart of the way Australia developed and functions as a modern nation' (Dodson, 1995a: 43).

Predominant responses to continuing disease patterns within the Indigenous population have focused on arguing the need for better provision of welfare services. The claim by Indigenous people of their right as citizens to better health provision is an important part of the effort to improve health standards and also, more broadly, of the struggle, underway since at least the 1950s, to claim effective citizenship. But these efforts may themselves remain inhibited within a too restrictive understanding of citizenship and political community. The second 'answer' to the question of Indigenous health, then, is that casting the question in terms essentially of welfare entitlements has proved an insufficient response to the alienation and exile of Aboriginal people within their own place; in degenerating into 'welfarism' it has effectively deepened that exile. But rights and citizenship are not reducible to welfare, far less *welfarism*. The second answer endeavours to address more directly some of the fundamental constructions of political community that continue the exclusion and dispossession of Aboriginal people as shaping Aboriginal ill-health. It is thus an effort to approach questions of self-determination more openly: it focuses not on welfare entitlements (which are themselves a function of citizenship) but on rights understood as the fundamental power to participate in the organisation of political community. Effective access to welfare entitlements is in part a consequence and a demonstration of this more fundamental power to participate.[3]

'Self-management' and 'self-determination' have themselves become policy terms within the health and welfare arena, and refer to various mechanisms to include Indigenous input into health administration. While important, such efforts have been limited in practice.[4] Significant improvement in health for Indigenous people is likely to depend upon the growth of a more far-reaching and open-ended sense of self-determination – one centred on Indigenous communities taking, and being recognised as having, responsibility for the on-going task of defining and pursuing their own well-being in interaction with the broader dynamics of Australian political institutions and concerns. Rather than the extending of a commodity from one to another, this is a process of negotiation and a means of listening to and working with difference, whether at grassroots level, in the operation of a particular clinic or health promotion programme, or at broader levels that may change social practices for non-indigenous as well as Indigenous people. 'Whether guided by self-determination, self-management, or their successors, the promulgation of policy and development of programs [require] a wider understanding of social change that acknowledges both traditional and conventional needs of Aborigines, in a society that contains both Aborigines and non-Aborigines' (Hunter, 1993: 264).

There is nothing new about this remedy. Aboriginal people have been publicly agitating for what, essentially, is a recognition of themselves as participants in shaping Australian political and social life since at least the 1930s. The Aboriginal Tent Embassy on the grounds of Parliament House in 1972 was a symbolic assertion of a real difference and a call for the mutual respect from which negotiation could begin. The calls throughout the 1980s and again since the beginning of the new century for a treaty between Indigenous and settler Australia are moved by a similar logic. The search for reconciliation can also presuppose the recognition of difference as a legitimate element of political community. There has been debate since at least the 1980s concerning possible forms of Indigenous self-government. The RCIADIC (1987–91), the most comprehensive inquiry into the lives of Aboriginal people, saw the self-determination and empowerment of Indigenous society as the fundamental means by which Aboriginal people could overcome the inequality and disadvantage which distort their lives. 'There is no other way. Only the Aboriginal people can, in the final analysis, assure their own future' (RCIADIC, 1991: Vol. 1: 16).

Since 1967, and more particularly since the mid-1970s, the Commonwealth Government has mounted policies aimed specifically at bringing Indigenous health to the same level as enjoyed by other Australians. Moreover, since the mid-1980s there has been unprecedented media attention given to Aboriginal issues, including health. It seems that 'millions' are spent annually on indigenous health but with very little result. The statistics of Aboriginal health are thus widely seen as 'mystifying because Australian taxpayers, over the past 20 years at least, have always provided generously for indigenous Australians'; and they are shocking 'not only because of the human tragedy but also because taxpayers simply have assumed a better return for their money' (Jones, *Northern Territory News*, 20 March 1994: 16). The obduracy of patterns of ill-health thus become not the consequence of a history of management, but another sign of the 'Aboriginal problem' – a graveyard of politicians, bureaucrats and well-intentioned liberals. 'Endemic poverty, trashed housing, unemployment and alcohol-related violence and despair are portrayed as aspects of an "Aboriginal problem" which seemingly defies resolution' (Kidd, 1997: xix).

Leaving aside the misleading politics of demands for equality of expenditure rather than equity of outcome, however, the appearance of vast expenditure on Aboriginal and Islander people is misleading. Comparison of government expenditure on Indigenous and non-Indigenous health is complex, and reliable figures only started emerging in the late 1990s. According to John Deeble's 1998 study, only approximately 63 cents per head is spent on Indigenous health care for every dollar outlaid on the health of other Australians, and 'only a portion of the sixty three cents is spent on culturally acceptable and effective services to Aboriginal people' (quoted in Hunter, 1999). This is because Aboriginal people are not accessing Medicare (the national medical rebate scheme) or government-supported pharmaceutical schemes. The 'model of short consultations in a private practice setting does not fit with the needs of Aboriginal people for holistic, comprehensive care in a culturally appropriate setting' (Hunter, 1999; see also Anderson, 1994). Specially targeted expenditure on Aboriginal health thus far has not come close to compensating for what they are missing in the way of primary health care services widely available to the general community. Not making use of general primary health care (for a variety of reasons), Indigenous people often wait until they are severely ill before seeking treatment, leading to a high rate of costly medical crisis interventions. Moreover the cost of delivery of many medical services in outback Australia, where a significant percentage of the Indigenous population live, is inevitably much higher than the cost of delivering the same service in an urban centre. Thus comparatively little is actually spent on Aboriginal health care, and little effective primary care is actually reaching Aboriginal people.

The actual quality of service delivery or of the welfare rights offered to Aboriginal people, and the monies expended on Aboriginal health, are further investigated in relation to Commonwealth health policies (pp. 182–8). But first it is important to consider briefly the more fundamental failure to accept Indigenous people as genuine interlocutors in political community. Both of the answers just considered to the 'question' of continuing Aboriginal ill-health have light to shed on the problem. The section following explores further both responses – which complement but are also in tension with each other – through a discussion of the construction of Aboriginal society as a lack and as a problem, and the twentieth century's predominant response to that problem: institutionalisation.

'The great Australian silence'

The 1992 Australian High Court decision on Aboriginal land rights, known as the 'Mabo decision', overturned the legal categorisation of Australia as 'empty land' (*terra nullius*) and recognised within Australian law the legal title to traditional lands of Australia's Indigenous people. The categorisation of Australia as *terra nullius* was established in 1788. *Terra nullius* was an international legal term signifying that the land in question belonged to no one, either because it was literally unoccupied or, as in the case of Australia, was not established as a form of possession in a manner recognisable to the colonisers through a system of local law or transformation by labour. The country was indeed seen to be populated, but by people who were not understood to constitute a 'society'. The doctrine of *terra nullius* acted as an erasure of Indigenous people as potential interlocutors, and as a powerful assertion of their total exclusion from negotiation, mutual interaction or 'the need to deal'. *Terra nullius* thus became both the international legal basis for the British assertion of sovereignty over the land of what became Australia and a statement of the legitimacy of British occupation. The two other forms by which sovereignty could be sought – conquest or treaty – were both in principle predicated upon the recognition of a society that was already in place, featuring a system of law, ownership of land and a form of political order. Territory acquired through conquest or treaty could thus be declared constitutionally subject to, in this instance, the British crown, while remaining the actual common law property of the colonised people. The recent high court debate over land rights was about whether Indigenous Australians could claim this common law title.

In terms of legal access to actual rights to land, the decision was highly conditional: the 'deepest significance of this decision on native title lies, not in its implications for property law', but in its profound implications for, and challenges to, Australian political and constitutional life (Dodson, 1995a: 96). This challenge is to both historical and contemporary conceptions of Australian political community and constitutional order. The judgment recognised that it was the 'dispossession [of Aboriginal people that] underwrote the development of the nation' (Brennan, in Dodson, 1995a: 43). Moreover, in recognising native title, the common law recognised and 'made room for a kind of law that had its roots outside the system' (Webber, 2000: 69). In so doing, the Mabo decision accepted Aboriginal society as a continuing (although by no means discrete) political and legal order. 'Mabo . . . said: "You have a place to engage, you have a place in this country and that place is guaranteed under the rule of law" ' (Pearson, in *Weekend Australian*, 8–9 November 1997: 26). The recognition of native title is thus

> about the co-existence of partially autonomous societies, each with its own system of law, that must in some fashion good or ill, relate to each other. Because of the challenges of adjustment – because of the sometimes profound differences of context and forms of social ordering – that process may only be achieved through mutual accommodation over the very long term. (Webber, 2000: 70)

It is now at least a legal and constitutional potential that 'Australian nationhood is no longer forged within an exclusively non-indigenous crucible' fuelled by 'a vision of a single people' but through a broader, more open, conception of participation (Webber, 2000: 77, 88).

The Mabo (and the Wik) decision also focused attention emphatically on a fundamental element of the greater history of Indigenous and non-Indigenous interaction and the colonisation of Australia. This is the issue of what Stanner called 'the great Australian silence' (1969: 18), that is, the settling over time of Australia by non-Aboriginals 'on the basis that there was no need to deal with the indigenous inhabitants or even acknowledge their laws, their rights or their interests', or indeed their existence (Nettheim, 1993: 104).

The means by which 'land' was recognised as 'property', crucial to the assertion of *terra nullius*, is significant here. For the British colonists, following Locke and, later, Tocqueville and other theorists of the state (as mentioned in Chapter 2), ownership of land was established by cultivation 'defined in terms specific to European agriculture' (Tully, 1995: 73). Australian Aboriginals were hunter-gatherers and, not being engaged in fixed agriculture, did not have a system of settled individual land ownership. Like the Amerindians they 'occupied but did not possess the land. It is by agriculture that man wins the soil' (Tocqueville, in Connolly, 2000: 185). Indigenous peoples were 'in a state of nature'. Stable property is a fundamental element of Lockean contractarianism. The need for protection of property and for resolution of disputes concerning it is one of the prime motivations for men to enter into contract, so establishing a system of laws, of magistrates and of sovereign powers. Moreover, a system of individual land ownership and sedentary agriculture is seen, in this account, as the basis of a surplus economy and an increasingly complex economic life. Property thus functions as an essential foundation of both political life and economic well-being – as enabling and underpinning 'civilisation' in the form of the state. Being by definition without property, Aborigines had thereby not entered a contract and so did not constitute a society. They were seen as a 'people without politics' (according to the anonymous anthropologist quoted in Langton, 1994: 132), without law or the supposedly civilising influence of a complex market economy, with 'neither nationhood nor territorial jurisdiction' (Tully, 1995: 72).

According to this powerful and pervasive account of political community, Indigenous peoples represent the prehistory of political life – the world before crossing the threshold of the social contract into the state. Here the imperial powers of Europe represent the highest and most developed point in a natural trajectory of human civilisation. They are at the endpoint – or almost there – where humanity meets its potential. Indigenous people are primitive waystations or *cul de sacs* which had already been overtaken, experiments that had not altogether borne fruit, dead water that now, given the opportunity, would naturally flow into the great stream of civilisation – or dry up. Moreover, through this vision of mounting stages of civilisation, and by virtue of the supposed economic inefficiency of hunter-gatherer life, it was – and often still is – presumed that Aboriginal people essentially *benefit* from the seizure of their lands and the destruction of their manner of life, for then they can be assimilated into civilisation. This indeed was explicitly part of the argument for removing mixed-race children from Aboriginal parents. While certainly not the only way of approaching Aboriginal peoples – some settlers resisted the violence towards and the exploitation of Indigenous people – it was the predominant way. Tully, commenting on Locke's justification of the colonisation of North America, points to a pattern equally relevant to the later colonisation of Australia. Locke's account replaces the long, painful history of conquest, destruction and betrayal of Indigenous Americans 'with the captivating picture of the inevitable and benign progress of modern constitutionalism' (1995: 78).

The picture of the progress of modern constitutionalism was only deepened by the emergence in the nineteenth century of social Darwinism. This doctrine elaborated a division of the human species into superior and inferior races in which 'the superior races have a right, because they have a duty . . . to civilise the inferior races' (Ferry, in Cowie, 1986: 47). The land 'offers itself not to the isolated, ignorant man of the first ages, but to man who has already mastered the most important secrets of nature, united to his fellows, and taught by the experience of fifty centuries' (Tocqueville, in Connolly, 2000: 185). Indigenous people were now believed to be a biologically as well a as socio-politically more primitive stage of human evolution – 'mankind in the chrysalis stage' (Sir James

Frazer, in Stanner, 1969: 35) which would naturally pass away when faced with the reality of modern man. Thus for almost a century it was believed that Aborigines would simply die out. Events appeared to bear out this presumption, with the severe depletion of the Indigenous population through introduced diseases, killings and enforced changes of lifestyle. The 'expected disappearance from the face of the earth [of Aboriginal peoples] was merely a case "following the order of the world, the lower race preparing a home for the higher"' (Dodson, 1993: 44, quoting Stanner). The full membership of Aborigines in the human race was a point of real anthropological, medical and popular debate. As a result there was relatively little official attention paid to understanding the circumstances of Aborigines, including their health status, for 'as long as the extinction of the aborigines was assumed to be inevitable (and as late as the 1930s the historian Hancock could still speak of their "predestined passing") no information could have had much more than a poignant irrelevance' (Stanner, 1969: 37–8).

After surveying histories of Australia written between the 1930s and the late 1960s, for example, Stanner concludes that 'inattention' to the Aboriginal community in Australian histories was 'a structural matter, a view from a window which has been carefully placed to exclude a whole quadrant of the landscape' (1969: 24). The Immigration Restriction Act was one of the first bills to be passed on federation and it formally inaugurated the raft of measures known as the White Australia policy. This policy, which remained in force until 1967, expressed a key social and political aspiration – an egalitarianism of white male workers from which Aboriginal people were by definition erased. The exclusion of Indigenous people from full legal citizenship and census-taking until overturned by referendum in 1967, after the great influxes of post-war migration, gives some indication of the political realities of this silence and the extent of Aboriginal powerlessness within the Australian community.

Terra nullius was a formal legal expression of this exclusion which formal legal citizenship did not override. Citizenship could stand as an assimilationist presumption, even after that goal had been officially repudiated. *Terra nullius* remained as an assertion that Aboriginal society had no political existence, no pattern of law or binding relationship within which 'rights' or indeed real community could be located, other than those conferred upon individual Aborigines by absorption into civilised ways. This stands in contrast to migrants, who had culture and politics – even if their source was elsewhere and often regarded with prejudice. Aborigines were those upon whose absence the presence of the settler society was founded and upon whose inferiority, evolutionary closure and natural disappearance from history the blossoming and vigour of Australian political life was predicated and justified. The significance of the Mabo and Wik decisions lies in the overturning, in the legal and constitutional spheres at least, of these presumptions.

This 'overlooking' and erasure of an Indigenous people does not mean that no attention has been paid to Aborigines. On the contrary, Aborigines have stood as exemplifications of shifting categories within the settler colonial culture – noble savages, vermin, children and, latterly in some quarters, victims. Their exclusion has constituted a very particular and compelling place, for it was precisely the 'failure' (however conceived) of Aboriginal people that legitimised white possession of the country. It is not surprising, then, that Indigenous people have been constituted as a lack, an incapacity and a 'problem' (this is evident in the high incarceration rates of Aboriginal juveniles for minor offences) – 'a doomed and primitive race who were not part of Australian society except as recipients of non-Aboriginal benevolence' (RCIADIC, 1991: Vol. 2: 5). At the same time, they are a threat and an otherness whose lawlessness and disruption is to be feared. How to handle this 'people as problem' has led over the past century to successive forms of institutionalisation.

'Invisibility' and institutionalisation have constituted the conditions within which Aborigines could pursue their well-being within the context of the dominant Australian society. The institutionalisation of Aboriginal people has proceeded since the mid-nineteenth century under a variety of policy settings and intentions – segregation, assimilation, integration – and, arguably, continued under more recent policies of self-determination. Institutionalisation frequently involved a process of centralisation, 'despite the small-group orientation of traditional Aboriginal societies' (Hunter, 1993: 259), with the location, size and composition of the community usually determined according to ease of administration by the state rather than clan or group affiliation. It enforced a 'change from small, semi-nomadic communities into large aggregations of people from many different areas [and so] led to a rapid increase of both communicable diseases and social tensions resulting in physical violence', as well as degraded dietary habits (Reid and Trompf, 1991: 385). The reserves were authoritarian in structure and not integrated into the broader economy.

The effect of institutionalisation has been to establish an astonishing degree of control over Indigenous people's lives by state institutions or bodies (such as missions) run in broad terms on behalf of the state. Over generations, this process has created conditions of extreme and enforced dependence. 'Diet, movement, employment, marriage, child-rearing arrangements, and the exercise of religious belief were all subject to the wishes of the mission or settlement custodians' (Reid and Trompf, 1991: 385). To give an example, a study of infant and child mortality between 1967 and 1969 in communities under Queensland Aboriginal Affairs Department's control found that malnutrition was the key factor in infant mortality and the chronic ill-health of the surviving children. The study drew attention to inadequate medical attention and 'defective social indices', such as income and housing. The official response included appointing liaison officers to target 'parental incompetence'. The liaison officer was to oversee health and hygiene but also to pursue rent arrears, ' "acquire a knowledge of all the individual residents", transmitting to head office "their names, where they live, how they care for their families, standard of housekeeping, work record, personal problems and difficulties, particular abilities and any other material that may be of value" ' (Departmental communication, quoted in Kidd, 1997: 261, 262). Parents deemed 'incompetent' might have their children removed. Not surprisingly, compliance with the liaison officers was low. 'Liaison officers . . . effectively acted as agents to advance the implementation of the state's assimilation policy at an individual level . . . the more "advanced" or "suitable" families were given access to the new housing and the more impoverished or destitute were passed over' (Kidd, 1997: 263).

The RCIADIC found that the level of control exercised over Aboriginal lives

> was no less brutal for the fact that the policies which achieved the control were often justified by their authors on humanitarian or paternalistic grounds . . . [Those whose deaths were investigated by the Commission] all had files – in many cases hundreds of pages of observations and moral and social judgements on them and their families; considerations of applications for basic rights, determinations about where they could live, where they could travel, who they could associate with, what possessions they could purchase, whether they could work and what, if any, wages they could receive or retain. Welfare officers, police court officials and countless other white bureaucrats, mostly unknown and rarely seen by the persons concerned, judged and determined their lives. The officials saw all, recorded all, judged all and yet knew nothing about the people whose lives they controlled. Aboriginal people were removed at the whim of others, crowded into settlements and missions and in impoverished camps on cattle stations. Always there were non-Aboriginal people giving orders, making decisions in which the opinions of the Aboriginal people were not sought nor, if volunteered, heeded. Aboriginal families could be separated, children removed if judged too light skinned, placed in homes or boarded out as servants of non-Aboriginal families . . . This control – these horrors of subjugation – were still occurring in the 1960s and for much of the 1970s. (1991: Vol. 2: 502–3)

Commonwealth Indigenous health policy – 1970s–2000s

Aboriginal people throughout the country were formally registered as Australian citizens and included in the census in 1967, following a national referendum. This was the result of increasing Aboriginal civil rights activism, growing sensitivity to issues of race relations within sectors of the non-indigenous electorate and increasing international debate on issues of colonisation and racism, with many newly independent states being sharply critical of those countries, like Australia, where Indigenous people were not full citizens. The decision was a clear win for those groups, in particular Indigenous groups, which had been fighting to overturn this particular assertion of black invisibility. For many Aborigines, this shift opened the way for '[i]deas of autonomy, self-determination and sovereignty [to become] central . . . In this new era the key issue became how Koories would exercise their rights to health care' (Anderson, 1994: 34). In 1971, Aboriginal people established the first Aboriginal Medical Service (AMS) in Sydney, staffed in part by Indigenous people and dedicated to serving their health needs. Aboriginal Medical Services, which aims to provide community controlled primary health care, has subsequently become one of the fundamental elements of Aboriginal health care throughout the country, with some hundreds in operation.

The crucial practical effect of the 1967 referendum was that it meant that, for the first time, the Commonwealth (rather than the state governments) had power to legislate on Aboriginal issues, extending to authority to override the states. Persistent and at times savage jurisdictional dispute is a standing feature of the Australian federal system. Up until 1967, 'Aboriginal Affairs' had been overwhelmingly the province of local state governments. After 1967, the fact of citizenship added another tier of government and funding – one regarded with deep suspicion by the states but which provided greater leverage to Indigenous groups pressing for change.

In practice, however, a more substantial focus by the Commonwealth Government on Aboriginal health did not emerge until after a change of federal government in 1972, with 'self-determination' for Aboriginal people being adopted as a policy goal by the new Labour Government. In 1973, the first National Plan for Aboriginal Health was released. This plan envisaged that within ten years Indigenous health would achieve levels broadly consistent with settler Australian health. State and territory governments, however, refused to endorse the plan. It is not surprising on any level, then, that despite some positive achievements the plan failed, and in doing so demonstrated issues that ever since have characterised government health policies for Aborigines. On administrative grounds, alone, the plan failed because of lack of coordination and cooperation among levels of government, and lack of commitment on the part of the federal government to push forward its policy goals against resistance from state or local governments; because of inadequate funding; because it did not have or provide tools with which to grasp the extent or nature of the problem; and because of the kind of medical intervention that, in the main, it was designed to provide. It is interesting to note, almost thirty years later, that the first paragraph of the most recent government report into Indigenous health states that 'the planning and delivery of health services for Indigenous Australians is characterised by a general lack of direction and poor coordination', with no delineation or agreement among different levels of government concerning their responsibilities (HRSC, 2000: 1).

In retrospect, the 1973 plan appears no more than a statement of intent. As was argued earlier, grappling with the nature of Indigenous ill-health involves engagement with Aborigines as people with whom political community is shared. This is a difficult and challenging process. But even at the technical-administrative level, one of the simplest tools necessary for coming to grips with Aboriginal ill-health – information on mortality and morbidity patterns and their social as well as medical contexts – has to a significant degree been unavailable. It is perhaps not surprising that, after decades during which the issue was ignored, there was little information on Aboriginal ill-health's extent. However, the first effort at a genuinely national database on Aboriginal health was not released until 1997, almost twenty-five years after the National Plan. Lack of information not only continues a level of ignorance about specific patterns of ill-health and disease, and about Aborigines' identification of their own health priorities, it buries the simple and evident connections between Aboriginal disease and Aboriginal history as well as information on the state of service delivery and the on-going experience of discrimination. Lack of reliable information also contributes to the powerful popular misconceptions that Aborigines are funded to a level well in excess of that of the 'ordinary' Australian and that continuing destitution and ill-health are a mysterious function of 'Aboriginality'. It allows the charade of government ministers regularly 'discovering' black living conditions and the attendant, perhaps genuine, expressions of shock, with little to indicate a clear outcome, and repeatedly blaming the persistence of poor living conditions on official and community ignorance.

Despite this somewhat disingenuous cycle of ignorance and shock, the broad sweep of Aboriginal health problems and solutions has not been obscure. The first major official inquiry into Indigenous health, undertaken by the House of Representatives Standing Committee on Aboriginal Affairs (HRSCAA) in 1979, attributed Aboriginal morbidity to unsatisfactory environmental and public health, their low socio-economic status and the cultural insensitivity of much health delivery. It emphasised provision of basic environmental health care, particularly safe water supplies, the need for Aborigines to be involved at all levels of health care and for their effective self-management of health and well-being (HRSCAA, 1979). These findings are notable in that they are consistent with the recommendations of all subsequent official inquiries into and major official statements concerning Indigenous health.

In the administrative domain, the division of planning, responsibility and funding between levels of government and across diverse departments and instrumentalities has been of immense detriment to Aboriginal health. While the Commonwealth has led policy development and provides the majority of the funding, health delivery remains primarily a state and territory responsibility, while the provision of the most basic services – water, sewerage and so on – has to a significant extent rested with local councils. The Commonwealth funds much of the provision of essential services, but plays no part in the actual allocation of funds on the ground. Accountability for expenditure appears vague.

According to Aboriginal health workers, clinics may have to deal with up to eighty different bureaucracies split among three levels of government. And the jealousy endemic in Australia's federal system has allowed lines of responsibility to blur and disappear. This fragmentation is compounded by the absence of an agreed plan or of close coordination among policy-making bodies. Thus, despite the 1973 plan, there was no coordinated strategy for actualising intentions articulated for Aboriginal health until the release of the first *National Aboriginal Health Strategy (NAHS)* in 1989. But the *Strategy* was not able to overcome the difficulties created by the fragmentation of responsibility, and the lack of long-term planning and accountability for outcomes.

The next *Strategy*, announced in 1994, was itself quietly abandoned less than two years after its adoption, leaving no clear trail of what had actually happened to many of the programmes planned or the monies promised. A case study of the 1994 *Strategy* by Access Economics called it a 'budgetary illusion' which created the impression of new programmes and major additional funding – and so either an image of social policy commitments or more 'waste on blacks', depending on your view – through the misleading representation of on-going running costs as 'new monies' (Access Economics, 1994). The 2000 HRSC report still warns that 'lack of clear delineation of responsibility [for] Indigenous health is . . . an incentive for the parties, particularly the States, to indulge wherever possible in shifting the onus for payment to [another] sector', while Recommendation 1 is still a call for the Commonwealth to actually accept responsibility for primary health care for Aborigines (HRSC, 2000: 2–3).[5]

Lack of coordination leads to buck-passing between funding bodies, confusion among those working directly with people's health and a convenient cover for dishonesty over funding. It leads also to intense competition for the too scarce 'Aboriginal health dollar' among different aspects of health, and to programmes working at crossed-purposes. Thus, providing better housing, a fundamental aspect of environmental health, 'has led in some communities to a decline in health status. This has resulted from a reduction in disposable income as a consequence of increased rental and utility charges and a decrease in funds for foodstuffs, in turn leading to undernutrition and greater susceptibility to infection' (Saggers and Gray, 1991: 392). Moreover, Commonwealth funding for housing and essential infrastructure for disadvantaged Indigenous communities comes under its indigenous health budget whereas similar services for non-indigenous communities are provided under a range of other budgets. This adds to the misleading impression that large sums of money are spent on Aboriginal health. With no clear lines of responsibility many programmes at federal and state level simply fail to eventuate, although by that time public sensitivity over the 'costs' of the Indigenous population will have been fed. The results of jurisdictional rivalry and subversion, of budgetary and electoral manipulation, of lack of coordination and accountability are regularly bemoaned as yet another dimension of the 'Aboriginal problem'.

As well as the impact of administrative fragmentation and sleight of hand on Aboriginal health delivery, government endeavours have also been limited by a general failure to approach Aboriginal understandings of what might constitute well-being and so, as a result, by the misplaced or inappropriate nature of much medical intervention. Building on a long history of approaching Aboriginal health as a policing matter, often aimed at protecting the white population from communicable diseases, the dominant contemporary approach has been one of 'medical problem solving' aimed at 'taking over' a particular moment of health. For example, one particular area of focus under the 1973 plan was infant mortality, where rates of death paralleled the worst recorded anywhere in the world. Results here demonstrate both the successes and the limitations of the dominant medical approaches to black health. Due to highly focused medical intervention, infant mortality rates fell significantly, particularly in rural areas. This has largely been the result of Western medical techniques taking over, holus-bolus, the actual delivery. So, for example, in some regions pregnant Aboriginal women are transported hundreds of kilometres to the nearest hospital for their confinement. It is not simply that this technique of delivery is deemed culturally inappropriate (and frightening) by many Aboriginal women, offending traditional women's law and isolating women from family support at a time of vulnerability; it also leaves the mortality rate, after almost thirty years of intervention, at two to three times the rate of settler infants (and maternal mortality at five times the rate of the general population). Moreover, 'such focused health interventions have not solved the problems of ill-health in Aboriginal children. Rather, they have changed the nature of the problem. The children of impoverished Aboriginal parents no longer die in infancy. Instead, many survive, but "fail to thrive"' (Saggers and Gray, 1991: 409). The Royal Commission into Aboriginal Deaths in Custody described the 'pleasing reduction in Aboriginal infant mortality' as an example of 'improving the indicator rather than improving the quality of life . . . What may appear on the basis of a particular indicator to be a real achievement may, in fact, reflect simply an improvement in one narrow area rather than any substantial improvement in the quality of life' (RCIADIC, 1991: Vol. 2: 51).[6]

The limitations of 'taking over' a moment of health in this way are a consequence of both cultural difference – the contexts of meaning within which people situate their lives, their family relationships and their well-being – and power: 'medical interventions are not value free . . . [or] limited to the organic realm. Medicine is an agent of cultural change . . . The body which enters the clinic is a product of organic and social processes which are so intertwined it's impossible to engage with, or intervene in, either realm without impacting on the other' (Anderson, 1994: 39, 40). 'Colonial' categories of Aboriginality still structure many health encounters for Indigenous people. The comatose diabetic, for example, is assumed by police and ambulance officers to be drunk and put in the lock-up where he dies from lack of medical attention. '[O]n a daily basis this tragedy is re-enacted, albeit on a more mundane level' (Anderson, 1994: 43). 'Experienced, skilled workers do make mistakes of this order when dealing with Koori people – not only because they lack technical knowledge but because their actions continue to be driven by a colonial view of Aboriginal Australia' (Anderson, 1994: 31). More broadly, an experience of health care which repeats the conditions of inequality, lack of autonomy and diminished self-respect which contribute to the original patterns of disease will work to negate the long-term value of the care provided.

Different beliefs and practices concerning the nature and causes of illness can profoundly influence the effectiveness of health care as well as contribute to the confusion of both parties and the alienation and humiliation of the patient. 'With the pervasive influence of Western medicine in Australia, it is easy to lose sight of the differing underlying health beliefs of sub-sections of the Australian population . . . Even among Aborigines living in cities and towns of south-eastern Australia current understandings represent an amalgam of Western and Aboriginal belief' (Thompson, 1989: 192). Aboriginal conceptions of health focus less on disease and intervention than on the dynamics of extended family and community well-being as part of a network of 'inter-relationships between people and land, people and creator beings, and between people, which ideally stipulates interdependence within and between each set of relationships' (*NAHS*, 1989: ix). Moreover, following a diabetic diet or finding time for dialysis can be difficult when you are living in the social and economic conditions of many Aborigines. 'Is Aunty's dietary change only to be achieved by persistently telling her how to eat better? How might our strategies change if we focus on the family and not the individual?' (Anderson 1994: 43). Ian Anderson emphasises the need for doctor and patient to establish a consensus on how they will, together, approach the alleviation of suffering. 'Doctors must see that the extent to which people incorporate medical advice is not the responsibility of the patient alone. It's a problem of the doctor–patient relationship'. For Anderson, a Koori medical practitioner trained in conventional Western medicine, health practices in a community of both Indigenous and non-Indigenous people must involve processes of mutual recognition and negotiation of 'healing strategies' (1994: 42).

In this context the operation of the community-managed Aboriginal Medical Service is particularly important. A loose national structure of the AMS has emerged, with the National Aboriginal Community Centre Health Organisation (NACCHO) formed in 1997 as a peak body for the services. NACCHO has been negotiating framework agreements with key parties in health management state by state to assist the AMS to tame the absurdly fractured jumble of bureaucracies with which it must deal. NACCHO is consulted but not deeply involved in policy or funding decisions at state or national level and could not be called an equal partner in Aboriginal health delivery. Nevertheless, NACCHO is emerging as a major resource for governments and for Indigenous health, with the potential to work as a mediating body between governments and mainstream health delivery on the one hand and an expanded form of Indigenous self-managed health services on the other.

Self-determination and citizenship

Questions of self-determination and self-management are repeatedly determined to lie at the heart of Indigenous ill-health. Reflecting this, self-management and self-determination have been the official policy orientations of federal health delivery programmes for the past twenty-five years. But what has self-determination meant? Clearly, it has meant different things in practice as well as in theory – too many to be considered fully here. For government administrative bodies, however, notions of self-determination seem often to presuppose either a model of a universally accessible space – that is, contemporary liberal notions of the universal man and citizenship – or, more mundanely, the protocols of bureaucratic meeting procedure. While certainly not without value, these models are neither neutral nor universal. Put differently, the structure of bureaucratic consultation tends to reflect bureaucratic norms, not Aboriginal communication patterns. Or notions of self-determination may emphasise models of development, which have 'emerged as a Western panacea for the inequalities continuing in the aftermath of decolonisation' (Hunter, 1993: 267). But either way and despite effort at consultation, the question becomes stuck in the confusion of trying to 'deliver' self-determination as a service. 'Regardless of the political rhetoric of opportunity and empowerment, under whatever policy or platform, the structuring of Aboriginal lives continues. To suggest that this will not occur in the era of self-determination and self-management denies the institutional reliance on such policies and programs' (Hunter, 1993: 267). Indeed, despite 'de-institutionalisation', it seems that

> the control remains just as effective today whatever may be the rhetoric of government . . . [Many Aboriginal people] would say that economic dependence upon government and the restrictions placed upon them by discriminatory practices achieve the same result – their lives are controlled by others who share neither their culture nor their perspective . . . because they have not shared their history. (RCIADIC, 1991: Vol. 2: 502)

Overviewing governmental social justice initiatives of the 1980s the then Aboriginal and Torres Strait Islander Social Justice Commissioner Mick Dodson observed that 'self-determination, considered as a component of the Commonwealth social justice policy . . . [has operated as] a welfare measure directed at Aboriginal and Torres Strait Islander peoples . . . [which] rests on a policy decision taken by the Commonwealth Government *about* us' (1993: 43). Two years later Dodson warned: '[A]s long as the relationship between the state and Indigenous people is caught in a dynamic of dependence, any policy, no matter how you dress it up, will perpetuate the violation of our rights as peoples' (Dodson, 1995b: 20). Dodson argued that self-determination in fact turns on 'the great unposed question dividing Indigenous from non-indigenous Australians . . . The essence of the matter goes to asking the question which has never been put to our people: Do you consent?' (1993: 51).

This paradox of administratively conceived (but underfunded) 'self-determination' turns the argument back to the two ways of responding to, and understanding the reasons for, Aboriginal persistent ill-health. The first is in terms of rights as *entitlements*: of the history of administrative measures and the need for improved service delivery and accountability. The second is in terms of rights as *mutuality*: of being recognised as a participant in the inevitably shared and uncertain processes of political and social life – of recognising Indigenous people as interlocutors who are both different and at the same time, as Aboriginal artist Sally Morgan pointed out, part of us (RCIADIC, 1991: Vol. 2: 44)[7]. The first response emphasises equitable access to essential social commodities; the second approaches Aborigines not as recipients but as participants in constructing not only their own but the broader political life of the country. This goes beyond the goal of cultural sensitivity to the recognition of a process of ongoing negotiation; beyond the distribution of material goods to the production of the categories and relationships of understanding, power and social order. It is here, in this difficult place, that the question of self-determination bites home. The two responses closely interweave (distribution of material goods, for example, naturally affects power, while real access to social capabilities is a matter of power). In so doing they touch on what may be the particular questions and challenges posed by Indigenous people to practices of citizenship and to notions of political community, at least within liberal states. That is, the issue of Indigenous health and rights to health care raises the question of how, in a liberal state, we understand the principles of 'participation' and 'consent', of how we construct statehood. It questions not 'Aboriginality' but the nature of political community.

Essentially, since 1967, the Australian population has been hedging around the issue of what citizenship for Aboriginal people might mean. Long-standing inadequate funding and a lack of government accountability and coordination, despite announced policy goals and commitments, not only raise questions about the operations of government, although these questions are pressing. These failings raise fundamental questions also about the capacity or the willingness of our political order to reach accommodations or to 'deal with'

Aboriginal people rather than simply reduce them to 'problem' categories, failure, lack and threat.

Dodson puts the case for effective, rather than simply formal, recognition of Indigenous people as citizens who have entitlements. 'Policies and programs which rest primarily on a perception of need and powerlessness subtly reinforce the powerlessness of the recipients . . . The recognition of entitlement is in itself an act of empowerment' (Dodson, 1993: 7). Effective citizenship and equal rights remain key goals. But they can also be ambiguous goals. With the slow repeal of much of the more draconian and exclusionary legislation and regulations throughout the country, Aborigines have been expected, as Aboriginal lawyer Noel Pearson suggests, to become simply 'black Australians'. Two elements of this expectation are relevant here. One is that models of citizenship can contain the assimilationist assumption (at times made explicit), referred to earlier:

> The policy of assimilation means that all Aborigines and part-Aborigines are expected to attain the same manner of living as other Australians and to live as members of a single Australian community enjoying the same rights and privileges, accepting the same responsibilities, observing the same customs and influenced by the same beliefs, as other Australians. (Native Welfare Conference, in RCIADIC, 1991: Vol. 2: 510)

This is a model of citizenship as sameness and of entitlements as rights to that sameness. For most Indigenous people (as well as other social groups) it offers only the appearance, not the real possibility, of 'entry'. It turns on the crucial understanding that Aboriginal people are themselves 'other, something outside this – people not in fact part of this nation . . . [and then it offers them] a chance to "fit in" . . . by abandoning their particularity' (RCIADIC, 1991: Vol. 2: 511). Its goal is to treat what is different as the same and so to deny the process of negotiation and accommodation of difference and identity. The practical effects of this approach can be seen again and again in the actual dynamics of settler Australians' 'consultation' with Aboriginal people.

Assimilation has been officially repudiated, but the new models of 'self-determination' remain obscure. Efforts to provide Indigenous Australians with their entitlements, with 'access and equity', are eroded by the uncertainty of the non-indigenous population and institutions of what to make of Indigenous difference – or rather, of what seems to some an opportunistic mix of difference and sameness. Different relationships to land – in a sense, the crucial original difference – remain one of the more evident and disturbing encounters, particularly since the Mabo decision opened the way for Indigenous people to make claims to native title on certain categories of land. Facing the uncertainty of negotiating mutually acceptable and co-existing land uses rather than the certainty of a single unitary title has proved highly unsettling for many non-indigenous organisations and people. A choice between two options – neither of which is likely to be viable – seems implicit in the insistence on certainty. Indigenous people can be different – they can take their land rights (carefully delimited to protect non-indigenous mining, farming, commercial and electoral interests) and go home to, as it were, the remnants to work out their own health and other problems. Or they can be just like 'us' and play by 'our' rules. Caught somewhere between these poles, and despite the efforts and successes of particular programmes, the broad operational understanding of Indigenous health care has remained stuck in 'charity', dependence and welfarism.

Underpinning the real policy, conceptual and practical difficulties of effectively repudiating assimilationist constructions of citizenship, participation and equity may be a second element in the expectation that Indigenous people will become 'black Australians'. This is the construction of the person and of political community – broadly liberal and to some extent Lockean constructions – upon which understanding of participation and consent are in part predicated. Here, as discussed in chapter 2, political community is imagined as ideally founded upon a universal public space which emerges literally or metaphorically out of the free agreement of rational people (the universal man) or through the operation of a universal proceduralism. 'Participation' thus tends to occur within boundaries already defined by particular and rather narrow models of the person and of community. But as the discussion of *terra nullius* suggested, the assertion of Australia as a state drew not on a slow process of accommodation with Aboriginal society but on classifying Aboriginal people as not rational, or incapable of political community or of the consent that, for liberal models of political community, underpins participation. The 'dispossession . . . [of the Aboriginal people] underwrote the development of the nation' (Brennan, in Dodson 1995a: 43) not only because the killing and quarantining of Indigenous people made their land available for settlers and their economic activity, but because the construction of the state and of citizenship was in significant ways predicated on the constitution of the natives as outcasts, inferior, beyond community. Aboriginal people's relationship to the scope of 'universal man', and to the forms of citizenship or self-determination still within the ambit of this figure, remains at best ambiguous.

The processes available to Indigenous people to take part in citizenship have too easily become, then, akin to charity or to policing. The Queensland liaison officers, policing every aspect of those Indigenous lives under their purview in the 1960s and 1970s, could quite reasonably have considered themselves to be assisting Aboriginal people to claim their entitlements, overcome their disadvantages and participate in modern life. Policies of self-determination have not been able effectively to step out of this dynamic. The HREOC, commenting on the Act of Parliament which provides the key legislative underpinning for Indigenous rights in Australia, noted: 'The Racial Discrimination Act provides for "special measures" to be taken to redress disadvantage.' However, as it stands the Act 'cannot adequately protect the cultural rights and the right to self deter-mination of Aboriginal and Torres Strait Islander people. The reliance on the special measure provisions of the Act to justify different treatment implies that at some point special measures should cease and mainstream policies apply' (HREOC, 1994: 9).

This is the ambivalence of claims to citizenship and participation; it is also the ambivalence of notions of rights – an ambivalence that this the present examination has approached by referring to rights as both a way of asking ques-tions and a form of answer which does not exhaust the question. Indigenous people claim citizenship, participation and rights – and doing so has made avail-able significant political leverage as well as some access to resources. Perhaps more fundamentally it has provided Aboriginal people with one way of articu-lating their suffering, their self-respect and their aspirations to be treated with respect and to shape their own lives. The practices, language and institutions of citizenship and rights are certainly not monolithic, despite the power and persistence of the dominant models. The operation of the courts system, for example, both indicates the limitations of this key set of frameworks and practices to respond, in its designated place and moment of action, to systemic alienation and marginalisation, and has provided one of the most potent levers by which Aboriginal people can stake their own claim in Australian political life. But what is being fought over is not entry into a community of sameness, where a 'problem' people seem to just fail to make the grade, but a shift in the dominant constructions of citizenship, participation and rights.

Participation as the acceptance of mutuality is important because it is a rejection of the subtle assertion of an exclusionary sameness as the basis of political community. It is important also as a reminder of the need to work *with* difference and not quarantine it 'elsewhere'. One response to have come from both some Indigenous and non-indigenous people to the question of self-determination has been to assume that once Aborigines are on their land their other problems, such as ill-health, will evaporate; or that once whites are out of the way, Aborigines will return naturally to their traditional ways. But even leaving aside those many Aborigines with no real access to traditional lands, Aboriginal societies are in radical transition and traditional customs are not necessarily simply there waiting to be recovered. Interpretations of Mabo, for example, can have an anachronistic element, seeming to require Aboriginal people to return to a state of 'otherness', but the judgment was a recognition, not of native title in 1788, but of its on-going vitality and place in contempo-rary Australian political life.

Self-determination, as Mick Dodson has pointed out, is a process. It is a process that does not flow simply from an original or foundational consent, but one that flows from the act of asking and listening, the work of negotiating 'every issue concerning the historical and present status, entitlements, treatment and aspirations of Aboriginal and Torres Strait Islander peoples . . . The right to self-determination is the right to make decisions' (Dodson, 1993: 41). Self-determination for Aborigines requires non-indigenous institutions and people to be prepared to enter the process that was originally denied – to negotiate, to accommodate Aboriginal people as part of the decision-making, to accept uncertainty of outcome and in some cases significant change in their own institutional patterns and practices. There is little sign of this preparedness in the current political climate in Australia, yet there is also a growing restlessness as evidence of pointless trauma, the violence of destructive policy and rifts between white and Indigenous accounts of the recent past become increasingly obvious and demanding of explanation.

While of great significance, the gaining of formal citizenship and the recognition of native title did not markedly affect health or education or custodial rates or indeed the life experiences of most Aboriginal people. The empowerment of some groups through, for example, gaining land rights does not automatically provide either the funds or the range of capacities needed to meet complex health needs. Claims to citizenship and real participation for Indigenous people, but also debate about the nature of citizenship, need to be pursued across each area of interaction. It is through the process of negotiating what self-determination might mean in regard to particular aspects of education, health, law, policing, land rights, and so on, that the practical constitution of intercommunal life in Australia can shift. Reconciliation, mutual respect or dialogue do not lay claim to an ideal or essential space of exchange; that requires the on-going effort to create workable spaces. In this sense rights as entitlements and as the mutual recognition that makes negotiation possible are entwined. The enjoyment of rights, like participation in political community, is ultimately a practical matter.

What is to be decided and how, are themselves part of the process of self-determination or dialogue between and within constituencies. Dialogue – the conversations within, across and among cultures – occurs in particular historical, political and practical contexts. But it can nevertheless be 'open' in the sense of having outcomes that are not heavily predetermined and if all parties involved are prepared to accept change. The concept of rights that operates (weakly) under forms of assimilation has required change only on the part of Indigenous people – if supposedly intended for 'their benefit'. For the rights that articulate self-determination, *all* parties must accept change. For non-indigenous society, structures and institutions, accommodation involves listening to and engaging with Indigenous people and social forms in a way that accepts the possibility of 'loss' of control and the fluidity that negotiation brings. That is, it involves 'respecting the human rights' of Indigenous people. 'If the demand [for forms of self-determination] far exceeds what governments and the broader community are prepared to accept as appropriate then so will be set the ambit for negotiation or determination of the issue' (RCIADIC, 1991: Vol. 2: 509). The assertion of Indigenous rights is the *entry* into such open-ended processes of accommodation; it does not resolve or order those processes. This does not mean that such processes of mutual adjustment are without institutional structure or context, providing not certainty, but some reliability of exchange and engagement. Nor does it mean that Aboriginal people just 'take the land' or continue unhindered with the levels of personal violence that have scarred their communities. Again in the words of Mick Dodson:

> while Indigenous peoples have the right to retain our culture, this is not an absolute 'context-free' right, irrespective of other factors ... The notion that 'universal human rights' provide a clear resolution for every situation is overly simplistic. There are different sets of rights at play and they will, at times, conflict. This debate has particular significance in Australia in relation to the recognition of customary law. No general rule provides a guide for which right has primacy. The competing considerations need to be balanced, *by all peoples concerned*, in respect of each site of conflict (Dodson, 1995a: 68).

There is nothing inevitable about the process of negotiation. And it is far from a meeting of equal parties. History provides good reason for ambivalence about trusting the processes of engagement, particularly, of course; for indigenous peoples. But nor might it be so easy to sidestep the challenges of living together without embedding patterns of marginalisation. An inability or a refusal to engage would not be cost-free, as interracial and intersocial conflicts around the globe, or simply the confinements of rigid and intolerant societies, scored with entrenched suffering, suggest. And 'relations of power are not the whole story. Arguments of justice, consistency of principle and moral appeal remain important (though by no means determinative) as indeed they have been throughout Australia's recent grappling with indigenous rights', while power is itself woven with questions of value (Webber, 2000: 74).

Entering conversations with Aboriginal communities and people, over health, policing, education, land, dance, music, family and so on, provides and demands the opportunity to open the door of Australia's political life in the broadest sense of the word, just as Mabo opened a space for a law that is outside, but now intertwined with, Australian common law. The slow process of gaining land rights has tentatively recognised Aboriginal people as having a 'special' place in the dynamics of Australian political life. This 'specialness' is being vigorously fought by those (such as the One Nation Party) who believe that egalitarian values, or community, demand sameness; but, if it continues, this development might rather mean more open and complex avenues of participation in political life for Australians more generally. To recognise Indigenous people as interlocutors on their own terms, in their own, various selves, also requires an acknowledgment of the history of the Australian state. That history, in its general sweep but also its particular, localised and diverse legacy of encounters, is a valuable shared resource for exchange. 'People draw upon [the national past] in their arguments and their claims, and as they do, they suggest what is most valuable, and what should be left behind' (Webber, 2000: 80). An apology is part of this, as could be a treaty process. An apology may be useful for the process of healing, to which many Aboriginal people refer; it would also explicitly recognise Aboriginal people as participants and recognise the fact and the character of the history to the conversation – theirs and (for what can sweepingly be called 'mainstream' Australia) ours.

Participation, or engagement, is intrinsically an open-ended ethic, with, in practice, multiple parties. This is not to say, however, that on a practical level there are no structures for situating dialogue, no mechanisms for moving forward or localised histories providing impetus and shaping pathways. Mutual accommodation is a lengthy, on-going and many-sided process that requires organs of interaction and collaboration, as well as flexibility (Webber, 2000). In the health arena, the AMS and the NACCHO were set up by Indigenous people to work with both Indigenous health needs and understandings and the health resources and systems of the wider community. Other local or national bodies may well emerge. The AMS was one of the first Indigenous institutional efforts to set out to assert effective self-determination within the context of Australian political and social systems. These bodies, with which there is already some history of negotiation, provide a place to start.[8]

The processes of negotiation are not purely a domestic Australian matter, as the Mabo case also reminds us. As a tenet of international law since the seventeenth century, the principle of *terra nullius* was part of that system which, certainly not without debate, articulated how to deal with difference within the ambit of the 'civilised' states of Christian Europe on the one hand – that is, through principles of non-interference in sovereign jurisdictions – and how to deal with the difference between these 'sovereign jurisdictions' and the 'less civilised' races or the 'lawless savages' on the other hand. *Terra nullius* has been intrinsic to the language and processes of colonisation and the history of the state system. It has not been a static principle. The high court decision which overturned its application in the Mabo case was, in the broadest sense, part of the on-going revolutions of the state system that are gestured to as imperialism, colonisation and the slow mutations of decolonisation. It was more directly part of the international legal and political conversation regarding indigeneity and what stand as the criteria and constitution of political community.

The majority judgment in that case drew partly on international legal norms and decisions which are now marked by decades of decolonisation. In so recognising Aborigines as a people or a political body, with a way of life and a law, this decision amended the standing of Indigenous people within common law: 'The High Court's judgement [recognising native title] . . . was, in itself, an act of reconciliation between two laws. It declared the common law of Australia and recognised what has always been true in the law of Indigenous Australians' (Dodson, 1993: 13). In fact the Mabo decision was a very public transaction between three laws that are not neatly distinct but evolving and historically interpenetrating: Australian common law, traditional and continuing Indigenous law and international law in the form, most importantly for this case, of the Convention on the Elimination of All Forms of Racial Discrimination,[9] as well as a body of case law. Thus, in this case, the appeal to or recognition of rights that predate the establishment of the state or the colony does not depend upon a claim to universalism or to 'man in nature' or a veil of ignorance, but rather recognises the process of negotiation and the need to deal across and between actual political communities that are the starting-point of rights as participation.

The challenge to re-work the practices of citizenship that Indigenous people present to Australian political life and non-indigenous people, to the liberal norms of the state and to the complex function of those norms in the operation of the state system, again underlines the paucity of arguments which remain closed within an opposition between citizenship rights and the 'rights of man', or the particularity of the state and the universal. The 'rights of man' have to a significant extent been part of the historical articulation of a dominant set of practices and a language of the state and the citizen – a set of practices in which various categories of people have had little or no effective place. At the same time 'citizenship' is not a settled category limited to black letter law within the allegedly clear confines of state jurisdictions. It is a slowly shifting set of transactions constituted and shaped by the changing dynamics of world politics and the state system, as well as by the lives of people, intersecting constituencies and the dynamics of social institutions and orders within states.

NOTES

1   'We are still the stereotyped welfare class of people as viewed by the Australian public. Sadly, deep down we view ourselves in a similar way . . . We are, with some exceptions, in every demeaning sense, largely dependent on our annual welfare handout' (Perkins, in Hunter, 1993: 264–5).

2   Different names are commonly used to refer to Aboriginal people from different regions. Names include Murri (north-eastern) and Koori (south-eastern). These are not clan or tribal names.

3   This tension between different dimensions of rights is central to a debate within the Indigenous community between those who advocate pursuit of political relationship with settler Australia through an emphasis on rights, and the rejection of that position, because of the welfare dependence with which it has become associated. This second view emphasises instead the assertion of and quest for economic self-determination, identifying economic power as key to survival.

4   As the preliminary Water Report noted: 'The consultation process with Aboriginal and Torres Strait Islander people . . . is a matter of serious concern. Much of the information

transmitted in technical discussions is either irrelevant or meaningless to people with a different cultural or historical experience. Despite this, [Indigenous] community councils are asked to make decisions on million dollar projects. Consultants employed to advise on projects are often not aware of the wider needs of the community. There is very little real opportunity for communities to negotiate alternative options' (HREOC, 1994: 11–12).

5　At the same time Aboriginal clinics and organisations are, rather ironically, given stringent accountability mechanisms.

6　'The construction of problems to fit solutions is particularly seductive for health, where the medicalisation of social problems appeals to both political and health care delivery systems' (Hunter, 1993: 266).

7　As Sally Morgan has said: 'In the telling [of our stories] we assert the validity of our own experiences and we call the silence of two hundred years a lie. And it is important to you, the listener, because like it or not, we are a part of you. We have to find a way of living together in this counting, and that will only come when our hearts, minds and wills are set towards reconciliation' (RCIADIC, 1991: Vol. 2: 44).

8　Many Aboriginal community councils and associations work effectively as a third tier of government. '[T]hey not only have the potential to establish and deliver essential services: in the fullest form they can operate as the medium of full community self-government' (Dodson, 1993: 59).

9　CERD was fully ratified and then incorporated into Australian domestic law in 1975, in the form of the Racial Discrimination Act. This Act played a key role in the judgment in Mabo.

7

Conclusion

What is the use of having a right of free speech if no one is listening. (Aboriginal artist Sally Morgan, Radio National, 10 November 1995)

THE TERRAIN OF human rights is broad and there are many ways of crossing it. Moreover, it is a terrain that is incoherent and contradictory, and full of both vehemence and uncertainty. This reflection on rights has sought to take a particular path across that broad and rocky terrain, particularly in regard to the promotion of human rights practices and approaches in international life – a life that does not start at the borders but one which in various ways includes us all. It argues for a shift in approach – a greater preparedness to reflect on some of the categories by which we construct our sense of human rights and some acknowledgment of the limits of our understanding, or even of our ignorance, of the complex life to which these categories, particularly that of the human, refer. The purpose of this questioning is not to reject outright classical perspectives and mechanisms or to elaborate a new vision of human rights. It is more simply to enable a better human rights practice – that is, to enable a rights practice which is more observant of and responsive to the spectrum of injury that we collectively inflict and endure, more open to engagement over the long term with the complexities of the actual social practices, institutions and circumstances in which many forms of abuse are embedded, and which is at the least oriented no less towards the reconstitution of social and political relationships and structures shaped by violence and humiliation than it is towards the condemnation of the perpetrators. It is to enable a practice that is less preoccupied with promoting a gilded vision of its own self-image as the truth and, while not abandoning tools and experience, more willing to listen to and work with others. It is these concerns that have been explored in the case studies.

The language of human rights has emerged as part of the ambiguous possibilities and shifting forms of the modern state – the state not solely imagined as contained within its borders but understood as part of the broader international dynamic by virtue of which borders and states, as such, exist. The transformations of this language of human rights, as of the forms of governance with which it is so intimately connected, are an on-going and largely unpredictable process. It is a language or a set of tools which can work in various ways and to various effects, and which has a complex, dense accumulation of traditions, debates and practices. What is meant by human rights in practice (and how widespread and functional the international standard in fact is) will evolve, if at all, not as a Western concept exported elsewhere, but through the pressures of interaction within and between communities caught up in the patterns of conflict that collective suffering reflects and generates. For this argument, the significance and much of the power in contemporary international life of concepts and practices of rights lie in their use as a means of articulating and recognising suffering, of questioning the use or generation of systemically imposed injury as a form of political organisation or a means of constructing community and, counterposed to the infliction of suffering, of enabling relationships of active respect.

Running through human rights practices and approaches, however, particularly in international 'rights talk', is the dominant model, or family of models, of rights, discussed in chapter 2. In this model, rights have been classically constructed in terms of the legally defined relationship between the individual and the state – the notional contract. Rights fulfil, in this construction, two functions. They stand as the fundamental (political) expression of the subject; and they act as those mechanisms that constrain infringements by the state (or the majority) on the individual's proper exercise of his or her freedoms and interests. Thus rights protect both the individual from incursions by the state and the individual's interests in the context of the state. This way of conceptualising human rights has been fundamental to the evolution and the project of the modern free-market liberal democratic state. It has provided a remarkably powerful framework for the characterisation of both the individual and political community and for the identification of abuse. Moreover it has to a significant extent shaped the terms in which general debate over human rights in international politics has been repeatedly cast, particularly the polarity of universal and relative values, of the 'rights of man' and the citizen's rights, and of political and economic (or social or cultural) rights.

In this construction of rights, the individual's freedoms or interests may be conceptualised as natural and as (notionally) pre-existing the state; rights are then understood as the exercise and protection of inherent attributes through the medium of the state, as flowing from the individual and transcending the state. Here the claims for human rights as the essential attributes and expression of the abstract universal individual are cast and aspirations for individual liberty or equality are spoken as ontological truths or natural destinations. Or rights may be seen more pragmatically as socially conditioned mechanisms not so much grounded in nature as located in the legal and political apparatus of the state or in agreements among states – as the legal and quasi-legal relationships by which citizens' claims for their freedoms or entitlements against each other or the state can be considered. Rights in this case stand as a broader field of entitlements and obligations of which 'human rights' comprise a subcategory. Thus the language of rights in this dominant family of models is, in very broad terms, characterised by two voices – an ontological universalist approach and a more utilitarian administrative emphasis on civic virtue. These two voices or positions can be understood as competing, as an ontological 'rights of man' versus a more utilitarian 'civil rights'. Or the legislative and utilitarian can be understood as an expression of an underlying ontology. (For example, Dworkin in *Taking Rights Seriously* (1977) argues for the integrity of legislation and principle.) Or the utilitarian approach can assume that it grasps, not a universal ontology of the human, but the principles of modern rational social progress. Within broadly liberal institutions, in practice at least, the two approaches often work in tandem.

The language of universal human rights imagines it is talking to and for all the world, calling on both the persistence of people's aspirations for non-violence or justice or compassion in the face of the experience of violence, exploitation or marginalisation, as well as on the historically hegemonic power of modern liberal democracies to back this claim. This category of the universal, however, is less an expression of the natural shape of things than part of the conceptual construction of the state and of specific models of citizenship. Within classical liberalism the rights of universal man are rights within a state just as the trope of universal man emerged as an imagined authoritative origin for the state. The contract is with the state, and the human rights of the individual are recognised and upheld by the duties of the state. Rights are conceived as precisely that means by which the sovereignty of the individual citizen within the state is in principle defined. But the sovereignty of the citizen rests upon the prior sovereignty of the state and its capacity to assert that sovereignty in the world. Within this language of rights the individual and the state are mutually constitutive fundamentals locked, at this level of abstraction at any rate, in a permanently circular relationship. The categories of the state and the individual produce each other. It is *this* construction of human rights which gives so much purchase to the question of whether rights belong to the individual (the 'rights of man') and are articulated only by the state or whether they are located primarily (or even solely) in the legal technologies of the state (the 'rights of the citizen'). It is this construction of rights which establishes and counterposes these two – and only these – sources of legitimate authority or origin for claims of rights.

This dominant construction of human rights establishes a quite particular way of imagining and constituting both the individual person and the political community or relationship. In so doing, it also highlights a narrow, if significant, range of political injury. The attributes and aspirations of the highly abstracted conceptualisation of the individual subject produced by this approach become the yardstick for the universal, but it is a yardstick that for many people – Indigenous youths in Australian jails or low-caste women in Bangladesh, for example, or children dying of diarrhoea across Africa – has proved in practice to have little to say. Moreover, as the discussion of Indigenous health in Australia indicates, as a basis for addressing equality in political community it can impose a subtle but powerful uniformity which further entrenches exclusion and abuse. Even the insight afforded by the figure of the autonomous self-interested individual into educated urban youths in Beijing demonstrating at the symbolic heart of state power can be flawed and misleading.

The state, as the other half of this partnership, is similarly abstracted and obscure. For much rights talk the form of the state is ideally one of a neutral rationality, a transparent container and mediator of the interests of citizens. The category of the state is regularly cast as intrinsically other than the broader social domain, which may be given its own special category of 'civil society' (a kind of community, however, to which it seems only politically 'advanced' societies can aspire). This radical bifurcation of state and society goes beyond the observation that the ending of a particular regime can remove the direct source of much violence or exploitation and allow a reconstitution of political life. Here the state occupies a position on a sliding scale between an ideal minimalism, where it protects the free flow of pre-given subjects and approaches a universalism of form, and an oppressive monolith, obstructing that free flow. But the discussion of both the Tiananmen Square killings and Aboriginal health suggests that the state is a multiple, dynamic reality with diverse and sometimes contradictory commitments, interests and inertias, that retains access to overwhelming force but is also deeply interwoven with many, perhaps almost all, aspects of life. In extreme forms, the figure of the 'state-as-tank', exemplified in much Western response to the Tiananmen massacre, can hinder our ability to understand or work to untie abuse. Certainly where abuse is concerned, this is a narrow, restrictive understanding of power, of political relationship, and of the place and mechanism of injury within it.

Or, in mirror-contrast to this divorce between state and society, for those strong communitarian perspectives which reject rights universalism and, for example, uphold the 'Asian Way', community is often understood as ultimately absorbed and bounded by the state. Thus the real and persistent difficulties of working across cultural and institutional differences are rewritten into an apparently philosophical confrontation between universal and relative truth. But, as was said in chapter 3, rather than being intrinsic to the nature of moral life, this particular confrontation seems to be rooted in, and a reflection on, the history of the Westphalian state and state system. As Walker suggests (1993), the idea of the sovereignty and legitimacy of the modern state, which in part emerged in response to the need to contain the violence of competing dogmatic claims to universal truth, itself works as a hinge between a conception of universality (whether the state is imagined as that political order founded upon a figure of universal man or as a neutral proceduralism that is everywhere efficacious) and a conception of differentiation – the particularity of territory, of culture, and of the exercise of power that define the state. The history of colonialism has further compounded this dynamic. It is here that the pseudo-choice of human rights as either a matter of abstract universalism or of relativism (neatly identified with the contours of the state) is claimed to be definitive.

Thus to step aside from the effort to ground once and for all an orientation towards non-injury, a respect for or even a cherishing of others in models of universality is to embrace neither relativism nor an ethical vacuum. The often rather parochial universals by which the modern citizen–individual is conceptualised are a mechanism for elaborating particular limits for particular kinds of political arrangement. They have value as such. But they do not do justice to the rich complexity of people,[1] nor should they be required to do so. Preoccupation with arriving at universals as fixed propositional truths, beyond the most general injunctions, may simply indicate a highly questionable belief in the pre-eminence of the conceptual domain, according to which what is most important in our interactions is an unvarying propositional product.

As well as the debate between universal and relative values, international rights talk often reflects a preoccupation with the contract between individual and state in other, more direct, ways. Certain kinds of abuse, particularly those that involve overt confrontation with arms of the state, are noted; systemic injury which is embedded in other patterns of social practice (as is the case with much abuse of women, for example) or reflects extreme social dislocation or an underresourced or incompetent rather than oppressive government, are relatively invisible or, if visible, draw little international response. Those widespread patterns of abuse which occur in the pursuit of another kind of free flow – that of capital and wealth creation – and which are frequently embedded as much or more in international economic dynamics as in structures of a particular state often sink into profound darkness.

Perhaps because it is assumed that we in the liberal democracies already know well enough what the person is and what constitutes proper political arrangements, human rights are often promoted internationally as a message from one state to another. Moreover the message of rights is often implicitly or explicitly a threat. It is not surprising that an understanding of rights which situates them finally and overwhelmingly in the relationship between individual and state (as moving from oppressive to transparent) sees success or failure at pressuring governments as the crucial test in the pursuit of rights. The often complex and obdurate problems around which abuse erupts most violently are referred for solution to what is assumed to be 'an achieved body of principles and norms and rules already codified in texts and traditions' (Walker, 1993: 50). This approach is liberal in principle but realist in method; explicit or implicit confrontation is its primary defining tool.

The liberal construction of rights, and of international relations, has produced not only an articulation of principles but an emphasis on rights regimes and a framework of UN mechanisms and international institution building to support these principles. Through standard-setting and monitoring activities, formal and informal regimes enable some work across states on the gradual processes by which national institutions and political processes take shape and are reconstituted to be undertaken. Shared mechanisms for broaching practical problems in even this most sensitive area become thinkable. Yet much of this work remains distant from the concrete social relationships within which human rights abuse is often embedded. Patterns of suffering and eruptions of violence can raise questions that are intimate to the life of a community. International regimes would need to step well beyond the realms of technocratic elite networking, valuable though this can sometimes be, to penetrate the patterns of legitimacy, the distributions of power, within the lives of the cooperating states and the communities and institutions within and between them, to have sustained impact on human rights observance.

This broadly liberal construction of rights, in practice often both contractarian and utilitarian, has generated a complex network of practices. To question its terms and seek to step aside from its claim to encompass both the human and the human community is not to dismiss the aspirations, the particular forms of freedom, justice and equality, to which it gives priority. And it is certainly not to make light of the emphasis on institution building or the legal and administrative technologies of rights, which are an essential element of working rights practices. Moreover the practices that have emerged under or might be claimed by the rubric of the liberal construction of human rights are not always simply reducible to its theoretical models and their general implications. The significance of the use of particular mechanisms or approaches can depend on their context and application as much as or more than upon their more broadly apparent range of inbuilt possibilities, inhibitions and exclusions. Rights are 'protean and irresolute signifiers, varying not only across time and culture, but across the other vectors of power whose crossing indeed they are sometimes deployed to effect' (Brown, 1995: 97). Tools can have a number of uses and be turned to a number of purposes; but in themselves they represent neither the truth nor error incarnate.

In practice, as Wendy Brown and others have argued, the contemporary institutional and legal architectures of human rights within liberal democratic states have provided an array of mechanisms which can produce varying, even contradictory effects: 'rights converge with powers of social stratification and lines of social demarcation in ways that extend as often as attenuate these powers and lines' (Brown, 1995: 98). The life conditions of many Indigenous people in Australia are one example of how the contemporary operation of rights mechanisms in one particular liberal democracy has failed to deal adequately with severe, life-endangering marginalisation. In this case, the evolving framework of rights has both at certain points compounded abuse and at others provided crucial means for responding to it.

In the international domain the dominant approach to the promotion of human rights rarely acknowledges that what has been accumulated is a problematic but substantial array of practices that may indeed prove valuable in particular circumstances.[2] On the contrary, the liberal construction of rights is repeatedly put forward as the definitive word on complex values such as freedom, justice or equality. There is little acknowledgment that this model of human rights, which claims so much, can produce systemic myopia as well as its own forms of abuse, or that the actual history of rights practices has been experienced in sharply different ways by people who at any given time were included or occluded by its terms. Stepping back from these architectures of rights, without negating them in blanket fashion, can allow us to weigh our purposes and our methods in pursuing rights enhancement.

This reflection on human rights has approached its subject in an open-ended way, and some things may be lost as well as gained by this. The open-endedness is part of the effort to take issues of human rights back to what are understood here as their most significant broad purposes and orientations. That is, to take them back to the articulation and recognition of suffering and the questions with which the systemic infliction of suffering can confront us – back to the breadth of questions of how we value each other in the dynamics of the contemporary world, or, more sparely, to a consideration of how we harm each other and how such knots of harm may be loosened or undone. The dominant models of human rights could be understood as one prominent part of a more heterogeneous set of answers to such questions – a Western modernist jurisprudential response, which is itself embedded in complex arrangements of social institutions, social procedures, enforcement mechanisms and training of citizens. In the breadth and complexity of their practice, these answers are not to be essentialised and captured as inherently good or bad; the primary point here, however, is that they do not exhaust the questions.

The approach taken in this argument also raises questions that have only been touched on here. One of the more pressing is the question of injury. This argument begins less with a positive principle of human rights than with suffering and injury. Yet as a category for political or social inquiry, suffering is difficult to contain. It is a core reality of and a familiar companion to every individual's life and perhaps, as one of Nadine Gordimer's character's comments in *The House Gun* (1998), the only real democracy – one avenue to the experience, in all its living complexity, of what we share. But when does suffering become also abuse? Is suffering that is inflicted and legitimised as a foundation or consequence of political organisation, or as a means of asserting the potency of others, abuse? What are the processes by which the experience of suffering comes to be regarded, by the sufferers and by others, as a matter for political action? According to what forces do the thresholds of the tolerable and of the political shift? Those who benefit from the patterns of others' suffering, or else who do not bear its consequences, can too easily assume familiarity with the boundaries of the tolerable and of the political. Recognition of the intolerable is a dynamic understanding that learns and revises. Yet this is not to say that abuse, or the infliction of suffering as an instrument of political life, is an easily malleable category that transforms lightly, without residue, from time and place. Rather it seems more likely to be one of the slow-changing bedrocks of the human landscape.

Human rights practices are not part of a progression to perfection, or its approximation, but a way of working with the systemic generation of suffering. They offer not so much an answer to the persistent problems of living together as a way of going about these problems in contemporary circumstances. The 'way we go about these problems' is indeed a matter of political institutions and structure and of the social practices in which the patterns on the water which we identify as our lives take shape. But despite the vital significance of political structure to generating or countering abuse, this does not mean that human rights can be finally secured by getting right some particular model of the system. Nor does respect for rights resolve in advance what valuing people might actually mean in particular circumstances. And nor does it automatically resolve issues of competing entitlements. In the epigraph to this chapter, the Aboriginal artist Sally Morgan points to the limits of the legal architectures of rights in a political, institutional and cultural context where there is insufficient emphasis on communication, exchange and listening, where what is different or unexpected may be encountered. To be recognised as a bearer of rights is in the first instance to be accepted as part of the effort to work out in practical terms and without violence what valuing people might mean in this circum-stance and life.

Countering abuse is a practical matter which involves specific institutional, and often legal, mechanisms – mechanisms that may often be broadly repeat-able from one cultural setting to others. Much of the accumulated practice of the liberal jurisprudential and administrative traditions can be relevant here. Nevertheless legal (and policing) solutions can prove disastrously insufficient. It seems hardly surprising, for example, that female infanticide in western China is hardly touched by legal prohibition. Nor has formal citizenship, bolstered by anti-discrimination legislation, proved a sufficient response to the marginalisa-tion and 'outcasting' of Indigenous Australians. Moreover, as the discussion of

Aboriginal health underlines, nor do welfare remedies necessarily make up what is lacking from formal, politico-legal solutions.

To the extent that notions of human rights are a way of grappling with how to live well together, with constructing relationships which do not rely upon injury, they are about community. Indeed part of the potency of the relativist position in its classic conflict with universalism is that relativism promises greater sensitivity to the contours of local realities and actual communities than does the often strident declaration of an irreducible morality. As with the category of 'human' in human rights, addressed in chapter 1, 'community' can be a paradoxical term in this discussion, for notions of human rights both appeal to and challenge the structure and experience of community.

On the one hand, rights practices more broadly can constitute mechanisms for building and sustaining particular kinds of communities – for establishing forms of participative civility, for asserting or claiming a role as interlocutor, or sufficient membership of the community as one's right to participate and to be recognised as a participant in a particular domain of interactions. Rights, Marx argued, are 'only exercised in community with others' and 'their content is participation in community' (1972: 39). 'For the historically disempowered, the conferring of rights is symbolic of all the denied aspects of their humanity: rights imply a respect that places one in the referential range of self and others, that elevates one's status from human body to social being' (Williams, in Brown, 1995: 96). In this sense rights practices are not grounded in and need not entail strong assertions of individualism, for in practice and fundamentally they involve the recognition of the mutuality of our lives – of being part of the 'referential range of self and others'.

Indeed human rights are sometimes defined as 'co-extensive with membership in the community', with the possession of rights defining 'recognition . . . as a member of our community' (Bernstein, 1993: 29). In practical terms, when people are working to encourage conditions in which rights practices are possible, or are endeavouring to establish particular rights practices by embedding certain kinds of activities, approaches and restraints, they are nearly always working within some form of bounded community. Particular rights make sense, then, within the referential field of a particular world of interaction. This is the grounded but also exclusionary sense of community that is usually equated with the state and its legal structures but which is certainly not limited to the state – the obligations to and from others who are part of a distinctive social or economic matrix, for whom you occupy a position, a set of agencies and of proper expectations. Rights as specific entitlements, established by law or custom or institutional practice, are defined, enforced and evolve through reference to such sets of relationships.

At the same time the notion and often the practices of human rights – and the recognition of abuse – problematise community and its sense of shared, if

articulated and differentiated, identities and its natural exclusions and boundaries. Confrontation with rights abuse can show us unexpectedly 'the face of the
victim', a face in which awareness of the borders of our interest or concern, or
of the barriers (of race, gender, class, ideology, nationality, and so on) by which
our identities are articulated and which are so often the sites of abuse is juxta-
posed uncomfortably with a recognition of connection or of a common vulnerability. Thus it can question our sense of ourselves and of others and the social
and political priorities and practices which are the matrix of those identities. It
can demand that we see ourselves through the eyes of the victim. When cast
in general terms such questions are rhetorical – a general affirmation of the
priority of people. But in practice they are searching, and answers to their
conundrums of identities, commonalities, distances and dangers rarely seem
easy or obvious.

In this sense the idea of human rights suggests the possibility of a participation that is not exclusionary and that goes beyond the lived experience of a
common life. It recognises the possibility of mutuality across division and
emphasises the reality, with effort, of communication and shared understanding. This may be in part why we often talk about 'recognising' human rights –
not because the rights in question are necessarily an interior commodity awaiting recognition but because we are seeing a connection, identifying a commonality, recognising some element of 'ourselves', and so entering the process
of relearning and reshaping 'ourselves'. It is a recognition of interconnectedness. This is a recognition more likely to shake and disturb our sense of the way
things are than it is to offer reassurance. But it may be the great value of the
mixed bag of human rights that it keeps raising unsettling questions around
its own fundamental categories of human and community (or relationship),
categories that are not fixed so easily into those of individual and state.

This is certainly not to reach for an all-inclusive universal community of
humanity. (It can be too easy, with such an imaginary universe in mind, to think
that we can speak for all being and so avoid the difficulty of speaking from our
own lives.) Rather, it is more simply an emphasis on linkage, on the potential for
and (if we are to counter or avoid abuse) the necessity of communication and
engagement with others, on the absolutely ordinary (and often unsuccessful)
work of enabling mutuality – community as process. Thus community and the
communication which is part of it are not only an effort to translate 'them' into
'us', the strange into the familiar – a bounded process – but an open-ended relationship, to which listening, openness to being changed and to catching echoes
of the foreign within the familiar, and preparedness to work with and accept
difference are fundamental.

In practice, working with human rights may often involve assisting the
emergence of strategies by which the excluded can speak more effectively to
the processes which shape their lives. A working human rights practice may

essentially operate as a way of recognising others as interlocutors, acknowledging interconnections and common vulnerabilites across divisions that do not go away. Such processes are not particularly a matter of sentiment. All the case studies, in one way or another, turn on this point. Progress for East Timor, for example, requires of the international financial, peace-building and aid community the mundane but difficult process of taking the time to work on the ground with the East Timorese, of drawing on accumulated knowledge of other cases while holding back the imposition of 'solutions'. The emphasis on reconcialition by some leading figures in East Timor at present – an emphasis not necessarily widely accepted among the broader population – is a reminder of the difficulty of acknowledging a threshold of mutuality, of appreciating that the real need to pursue justice may occur in a context where violence has been a shared (if profoundly unequal) reality, and that this too must in some way be worked with. To repeat the 'international analogy' of chapter 1, this second sense of 'community' is a reminder that divisions are within as much as between communities, particularly that community which is the state. It is a reminder, too, when the state is taken as the defining community, as it often is for questions of rights, that states are shaped by histories and patterns of interaction that stretch well beyond the singularities of place, culture and political arrangement. The condition of Aboriginal health, for example, pulls on these different strands of community by highlighting the problem of the systemic marginalisation of indigenous populations within the mechanisms of citizenship, the questions this poses for the construction of citizenship, and the place of this quandary within the broader international dynamic of colonisation and decolonisation. Moving forward on questions around the status of Indigenous people in Australia is also often cast in terms of reconciliation. In this case it is important that any act of reconciliation is not another effort at final absorption and closure but the recognition that citizenship can be constituted through an on-going process of exchange.

The defining orientation to working with human rights abuse needs to be one capable of sustained work on reconstituting social and political relationships. Threats and punitive measures may be appropriate tactics – if you are in a position to threaten successfully, in a carefully targeted manner for a definite goal, if the situation of abuse is clear-cut, if the specific content of such measures is relevant to the nature of the abuse and the balance of forces within the state or the situation, and most importantly if the measures do not simply impose fresh abuse. And confrontation is often necessary. However, if the goal of the promotion of human rights is actually to bring about change in abusive practices and structures, confrontation can only be one moment in a much broader network which is not essentially confrontational or punitive but which engages directly with the institutions and practices at stake – at a structural level, to the extent that is possible, but also with the tissue of relationships, identities and tasks that give body to structure, that embed and reshape it. Unless it is purely a matter of exerting preponderant force at the crucial moment, even confrontation needs a context, some shared recognition of exchange, in which the weight of injury can be laid bare. Abuse is not 'their' problem for any more than a moment – the 'us' and 'them' of the systemic infliction of suffering is not fixed in absolute terms. Human rights rhetoric sometimes seems to suggest that only if enough pressure were brought to bear, oppressive regimes would come to an end and the problem of abuse would disappear. But the formal end of a particular regime (the withdrawal of the Indonesian military and sovereignty from East Timor, for example) leaves still the question of how lives and identities structured by violence and the logic of enmity are rebuilt. Declaratory standard setting, too, leaves this dimension untouched.

Thus, as the discussion of the Tiananmen killings and in different ways all three case studies argue, even when culpability is clear and specific, and condemnation and threats warranted and in some ways effective, the need for the laborious, long-term work with those complex institutions making up the state or shaping society remains. This may be the work that most enables and underlies long-term change in abusive practices within and across states, that may shift the fabric of possibilities from which responses to specific patterns of injury emerge, and so itself may contribute to the glacial movements of our political, economic and cultural arrangements. There is certainly significant scope for such work. Many societies are marked by similar and recurrent patterns of grave abuse, for example, relating to indigenous peoples, to ethnic or religious minorities, to women, or to prisons, police, labour conditions, to people displaced through industrialisation, refugees, and so on. These repeated sites of injury can be amenable to more cooperative, multi-levelled, enmeshed and tactical ways of working with rights. While such an approach is hardly novel, it could become more the heart of an international human rights practice. Although highly sensitive (how many governments are happy to reveal the state of their prisons or the practices of their police forces?) such ventures need not be so persistently structured by the dynamics of contending sovereignties. Nor need this be essentially 'welfare' work that avoids the 'hard' questions. It is rather to seek the hard questions of the production and distributions of power in and through the mechanisms of actual working and living arrangements – our own and others' – to recognise patterns of abuse and to support or strengthen those means for questioning or resisting violence, humiliation and marginalisation that are to hand, not as a transmission from those who 'have' to those who 'have not' but as an exchange on what are often common problems.

Such an approach could not deal directly with some crucial forms or occasions of rights violations – it is not equipped for the outburst of extensive slaughter in Rwanda, Kosovo, East Timor, even Tiananmen. As with other approaches to rights, it is not an answer that wipes away the problem of abuse. But while often identified with the moment of greatest violence, rights violations are embedded in a complex tissue of relationships and circumstances. While the explosion of violence calls forth a necessarily very narrow range of responses, the capacity for political and social change rests more with the formal and informal institutional frameworks and potentials that pattern all levels of collective life. To return to the example of Tiananmen, a more extensive and denser history of international engagement across many levels of institutional life in China could have shifted somewhat the context of that particular confrontation, both within China and internationally.

Such an approach would require a greater commitment of resources to the pursuit of human rights than is the norm. But it points to what is both a workable alternative and complement to the present narrow focus on either half-hearted and inconsistent confrontation of governments or standard setting, when that is not underpinned by substantial work at the site of abuse. Closer engagement with specific communities, institutions and practices could provide a localised *as well as* a more general vocabulary in which human rights practices came to be meaningful. For those governed by a violent rule, it could provide a more informed and organised basis upon which to resist the coercive exercise of power and an effective connection with a wider range of interested international bodies. It could reduce the chances of destructive and careless choices, such as were taken by a number of governments in regard to East Tim- or in 1975, as well as to Beijing in 1989. Perhaps it could provide a more seasoned practical and conceptual underpinning to the international rights debates and measures that now circulate at somewhat ethereal levels of government and international agency and are so easily enmired in versions of us versus them.

The ideas, norms and practices that underpin understandings of rights and of abuse are situated within a shifting construction of community and person – established not only by legal requirement but within a climate of political and economic relationships and of what we think, at the least, we owe one another. In some respects this matrix of expectations and relationships can change surprisingly rapidly on different fronts. In China, for example, as Ann Kent (1993) makes clear, the popular expectation of fundamental material security – people's right to subsistence – has been undermined in the process of economic modernisation with significant and complex implications for people's relationship with each other and to the government. In the English-speaking world, the norms that balanced company profitability and employment, suggesting when companies had a 'right' to lay off competent workers or when workers had a 'right' to continued employment, have shifted considerably, again with extensive ramifications for social organisation. Progress on land rights, but also the accumulation of stories of separation, loss, injury and survival – voices bearing the effects of decades of the administration of Aboriginal people – have shifted the exchange between settler and Aboriginal Australians. Within western societies the location of human rights so assertively in a figure of the individual, with society as a neutral form around the content of individual choice rather than a densely constructed field of possibility, has marked deeply many domestic human rights controversies, and has arguably limited our capacity for response.

Ideas and practices of human rights raise the question of what we value in political community and interaction; indeed they are a way of asking that question. This is not a reference to an ideal speech moment, nor is it simply diplomatic exchange between government elites and the powerful asserting their role as spokespersons of their culture. Rather it could be imagined as one part of a vast, complex and immensely difficult 'conversation', within each life, with each other, with our pasts, about how we live our collective lives – a conversation articulated with action, resistances and structures as well as words, and across many dimensions of our own and others' societies. To emphasise human rights as a form of question is to recognise that our understanding of the human and of community is limited, (indeed our official grasp of these categories is narrow and rigid) historically grounded and shifting. Or, to put it more positively, it is to realise that these fundamental categories by which we are so deeply shaped remain open-ended and exploratory. One value of this orientation is receptivity to the experience and lives of others. Answers to the questions raised in such a 'conversation' are not given or final, but made, well or badly and again and again, in the institutions and practical values of our common life.

NOTES

1   'What is the language of human rights – there is no one language. No one language can encapsulate these questions. We have some language for legal rights, less for rights as social beings, almost none for rights as spiritual beings' (Smitu Kothari, Indian human rights activist and commentator, in conversation, Melbourne, 1995).

2   There are exceptions to this. For example, some NGOs endeavour to use precisely this approach, working together with particular governments or institutions on, for example, prison reform.

REFERENCES

Aarons, M. and Domm, R. (1992), *East Timor: A Western Made Tragedy*, Left Book Club, Sydney.

Access Economics (1994), *Budgetary Illusion in Australian Federal Politics – the National Aboriginal Health Strategy*, R. Kilham, Briefing Paper for the Australian Medical Association, Canberra.

——(1995), *Federal Government Funding for Indigenous Health*, R. Kilham, briefing paper for the Australian Medical Association and the Australian Pharmeceutical Manufacturers' Association, Canberra.

Aditjondro, G. J. (1994), *East Timor: An Indonesian Intellectual Speaks Out*, ed. H. Feith, E. Baulch and P. Walsh, Australian Council for Overseas Aid, Sydney.

Age (1994), 'MPs Slam Blacks' Living Conditions', 29 March: 2.

AIHWJ (*Aboriginal and Islander Health Workers' Journal*) (1997), 'The Health and Welfare of Australia's Aboriginal and Torres Strait Islander Peoples', 21, 3: 9.

Alatas, A. (1993), 'Address to the Second World Conference on Human Rights', Vienna.

Anderson, B. R. (1995), 'East Timor and Indonesia: Some Implications' in P. Carey and G. C. Bentley (eds), *East Timor at the Crossroads: The Forging of a Nation*, Cassell, London.

Anderson, I. (1994), 'Towards a Koori Healing Practice' in *Voices From the Land: 1993 Boyer Lectures*, ABC Books, Sydney.

Araujo, A. 'East Timor: To Be or Not to Be a X(B)anana Republic', *The Jakarta Post*, Online Special, available: http://www.thejakartapost.co./special/os.asp (accessed 6 February 2001).

Australian Bureau of Statistics-Australian Institute of Health and Welfare (1997), *ABS Catalogue No. 4704.0/AIHW Catalogue No. IHW2*, Australian Government Publishing Service, Canberra.

Barme, G. (1990), 'Liu Xiaobo and the Protest Movement of 1989', in G. Hicks (ed.), *The Broken Mirror: China After Tiananmen*, Longman, Harlow, Essex.

——Hinton, C., and Gordon, R. (1995), *The Gates of Heavenly Peace* (Documentary), Independent Television Service, USA.

Bergere, M.-C. (1992), 'Tiananmen 1989: Background and Consequences' in M. Dassu and T. Saich (eds), *The Reform Decade in China*, Kegan Paul International, London.

Bernstein, J. (1993), 'The Theory and Practice of Human Rights' in S. Whitfield (ed.), *After the Event: Human Rights and their Future in China*, Wellsweep, London.

Bleiker, R. and McGibbon, R. (forthcoming), 'Timor-Oriental: Le Combat pour la Paix et pour la Réconciliation' (East-Timor: The Struggle for Peace and Reconciliation), trans. G. Thompson and T. Ruyer, *Cultures et Conflits*, 40.

Booth, K. (1995), 'Human Wrongs and International Relations', *International Affairs*, 71, 1: 103–26.

——(1999), 'Three Tyrannies' in T. Dunne and N. J. Wheeler (eds), *Human Rights in Global Politics*, Cambridge University Press, Cambridge.

References

Brown, C. (1999), 'Universal Human Rights: A Critique' in T. Dunne and N. J. Wheeler (eds), *Human Rights in Global Politics*, Cambridge University Press, Cambridge.

Brown, W. (1995), *States of Injury: Power and Freedom in Late Modernity*, Princeton University Press, Princeton, NJ.

Bull, H. (1977), *The Anarchical Society: A Study of Order in World Politics*, Macmillan, London.

——(1979), 'Human Rights and World Politics' in R. Pettman (ed.), *Moral Claims in World Affairs*, Australian National University Press, Canberra.

Butterfield, H. and Wight, M. (1966), *Diplomatic Investigations*, Allen & Unwin, London.

Byrnes, M. (1990), 'The Death of a People's Army' in G. Hicks (ed.), *The Broken Mirror: China After Tiananmen*, Longman, Harlow, Essex.

Carr, E. H. (1970), *The Twenty Years' Crisis, 1919–1939: An Introduction to the Study of International Relations*, Macmillan, London [1946].

CCJDP (The Catholic Commission for Justice, Development and Peace) (1993), *Just Reading No. 2, The Church and East Timor*, CCJDP, Melbourne.

Chen Xianda (1992), 'The Social System and Human Rights', *Qiushi*, 7 (trans. David Bray).

Chua, B. H. (1992), 'Australian and Asian Perceptions of Human Rights' in P. Van Ness, I. Russell and B. H. Chua (eds), *Australian Human Rights Diplomacy*, Australian Foreign Policy Papers, Research School of Pacific Studies, Australian National University, Canberra.

Cixous, H. (1993), 'We Who Are Free, Are We Free?' in B. Johnson (ed.), *Freedom and Interpretation: The Oxford Amnesty Lectures 1992*, Basic Books, New York.

Cohen, J. A. (1990), 'Tiananmen and the Rule of Law' in G. Hicks (ed.), *The Broken Mirror: China After Tiananmen*, Longman, Harlow, Essex.

Cohen, S. (2001), *States of Denial: Knowing about Atrocities and Suffering*, Polity Press, Cambridge.

Connolly, W. E. (1993), *The Augustinian Imperative: A Reflection on the Politics of Morality*, Sage Publications, California.

——(1995), *The Ethos of Pluralisation*, University of Minnesota Press, Minneapolis.

——(2000), 'The Liberal Image of the Nation' in D. Ivison, P. Patton and W. Sanders (eds), *Political Theory and the Rights of Indigenous Peoples*, Cambridge University Press, Cambridge.

Cowie, H. R. (ed.) (1986), *Imperialism and Race Relations*, Nelson, Melbourne.

Cox, R. W. (1981), 'Social Forces, States and World Orders: Beyond International Relations Theory', *Millenium*, 10: 126–55.

Cranston, M. (1973), *What Are Human Rights?* Bodley Head, London.

Crouch, H. (2000), 'The TNI and East Timor Policy' in J. J. Fox and D. B. Soares (eds), *Out of the Ashes: Destruction and Reconstruction of East Timor*, Crawford House Publishing, Adelaide.

Cullen, R. and Fu, H. L. (1998), 'People's Republic of China' in C. Saunders and G. Hassall (eds), *Asia-Pacific Constitutional Yearbook*, Centre for Comparative Constitutional Studies, Melbourne.

David, C.-P. (1999), 'Does Peacebuilding Build Peace?', *Security Dialogue*, 30, 1: 25–41.

Dittmer, L. (1989), 'The Tiananmen Massacre', *Problems of Communism*, September–October: 2–15.

Dodson, M. (1993), *First Report of the Aboriginal and Torres Strait Islander Social Justice Commission*, Australian Government Publishing Service, Canberra.

——(1995a), *Third Report of the Aboriginal and Torres Strait Islander Social Justice Commission*, Australian Government Publishing Service, Canberra.

——(1995b), 'Adequacy of the Protection for the Rights of Indigenous Peoples', *The Aboriginal and Islander Health Worker Journal*, 19, 2, March–April.

——(1995c), *Indigenous Social Justice: Strategies and Recommendations. Submission to the Parliament by the Aboriginal and Torres Strait Islander Social Justice Commission*, Vol. 1, Office of the Aboriginal and Torres Strait Islander Social Justice Commission, Sydney.

Donnelly, J. (1986), 'International Human Rights: A Regime Analysis', *International Organisation*, 40, 3.

——(1989), *Universal Human Rights in Theory and Practice*, Cornell University Press, Ithaca, NY.

——(1999), 'The Social Construction of International Human Rights' in T. Dunne and N. J. Wheeler (eds), *Human Rights in Global Politics*, Cambridge University Press, Cambridge.

Dunn, J. (1983), *Timor: A People Betrayed*, Jacaranda Press, Milton, Brisbane.

——(2001), 'Crimes Against Humanity in East Timor, January to October 1999', available: http://www.smh.com.au (accessed 28 April 2001).

Dunne, T. and Wheeler, N. J. (eds) (1999), *Human Rights in Global Politics*, Cambridge University Press, Cambridge.

Dworkin, R. (1977), *Taking Rights Seriously*, Harvard University Press, Cambridge, MA.

——(1984), 'Rights as Trumps' in J. Waldron (ed.), *Theories of Rights*, Oxford University Press, Oxford.

Fromm, E. (1960), *Fear of Freedom*, Routledge & Kegan Paul, London.

——(1977), *The Anatomy of Human Destructiveness*, Penguin, Harmondsworth.

Gadjah Mada University Research Centre for Village and Regional Development (1991), *East Timor: The Impact of Integration*, trans. and published by the Indonesia Resources and Information Programme.

Garnett, J. C. (1992), 'States, State-Centric Perspectives and Interdependence Theory' in J. Baylis and N. J. Rengger (eds), *Dilemmas of World Politics: International Issues in a Changing World*, Oxford University Press, Clarendon.

Gordimer, N. (1998), *The House Gun*, Farrar, Straus & Giroux, New York.

Gordon, C. (1991), 'Governmental Rationality: An Introduction' in G. Burchell, C. Gordon and P. Miller (eds), *The Foucault Effect: Studies in Governmentality*, Harvester Wheatsheaf, London.

Gowers, A. (2001), Third Country Migrants and the European Union, MA dissertation, University of Queensland.

Grossman, D. (1995), *On Killing: The Psychological Cost of Learning to Kill in War and Society*, Little, Brown & Co., New York.

Gusmao, X. (2000), *To Resist Is to Win! The Autobiography of Xanana Gusmao*, Aurora Books, Richmond, Victoria.

Hanlon, J. (2001), 'Can East Timor Survive the Aid Industry?', *La'o Hamutuk* (The East Timor Institute for Reconstruction and Monitoring) 2, 3, available: http://www.etan.org./lh/bulletinv2n3.html

214

References

Hao, Y. F. (1999), 'From Rule of Man to Rule of Law: An Unintended Consequence of Corruption in China in the 1990s', *Journal of Contemporary China*, 8, 22: 405–23.

Hicks, G. (ed.) (1990), *The Broken Mirror: China After Tiananmen*, Longman, Harlow, Essex.

Hirst, P. (1985), 'Law, Socialism and Rights' in P. Carter and M. Collison (eds), *Radical Issues in Criminology*, Barnes & Noble, New Jersey.

Hobbes, T. (1968), *Leviathan*, ed. C. B. Macpherson, Pelican Classics, Harmondsworth, Middlesex.

Holquist, M. (1990), *Dialogism: Bakhtin and his World*, Routledge, London.

HREOC (Human Rights and Equal Opportunity Commission) (1994), *Water: A Report on the Provision of Water and Sanitation to Aboriginal and Torres Strait Islander Communities: Brief for Governments and Service Providers* (Federal Race Discrimination Commissioner: Irene Moss), HREOC, Sydney.

——(1997), *Bringing Them Home: Report of the National Inquiry into the Separation of Aboriginal and Torres Strait Islander Children from their Families* (Commissioner: Ronald Wilson), HREOC, Sydney.

HRSC (House of Representatives Standing Committee on Family and Community Affairs) (2000), *Health Is Life: Report on the Inquiry into Indigenous Health*, Australian Government Publishing Service, Canberra.

HRSCAA (House of Representatives Standing Committee on Aboriginal Affairs) (1979), *Report into Aboriginal Health*, Australian Government Publishing Service, Canberra.

Human Rights Watch-Asia (formerly Asia Watch) (1994), *The Limits to Openness: Human Rights in Indonesia and East Timor*, by Sidney Jones for Human Rights Watch, New York.

Hunter, E. (1993), *Aboriginal Health and History: Power and Prejudice in Remote Australia*, Cambridge University Press, Cambridge.

Hunter, P. (1999), Keynote Speech, National Rural Health Conference, March, Adelaide.

Huyse, L. (1998), 'Transitional Justice' in P. Harris and Ben Reilly (eds), *Democracy and Deep-Rooted Conflict: Options for Negotiators*, Institute for Democracy and Electoral Assistance, Stockholm.

IMF (2000), 'East Timor: Establishing the Foundations of Sound Economic Management', by L. Valdivieso, E. Toshihide, L. V. Mendonca, S. Tareq and A. Lopez-Mejia, available: http://www.imf.org/external/pubs/ft/Etimor/index.htm

Indonesian Commission of Investigation into Human Rights Violations, 'News Special', available: http://www.smh.com.au (accessed 31 January 2000).

Johnson, C. (1990), Foreword to G. Hicks (ed.), *The Broken Mirror: China After Tiananmen*, Longman, Harlow, Essex.

Jones, A. (1994), 'Aborigines Still Deprived Despite Millions', *The Northern Territory News*, 20 March.

Kaldor, M. (1998), 'Reconceptualising Organised Violence' in D. Archibugi, D. Held and M. Kohler (eds), *Re-imagining Political Community*, Polity Press, Cambridge.

Kamenka, E. and Tay, E.-S. (eds) (1978), *Ideas and Ideologies: Human Rights*, Arnold, Port Melbourne.

Kelly, D. (1990), 'Chinese Intellectuals in the 1989 Democracy Movement' in G. Hicks (ed.), *The Broken Mirror: China After Tiananmen*, Longman, London.

References

Kelly, T. (1993), *An Expanding Theology*, E. J. Dwyer, Newtown, Australia.

Keohane, R. O. (1984), *After Hegemony: Cooperation and Discord in the Political Economy*, Princeton University Press, Princeton, NJ.

——and Nye, J. S. (1987), 'Power and Interdependence Revisited', *International Organisation*, 41, 4: 725–53.

Kent, A. (1993), *Between Freedom and Subsistence: China and Human Rights*, Oxford University Press, Hong Kong.

Kidd, R. (1997), *The Way We Civilise: Aboriginal Affairs – the Untold Story*, University of Queensland Press, St Lucia, Queensland.

——(2000), *Black Lives, Government Lies*, University of New South Wales Press, Sydney.

Kingsbury, D. (2000), 'East Timor to 1999' in D. Kingsbury (ed.), *Guns and Ballot Boxes: East Timor's Vote for Independence*, Monash Asia Institute, Victoria.

Kothari, R. (1991), 'Human Rights: A Movement in Search of a Theory' in S. Kothari and H. Sethi (eds), *Rethinking Human Rights: Challenges for Theory and Action*, Lokayan, Delhi.

Langton, M. (1994), 'Indigenous Self-Government and Self-Determination' in C. Fletcher (ed.), *Aboriginal Self-Determination in Australia*, Aboriginal Studies Press, Canberra.

Leys, S. (1990), 'After the Massacres' in G. Hicks (ed.), *The Broken Mirror: China After Tiananmen*, Longman, Harlow, Essex.

Li Lin and Zhu Xiaoqing (1992), 'An Outline of Discussions on Questions of Human Rights Since the Third Plenum of the Eleventh Central Committee Meeting of the Communist Party of China' in Cai Bin (ed.), *Contemporary Human Rights*, trans. David Bray, Chinese Social Sciences Press, Beijing.

Linklater, A. (1998), *The Transformation of Political Community*, Polity Press, Cambridge.

Liu Huaqiu (1993), Address to the World Conference on Human Rights (translation), June, Vienna.

Locke, J. (1966), *Two Treatises on Civil Government*, Everyman's Library, London.

London, M. (1990), 'The Romance of Realpolitik' in G. Hicks (ed.), *The Broken Mirror: China After Tiananmen*, Longman, Harlow, Essex.

Mabo v. The State of Queensland (no. 2) (1992), *Commonwealth Law Reports*, Vol. 175.

Macartney, J. (1990), 'The Students: Heroes, Pawns or Powerbrokers?' in G. Hicks (ed.), *The Broken Mirror: China After Tiananmen*, Longman, Harlow, Essex.

McCormick, B. L. (1990), *Political Reform in Post-Mao China: Democracy and Bureaucracy in a Leninist State*, University of California Press, Berkeley.

McGurn (1990), 'The US and China: Sanctioning Tiananmen Square' in G. Hicks (ed.), *The Broken Mirror: China After Tiananmen*, Longman, Harlow, Essex.

Marx, K. (1972), 'The Jewish Question' in R. C. Tucker (ed.), *The Marx-Engels Reader*, Norton, New York.

Minogue, K. (1989), 'The History of the Idea of Human Rights' in W. Laqueur and B. Rubin (eds), *The Human Rights Reader*, Meridian, New York.

Mirsky, J. (1997), 'China: The Defining Moment', *The New York Review of Books*, 9 January.

Mohamad, G. (1993), 'Notes on the Issue of Human Rights', unpublished paper presented to the International Seminar on Human Rights, Jakarta organised by *The Jakarta Post*.

——(1994), *Sidelines: Writings from Tempo, Indonesia's Banned Magazine*, Hyland House in association with Monash University, South Melbourne.

References

——(1995), Address to the Australian Institute of International Affairs (unpublished), Brisbane.

Morgenthau, H. (1978), *Politics Among Nations: The Struggle for Power and Peace*, 5th edition, revised, Knopf, New York.

Muzaffar, C. (1993), *Human Rights and the New World Order*, Just World Trust, Penang.

NAHS (1989), (*National Aboriginal Health Strategy*), Commonwealth Government Printing Service, Canberra.

Nandy, A. (1983), *The Intimate Enemy: Loss and Recovery of Self Under Colonialism*. Oxford University Press, New Delhi.

——(1998), 'A New Cosmopolitanism: Toward a Dialogue of Asian Civilizations' in K. H. Chen (ed.), *Trajectories: InterAsian Cultural Studies*, Routledge, London.

Nathan, A. (1989), 'Chinese Democracy in 1989: Continuity and Change', *Problems of Communism*, September–October: 16–29.

——(1990), *China in Crisis: Dilemmas of Reform and Prospects for Democracy*, Columbia University Press, New York.

——(1991), 'Tiananmen and the Cosmos', *The New Republic*, 29 July: 31–6.

——(1993), 'Chinese Democracy: The Lessons of Failure', *Journal of Contemporary China*, 4, Fall: 3–13.

——and Link, P. (eds) (2001), *The Tiananmen Papers*, Little, Brown & Co., London.

Nettheim, G. (1993), '"The Consent of the Natives": Mabo and Indigenous Political Rights' in *Essays on the Mabo Decision*, Law Book Company, Sydney.

O'Brien, K. J. (1999), 'Hunting for Political Change' in *The China Journal*, 41, January: 159–69.

Okensberg, M., Sullivan, L. and Lambert, M. (eds) (1990), *Beijing Spring, 1980: Confrontation and Conflict. The Basic Documents*, M. E. Sharpe, New York.

Ong, W. (1982), *Orality and Literacy: The Technologising of the Word*, Methuen, New York.

Parekh, B. (1999), 'Non-Ethnocentric Universalism' in T. Dunne and N. J. Wheeler (eds), *Human Rights in Global Politics*, Cambridge University Press, Cambridge.

Paris, R. (1997), 'Peacebuilding and the Limits of Liberal Internationalism', *International Security*, 22, 2: 54–89.

Pearson, N. (1994), 'Mabo: Towards Respecting Equality and Difference' in *Voices From the Land: 1993 Boyer Lectures*, ABC Books, Sydney.

——(1997), 'Bad Blood Rising', *Weekend Australian*, 8–9 November: 26.

——(2000), 'The Light on the Hill', Ben Chifley Memorial Lecture (unpublished), 12 August, Bathurst.

Peterson, V. S. (1990), 'Whose Rights? A Critique of the "Givens" in Human Rights Discourse', *Alternatives*, 15: 303–44.

Pettman, R. (ed.) (1979), *Moral Claims in World Affairs*, Australian National University Press, Canberra.

——(1991), *International Politics*, Longman Chesire, Melbourne.

Pilger, J. (1994), 'East Timor, A Land of Crosses', *New Internationalist*, 253, March.

Prybyla, J. S. (1990), 'China's Socialist Economy: A Broken System' in G. Hicks (ed.), *The Broken Mirror: China After Tiananmen*, Longman, Harlow, Essex.

Pye, L. (1990), 'Tiannamen and Chinese Poritical Culture: The Escalalation of Confrontation' in G. Hicks (ed), *The Broken Mirror: China After Tiannamen*, Longman, Harlow, Essex.

References

Raby, G. (1990), 'China: The Neither This Nor That Economy' Australian Department of Foreign Affairs and Trade (unpublished briefing paper).

Ramos-Horta, J. (1987), *Funu: The Unfinished Saga of East Timor*, Red Sea Press, Inc., New Jersey.

Rawls, J. (1971), *A Theory of Justice*, Harvard University Press, Cambridge, MA.

RCIADIC (Royal Commission into Aboriginal Deaths in Custody) (1991), *The National Report*, Vols 1, 2, 4 and 5.

Reeve, D. (1996), 'Indonesia' in A. Milner and M. Quilty (eds), *Communities of Thought*, Oxford University Press, Melbourne.

Reid, J. and Trompf, P. (eds) (1991), *The Health of Aboriginal Australia*, Harcourt Brace Jovanovich, Marrickville, NSW.

Rodan, G. and Hewison, K. (1996), 'A "Clash of Cultures" or the Convergence of Political Ideology?' in R. Robison (ed.), *Pathways to Asia: The Politics of Engagement*, Allen & Unwin, St Leonards, Australia.

Rorty, R. (1989), *Contingency, Irony and Solidarity*, Cambridge University Press, Cambridge.

——(1993), 'Human Rights, Rationality and Sentimentality' in S. Shute and S. Hurley (eds), *On Human Rights: The Oxford Amnesty Lectures 1993*, Basic Books, New York.

Saggers, S. and Gray, D. (1991), 'Policy and Practice in Aboriginal Health' in J. Reid and P. Trompf (eds), *The Health of Aboriginal Australia*, Harcourt Brace Jovanovich, Marrickville, NSW.

Saich, T. (1992), 'The Reform Decade in China: The Limits to Revolution from Above' in M. Dassu and T. Saich (eds), *The Reform Decade in China*, Kegan Paul International, London.

Saldhana, J. M. D. S. (1994), *The Political Economy of East Timor Development*, Pustaka Sinar Harapan, Jakarta.

Scarry, E. (1985), *The Body in Pain: The Making and Unmaking of the World*, Oxford University Press, New York.

Schwarz, A. (1994), *A Nation in Waiting: Indonesia in the 1990s*, Allen & Unwin, St Leonards, Australia.

Seymour, J. D. (1993), 'What the Agenda Has Been Missing' in S. Whitfield (ed.), *After the Event; Human Rights and their Future in China*, Wellsweep, London.

Shi, T. J. (1997), *Political Participation in Beijing*, Harvard University Press, Cambridge, MA.

——(2000), 'Cultural Values and Democracy in the People's Republic of China', *The China Quarterly*, 162, June: 540–59.

Shue, H. (1980), *Basic Rights: Subsistence, Affluence and US Foreign Policy*, Princeton University Press, Princeton, NJ.

Stanner, W. E. H. (1969), *After the Dreaming: 1968 Boyer Lectures*, Australian Broadcasting Commission, Sydney.

State Council of the People's Republic of China (1991), *Human Rights in China*, PRC Information Office, Beijing.

Tanner, M. S. (1998), *The Politics of Lawmaking in Post-Mao China: Institutions, Processes, and Democratic Prospects*, Oxford University Press, Oxford.

Taudevin, L. (2000), 'The Economic Viability of East Timor Using Indonesian Achievements as a Benchmark' in L. Taudevin and J. Lee (eds), *East Timor: Making Amends?*, Oxford Press, Sydney.

Taylor, C. (1992), *Multiculturalism and 'The Politics of Recognition'*, Princeton University Press, Princeton, NJ.

Taylor, J. G. (1995), 'Decolonisation, Independence and Invasion' in CIIR-IPJET (eds), *International Law and the Question of East Timor*, Catholic Institute for International Relations-International Platform for East Timor, London and The Netherlands.

Thompson, Neil J. (1989), 'Aboriginal Health: A Socio-Cultural Perspective' in G. M. Lupton and J. M. Najman (eds), *Sociology of Health and Illness: Australian Readings*, Macmillan, South Melbourne.

——(1991), 'Recent Trends in Aboriginal Mortality', *The Medical Journal of Australia*, 154, February 18.

Tingle, L. (1994), 'The High Ground on Black Health', *Weekend Australian*, 12–13 February: 3.

Todorov, T. (1987), *Literature and its Theorists*, trans. C. Porter, Cornell University Press, Ithaca, NY.

Tugendhat, E. (1994), 'The Moral Dilemma in the Resue of Refugees', paper presented to the conference *Rescue*, The New School, New York, November. .

Tully, J. (1995), *Strange Multiplicity: Constitutionalism in an Age of Diversity*, Cambridge University Press, Cambridge.

——(ed.) (1991), *Pufendorf – On the Duty of Man and Citizen According to Natural Law*, Cambridge University Press, Cambridge.

Turner, B. S. (1993), 'Outline of a Theory of Human Rights' in B. S. Turner (ed.), *Citizenship and Social Theory*, Sage, London.

Van Ness, P., Russell, I. and Chua, B.-H. (1992), *Australian Human Rights Diplomacy*, Australian Foreign Policy Papers, Research School of Pacific Studies, Australian National University, Canberra.

——(1992), 'Human Rights and International Relations in East Asia', *Asian Studies Review*, 16 January: 43–52.

Vincent, R. J. (1986), *Human Rights and International Relations*, Cambridge University Press, Cambridge.

Viviani, N. (1976), 'Australians and the Timor Issue', *Australian Outlook*, August: 198–224.

Walder, A. G. (1996), 'Workers, Managers and the State: The Reform Era and the Crisis of 1989' in B. Hook (ed.), *The Indivdual and the State in China*, Clarendon Press, Oxford.

Walker, R. B. J. (1993), *Inside/Outside: International Relations as Political Theory*, Cambridge University Press, Cambridge.

Waltz, K. (1979), *Theory of Interntional Politics*, Addison-Wesley, Reading, MA.

Webber, J. (2000), 'Mabo and Australian Constitutionalism' in D. Ivison, P. Patton and W. Sanders (eds), *Political Theory and the Rights of Indigenous Peoples*, Cambridge University Press, Cambridge.

Wik Peoples v. *The State of Queensland and Others* (1996), *Commonwealth Law Reports*, Vol. 1.

References

Wittgenstein, L. (1977), *On Certainty*, ed. G. E. M. Anscombe and G. H. von Wright Blackwell, Oxford.

——(1978), *Philosophical Investigations*, trans. G. E. M. Anscombe, Blackwell, Oxford.

Wong Kan Seng (1993), Address to the World Conference on Human Rights, Vienna, June.

Xia Yong (1993), *The Origin of Human Rights Conceptions*, trans. D. Bray, Chinese Political Science and Law Publishing House, Beijing.

Yi Mu and Thompson, M. V. (1989), *Crisis at Tiananmen: Reform and Reality in Modern China*, China Books and Periodicals, San Francisco, CA.

INDEX

Note: an 'n' after a page number denotes a footnote.

Lightning Source UK Ltd.
Milton Keynes UK
11 February 2010

149865UK00001B/9/P